THE POVERTY OF RICHES

The Poverty of Riches

St. Francis of Assisi Reconsidered

KENNETH BAXTER WOLF

OXFORD
UNIVERSITY PRESS

2003

OXFORD

UNIVERSITY PRESS

Oxford   New York
Auckland   Bangkok   Buenos Aires   Cape Town   Chennai
Dar es Salaam   Delhi   Hong Kong   Istanbul   Karachi   Kolkata
Kuala Lumpur   Madrid   Melbourne   Mexico City   Mumbai
Nairobi   São Paolo   Shanghai   Taipei   Tokyo   Toronto

Copyright © 2003 by Oxford University Press, Inc.

Published by Oxford University Press, Inc.
198 Madison Avenue, New York New York 10016

www.oup.com

Oxford is a registered trademark of Oxford University Press

Library of Congress Cataloging-in-Publication Data
Wolf, Kenneth Baxter, 1957–
The poverty of riches : St. Francis of Assisi reconsidered /
Kenneth Baxter Wolf.
   p. cm. — (Oxford studies in historical theology)
Includes bibliographical references and index.
ISBN 0-19-515808-3
1. Francis, of Assisi, Saint, 1182–1226.   I. Title.   II. Series.
BX4700.F6 W585 2002
271'.302—dc21   2002015407

9 8 7 6 5 4 3 2 1

Printed in the United States of America
on acid-free paper

für

Friederike Liese-Lotte von Franqué,

die mein Herz ebenso erfüllt wie Franziskus meinen Geist.

Preface

The idea for this book has been a part of me for a long time, at least since my graduate school days at Stanford in the early 1980s, when I first began to sift through Franciscan history in search of a viable dissertation topic. As it turned out, other saints intervened, and fifteen years passed before I found my way back to *il Poverello*. It seems as though I should be able to recall the exact moment when the coin dropped and I finally figured out what it was that had been bothering me about Francis all those years. I only know that I was already formulating the questions on which this book is based when I shared them with Robert McAfee Brown at his home in Palo Alto in early 1994. A timely invitation by my friend John Williams to speak at the University of Pittsburgh a year later gave me the opportunity to organize and present my thoughts on Francis and his "holy poverty" for the first time. I remember the energy that infused the audience that cold February afternoon in the "Cathedral of Learning." Everyone present seemed to have something eye-opening to say about the presentation. I returned to California convinced that I was on to something that would resonate with scholars from all across the academic spectrum.

I relived that experience many times with audiences in Kalamazoo (1996), Santa Barbara (1997), Knoxville (1998), Pasadena (1998), St. Louis (2001) and, of course, Claremont (1996, 1998, 2000, 2001). Each time, I learned a little more from the wide-ranging responses generated by my ideas. Over the same period of time, I subjected the thesis of this book, in one form or another, to the scrutiny of hundreds of students and more than a dozen scholars, including Peter Brown, Giles Constable, Sharon Farmer, Jim Powell, Tom Noble, Tom Burman, Richard Hecht, Kees Bolle, David Raizman, Betsy Perry, Jerry Irish, George Gorse, Bill Whedbee, Robin Walz, and Rick Wolf, each of whose reactions and comments contributed something to the final shape of this project. Most significant of all have been the suggestions made by my mentor, Gavin Langmuir, who, even after all these years, still reads and improves everything that I write. Although neither Vincent Learnihan nor Bob Wolf lived to see this project through to its completion, both deserve to be acknowledged for their encouragement, despite their misgivings about the thesis.

Contents

Note on Translations and Previous Scholarship

For the sake of convenient cross-referencing, I have chosen to make use of the highly literal translations of the Franciscan sources found in the recent English edition of the Francis corpus, prepared by Regis J. Armstrong, J. A. Wayne Hellmann, and William J. Short under the title *Francis of Assisi: Early Documents* (New York: New City Press, 1999–2001). In some cases I have made slight changes in the wording with an eye to clarity and more conventional English usage.

For the sake of maximizing the accessibility of this study, I have, with very few exceptions, confined the views of previous scholars to the endnotes.

THE POVERTY OF RICHES

Unde accidit ut frater quidam cuidam pauperi eleemosynam postulanti verbum invectionis inferret dicens: Vide ne forte sis dives et simules paupertatem.

—Thomas of Celano, *The Life of St. Francis* 76

Introduction

Francis of Assisi is arguably the most attractive saint that the Catholic Church has ever produced. In the two short decades that separated his conversion from his death in 1226, he managed to capture the imagination of Latin Christendom as no living saint had ever done before. No one, it seemed, had lived a life in closer harmony with the Gospels, making Francis, in the eyes of many of his contemporaries, nothing less than an *alter Christus*: a second Christ. Despite the controversies that tore the Franciscan order apart after Francis's death, his personal reputation as a saint only grew. Even the scathing criticisms directed at the friars in the later Middle Ages seemed only to add to his stature as the perfect founder of an all-too-imperfect order. It is significant, in this regard, that Protestant opinions about this particular Catholic saint ranged from hailing him as a pioneer in the return to the gospel roots of Christianity to criticizing his cult for diverting too much attention away from Christ himself. Francis's high "approval ratings" have continued unabated into modern times, as evidenced not only by the sheer quantity of books written about Francis over the last century but by their consistently pious quality. Even secular scholars, bent on approaching the saint from a more detached historical perspective, have invariably, if inadvertently, left Francis on the pedestal where they found him.[1]

The point of this newest addition to the Francis bibliography is not to add to the adulation that has surrounded—indeed enshrouded—Francis for almost eight hundred years. Instead its purpose is to take a close, critical look at the particular kind of sanctity that he, more than any other Christian saint, embodied: a sanctity based first and foremost on the deliberate pursuit of poverty. My point of departure is a series of simple but hitherto unasked questions about the precise nature of Francis's poverty.[2] How did he go about transforming himself from a rich man into a poor one? How successful was

3

he? How did his self-imposed poverty compare to the involuntary poverty of the poor people whom he met in and around Assisi?[3] What did poor people of this type get out of their contact with Francis? What did Francis get out of his contact with them?

As I probe the earliest Franciscan sources for answers to these questions, it will quickly become apparent that no matter how much Francis, dressed in his soiled tunic and begging for food, may have resembled the poor in appearance and behavior, he never actually succeeded in becoming poor. For when Francis, on that fateful day in the bishop's chamber, suddenly removed his clothes and handed them over to his disgruntled father, he did so with the expectation that by renouncing his patrimony here on earth he would become the heir to an even greater, albeit spiritual, fortune in heaven. Moreover, in his pursuit of these heavenly treasures, Francis managed to win the admiration and even veneration of other Christians whom he made feel guilty about their own involvement in this world, thus transforming himself into one of the most influential men of his day.[4] This spiritually beneficial, socially powerful kind of poverty based on a deliberate "divestment" from this world and "investment" in the next was not the kind that the ordinary poor people of Assisi knew. On the contrary, their poverty was seen by their contemporaries as, at best, a harsh reminder of the transitory nature of earthly possessions and, at worst, a symptom of their moral turpitude.[5]

Francis's extreme love of poverty, pursued for the sake of his own spiritual progress, did surprisingly little to elevate anyone's opinion of the other kind of poverty.[6] On the contrary, to the extent that early thirteenth-century society endorsed Francis's "holy poverty" as the most reliable road to Christian perfection, it potentially made the lives of those suffering from involuntary poverty even more difficult. For one thing, Francis could not help but attract the attention of almsgivers, many of whom appreciated the vicarious spiritual advantages of supporting him in his quest for perfect poverty, as opposed to trying to alleviate the poverty of someone who did not want to be poor. Second, if the kind of "spiritual economy" that Francis epitomized, based as it was on deliberate divestment from this world and investment in the next, required that a Christian have something invested in this world in the first place, how were the poor expected to compete with the rich for entrance into the next life? What were they to give up in order to prove that they were ready to leave this world behind?[7] Under these circumstances, the poor of Assisi inevitably found their role in the drama of salvation reduced to that of providing models for Christians of means like Francis to imitate, models of what—from the perspective of an affluent Umbrian burgher—a life detached from the things of this world would look like.[8] But the similarities between the poverty of the poor and poverty of the rich could never be more than superficial, for in a religious tradition where sacrifice meant little or nothing unless it was undertaken voluntarily, it was not at all obvious how the plight of the *poor* poor (as opposed to the formerly *rich* poor) was to be alleviated in the next world.[9]

It is from this iconoclastic perspective that I propose to reconsider the life of St. Francis to see what can be learned about this underappreciated side of voluntary poverty as an avenue toward Christian perfection.[10] This study is divided into two parts, each of which has a very different purpose and tone. The first is a four-part "think piece" aimed at problematizing this traditionally unproblematic saint by laying bare the ironies and contradictions inherent within the idea of holy poverty as preserved in the earliest Franciscan literature. In the second, more analytic part, I attempt to locate the idea of "holy poverty" in the Latin Christian world of the late twelfth and early thirteenth centuries by considering it in light of four different historical contexts that, taken together, help us to account for its distinctive contours. The first of these treats Francis's poverty as a function of his own distinctive manner of imitating Christ; that is, his *imitatio Christi*. The second places Francis's *imitatio Christi* within the broader context of the history of Christian sanctity, in particular as it relates to the longstanding tension between a life of withdrawal from the world with an eye to one's own spiritual development (*vita passiva*) and a life of service to the spiritual and physical needs of other people living in the world (*vita activa*). The third compares Francis with other urban saints in Italy at this time who experimented with their own distinctive forms of holy poverty. Finally, the fourth explores the effect that Francis's preconversion identity as the son of a prosperous merchant had on the shape of his distinctive spiritual regimen and on the composition of his audience.

Any attempt to recover the historical Francis of Assisi and his actual relationship to poverty is hampered from the outset by problems related to the sources. First, the modest corpus of Francis's own works that has come down to us contains very little in the way of conventional autobiographical information, virtually all of which is confined to his brief *Testament*. Second, although Francis inspired a large number of biographies, even the earliest of them were written after the great watershed of his death by men who were more concerned with confirming his claim to sanctity than they were with capturing the actual details of his life. As a result we are left, as is typically the case when dealing with saints, with an image shaped as much by timeless hagiographic expectations as by specific historical data.[11] But beyond the usual limitations associated with hagiographical sources, it is important to keep in mind that the earliest and most reliable lives of Francis were written against a historical backdrop of intermittent, often intense controversy about the very meaning of poverty as it pertained to the Order of Friars Minor.

In the appendix to this study, I offer the interested reader a detailed assessment of each of the earliest biographies, in particular: Thomas of Celano's *Life of St. Francis* and his *Remembrance of the Desire of a Soul*, the *Anonymous of Perugia*, the *Legend of the Three Companions*, the *Assisi Compilation*, and Bonaventure's *Major Life of St. Francis*. In each case, I locate the work, to the extent that it is possible to do so, within the context of the famous Franciscan poverty debates. For the purposes of this book, however, I have chosen to suspend judgment about the historicity of any piece of information about Francis's life contained in these sources, in the hope of focusing the reader's attention more on the *idea* of St. Francis as captured, or constructed, by his hagiographers. Though this kind of approach sidesteps important, if ultimately unanswerable, questions as to the accuracy with which the individual biographers depicted Francis's actual views on poverty, it does allow us to say important things about Franciscan poverty as an idea within the collective *mentalité* of the world inhabited by the authors and, by extension, their patrons and their readers.[12]

ST. FRANCIS AND THE IRONY
OF HOLY POVERTY

It would never have occurred to the earliest biographers of Francis to question either the ultimate success of his quest for perfect poverty or its implications for the spiritual welfare of the ordinary poor. As focused as they were on the extraordinary level of faith required for a man who had everything in this world to give it all up for the promise of even more in the next world, they never stopped to ask whether the theological and social rewards that came with such a willful pursuit of poverty might actually have compromised it in the process. Nor were they likely to recognize that so much emphasis on volition as a key ingredient of holy poverty posed very real obstacles for the salvation of Christians whose poverty was a function of circumstances beyond their control. In the second part of this study, I will explore a number of contextual factors that, taken together, help explain how the biographers could have missed these imperfections in Francis's perfect poverty. In this first part, I simply want to engage in some creative anachronism by juxtaposing the poverty of St. Francis and the poverty of the other kind of poor, so as to get a broader sense of the implications of "holy poverty" as a spiritual discipline.

Of the four chapters that follow, the first three rely primarily on the early biographies of Francis, approaching the ironies in the Franciscan conception of poverty from three different points of departure. In the first, I explore Francis's interaction and identification with lepers, who, as the quintessential social outcasts of his time, provided him with an ideal model for rejecting the world. In the second, I treat the saint's choice of clothing, from his youth as the child of an affluent cloth merchant up to the point when he finally decided which costume made the most sense for his new life of poverty. In the third,

I consider Francis's own conception of poverty as a spiritual discipline in light of his interactions with people afflicted with poverty of the usual kind. The fourth chapter is also focused on Francis's fascination with poverty, but it moves beyond the realm of the biographies themselves to consider a contemporary allegory depicting the "marriage" between Francis and "Lady Poverty."

St. Francis and the Leper

Sometime in September 1226, only a few weeks before he died, a blind and bedridden Francis dictated his *Testament*, in which he recalled the circumstances that had led to his conversion some two decades before. "The Lord gave me, Brother Francis, to begin doing penance in this way: for when I was in sin, it seemed too bitter for me to see lepers. Then the Lord Himself led me among them and I showed mercy to them. And when I left them, what had seemed bitter to me before was turned into a sweetness of soul and body. Afterwards I delayed a little and left the world."[1] From Francis's perspective, in other words, his change of heart with regard to leprosy was the defining moment in his conversion process.

The earliest biographers understood the importance of leprosy in Francis's spiritual development and felt compelled to elaborate on the volte-face described in the *Testament*. In his *Life of St. Francis*, written less than two and a half years later, Thomas of Celano reported that "the sight of lepers was so bitter to [Francis] that in the days of his vanity when he saw their houses even two miles away, he would cover his nose with his hands." But after he had "started thinking of holy and useful matters . . . he met a leper one day. Made stronger than himself, he came up and kissed him." As a result, "he began to consider himself less and less, until by the mercy of the Redeemer, he came to complete victory over himself."[2] From that point on, "the holy lover of profound humility moved to the lepers and stayed with them. For God's sake he served all of them with great love. He washed all the filth from them, and even cleaned out the pus from their sores."[3] The version of the same story recorded in the *Legend of the Three Companions* has Francis on horseback when he meets the leper.[4] Dismounting, he gives the leper a coin and kisses his hand. "After a few days," the *Legend* tells us, "he moved to a hospice of lepers, taking with him a large sum of money. Calling them together, he gave them alms as he kissed the hand of each." When Thomas of Celano revisited this episode in his *Remembrance of the Desire of a Soul*, he borrowed details from the *Legend* but added one more twist: after kissing the leper and remounting his horse, Francis looks back only to find that the leper has disappeared.[5]

Francis was not the first Christian saint to kiss a leper. Martin of Tours (d. 397) did the same on one occasion as he was passing through the city gates of Paris.[6] Not surprisingly, given the popularity of the *Life of St. Martin*, we find the leper-kissing motif trickling down through Latin hagiography, with appearances, for instance, in the *Lives* of Sts. Radegund (d. 587), Robert the Pious (d. 1031), and Hugh of Lincoln (d. 1200).[7] But Francis seems to have been the first saint whose conversion to a religious life was actually occasioned by kissing a leper. What was it about that kiss that made it possible for Francis and his biographers to invest it with such spiritual significance?[8]

The "bitterness" that the sight of lepers evoked in Francis before his conversion was a reaction that he shared with his culture as a whole. It was not simply the horrifying symptoms associated with the disease that made medieval Christians like Francis shudder at the very thought of it.[9] At least as frightening as its physical characteristics were the moral implications that attended its contraction. For leprosy was, from a medieval Christian point of view, more than simply a disease of the body. It was a disease of the soul.[10]

Part of the association in the Christian mind between sin and leprosy was simply a product of an overly empirical conception of divine justice. To be afflicted with such a terrible malady one must have committed a truly heinous sin. Indeed there are some biblical cases of leprosy being used by God as a form of punishment. We read, for instance, that Miriam, the sister of Moses, became "leprous, white as snow," when she offended the Lord by claiming that she and Aaron were the equals of Moses in God's eyes.[11] Similarly Elisha's servant Gehazi was punished with leprosy for his greed in accepting the gifts of the Syrian Naaman, whom Elisha had just cured of the same disease.[12] Finally King Azariah of Judah was stricken with leprosy for failing to put an end to the illicit sacrifices of his people.[13] But such direct connections between sinfulness and leprosy are not the scriptural norm. More often than not, leprosy in the Bible is depicted simply as a kind of "uncleanness," requiring not moral rectification but ritual purification to remove it. This is certainly the case in Leviticus 13, the principal biblical source of information about the disease and its victims. It also applies to the accounts of leper healings in the Gospels.[14]

More significant than the Bible as a source of linkages between leprosy and sin are the writings of Christian moralists who, in their efforts to instill in their audiences a healthy fear of moral turpitude, held up leprosy as a metaphor for sinfulness.[15] Such exegetes described sinners as "moral lepers" whose souls were suffering from an invisible form of decay every bit as hideous, in its own way, as the visible effects of physical leprosy. The most detailed and graphic of these descriptions of moral leprosy is to be found in the second book of the *Peristephanon*, composed by the Latin poet Prudentius (d. c. 410). Here St. Lawrence, resisting the efforts of a pagan Roman prefect to subvert his devotion to Christ, criticizes the courtiers around him, who "though strong in body" were nonetheless "corrupted by an inner leprosy."

> Here is one who takes pride in his silk, puffed up as he goes about in his chariot, while inside a watery dropsy bloats him with its invisible poison. Here is another whose greed has left him with his hands bent back, his palms folded over, unable to relax his tendons. This one's fetid lust has dragged him into the company of whores, staining him with mud and filth as he begs for their foul and disgusting services. And that one, seething with ambition and burning in his thirst for honor, is he not panting with an inner fever and raging with fire in his veins? He who lacks the self-control to be silent, itching to betray secrets, is simply scratching at his passions and itching in his heart. What shall I say about the swelling of scrofulous tumors in their envy-filled breasts? What of the festering black-and-blue sores of their malice? . . . [If you could see these same ones in the next life,] you would see their bodies covered with rags, their noses full of mucus, their chins wet with saliva, their eyes half-blinded by matter.[16]

"There is nothing more foul than a sinner," concluded St. Lawrence, "nothing more leprous or putrid. The scars of his sins keep bleeding and they stink like the pit of hell."

That this close association between sin and leprosy was alive and well closer to Francis's own day is evidenced by Richard of St. Victor's (d. 1173) observation that there are many "within the very bosom of the church, whom the leprosy of vices has disfigured and whom the contagion of sin has stained, just like the leper." Richard's list of such moral lepers included, among others, fornicators, concubines, adulterers, avaricious people, usurers, false witnesses, and perjurers. All, in fact, who are "separated from God by their own fault, are judged to be leprous and are to be separated spiritually from the assembly of the faithful by priests who know and observe divine law."[17] The early Franciscan preacher Anthony of Padua (d. 1231) linked each of the ten different kinds of leprosy that he was able to identify in the Old Testament to a particular type of sin: hypocrisy, ambition, lust, graft and usury, envy, impurity of thought, open iniquity, disorder of life, abandonment of the Christian faith, and discord.[18] When Louis IX (d. 1270) observed that "there is no leprosy as ugly as the leprosy of being in mortal sin,"[19] he, like Richard and Anthony, was simply expressing a longstanding Christian predilection for using leprosy as a "visual aid" for Christians who had difficulty imagining the spiritually disfiguring effects of their own sins.

Technically speaking, of course, none of this had anything to do with people who actually suffered from physical leprosy. But to the extent that these didactic exercises reinforced popular associations between leprosy and sinfulness, they subtly contributed to and tended to reinforce the idea that physical leprosy was an external, visible punishment for sin.

Given the moral dimensions of the disease, it is hardly surprising that the mode of contact imagined most likely to transmit leprosy was sexual intercourse.[20] This ancient notion about leprosy was only reinforced by the Christian predilection for relegating most forms of sexual contact to the category of mortal sin.[21] The venereal nature of the disease evolved in the Christian mind to the point where its victims were actually regarded as suffering from insatiable sexual appetites, further reinforcing the moral dimensions of the disease. It was as if lepers had already been consigned to a preliminary form of hell, forced to endure a punishment that caricatured the very sins that would ultimately lead them there.

Attitudes such as these explain why, from the moment a person was diagnosed as having leprosy, he or she was immediately removed from normal social intercourse and either confined to a leprosarium (if the leper had the means to pay for admittance into one) or simply escorted out of town. From a legal perspective, these people were not simply outcasts. They were considered already to have died.[22] From a social perspective, such a life bereft of normal interpersonal contact would have seemed to many to have been a fate worse than death, particularly for people—like the nobles and burghers of a city like Assisi—whose standing in their communities was built on such interaction.

This litany of negative images associated with the disease was partially offset by the traditional identification of Job and Lazarus as lepers. "Afflicted with loathsome sores from the sole of his foot to the crown of his head," Job provided an important counterexample of a man struck with leprosy despite an unblemished relationship with God.[23] Likewise Lazarus, who ended his life as "a poor man full of sores," nevertheless found himself elevated to the bosom of Abraham.[24] Job's explicit resignation to his fate and Lazarus's implicit one[25] suggested to some that, for all its physical horror, leprosy could be seen as a valuable lesson, even a gift from God, designed to drive home the importance of setting one's sights on the next world rather than on this one.

Beyond Job and Lazarus as models of sinless leprosy, medieval exegetes sometimes depicted Christ himself as a leper, in an effort to underscore his chosen earthly status as an outcast. Jerome fostered this association by his choice of language when he translated Isaiah 53:3–4 into Latin: "Truly [the Messiah] has borne our infirmities and carried our sorrows: and we have thought him as it were a leper, as one struck by God and humiliated."[26] Hagiographers of the thirteenth century were aware of and comfortable with this notion. In his *Dialogue of Miracles*, written about 1223, Caesarius of Heisterbach told of a holy bishop who ministered to a leper, only to find that he was in fact assisting Christ in disguise.[27] As already mentioned, Thomas of Celano hinted at the same association when, in the *Remembrance*, he had the leper vanish after Francis's fateful kiss. Bonaventure, who borrowed the "disappearing leper" episode for his *Major Legend*, made the identification with Christ explicit by adding that Francis, who had never been able to stand the sight of lepers, ultimately tended to them "because of Christ crucified, who according to the text of the prophet appeared despised as a leper."[28]

This sketch of medieval Christian ideas about leprosy allows an appreciation of the impact of Francis's kiss at a number of different levels. First of all, the leper served as a symbolic antithesis to the lifestyle that was Francis's birthright as the son of a prosperous merchant. By embracing the leper, Francis was quite literally embracing the life of the quintessential social outcast, demonstrating to his peer group that he placed no value whatsoever on the things that were important to them—the things that used to be even more important to him. For, as Thomas of Celano observed, before his conversion Francis had distinguished himself precisely in the zeal with which he pursued such "vanities." "He was an object of admiration to all, and he endeavored to surpass others in his flamboyant display of vain accomplishments: wit, curiosity, practical jokes and foolish talk, songs, and soft and flowing garments."[29] If Francis, in his youth, had made a point of "surpassing" his peers in conspicuous consumption and studied frivolity, it made sense that his conversion should entail the adoption of an equally extreme yet absolutely opposite lifestyle.

Second, the leper's rotting body served as a metaphor for the state of Francis's own soul prior to his conversion. Thus when Francis embraced the leper, he not only embraced an alternative, oppositional lifestyle; he also made manifest his own profound realization that his soul, infected by the worldly life that he had led as a youth, was as leprous as the body of the one he kissed. As Thomas observed early in his account of Francis's conversion process, Francis "could no longer delay, for by then a fatal disease had spread everywhere and infected the limbs of so many that, were the doctor to delay just a little, it would stifle breath and snatch life away."[30] So we find Francis taking the moralists at their word and deciding that it was in fact he, with his leprous soul, who really deserved to be ostracized.[31]

Finally Francis's embrace of the leper allowed him to dramatize his rejection of the corrupt world that had been prepared for him in a way that highlighted his own identification with Jesus, whose very Incarnation could be seen, with the help of Jerome's translation, as a form of leprosy.

But what about the leper in all of this? What did the leper get out of his contact with Francis? According to the *Testament*, he was the beneficiary of unspecified acts of mercy. In the *Life of St. Francis*, he had the matter washed from his sores and received a kiss. In the *Legend of the Three Companions*, the kiss came with a coin. In none of the accounts, however, do we hear of the leper being healed. Francis's kiss did not have the thaumaturgical effect of Martin's, which, according to his biographer, resulted in the leper at the gates of Paris being "instantly cleansed."[32] Why not? One explanation is that Francis, at the time he met the leper, had only just begun to "leave the world" and had not yet developed the power to heal. For indeed later in his life, and particularly after his death, Francis would prove himself quite capable of healing any number of different maladies, including leprosy.[33] But beyond this basic question of capability it is important to realize that, from a narrative perspective, the point of Francis's initial encounter with the leper was not to provide an occasion for the exercise of supernatural power. Nor was it to counsel the leper on how he might turn his physical affliction into a spiritual advantage by reminding him of Job and Lazarus. The point was for Francis to demonstrate a healthy disdain for the things of the world that were his birth-right by acknowledging his own kind of "leprosy" and willingly assuming the life of a leper. If anyone was to be "healed" by the kiss, in other words, it was not to be the leper. It was to be Francis, whose sudden recognition that his soul was leprous was, as the *Testament* reveals, absolutely pivotal to his spiritual transformation.[34]

Opting for the company of physical lepers over the company of the moral lepers that had been his companions up to that point in his life gave Francis an enormous amount of moral clout among his peers. By interpreting his own previous lifestyle as a kind of leprosy and driving home the point by associating with physical lepers as if they were somehow safer companions, Francis struck a chord that resonated with the members of his social class. A handful of them responded to the guilt that Francis's example ignited in them by becoming "lepers" themselves. Others, less certain about how to deal with the spiritual choices that Francis seemed to be laying before them, applauded his efforts from a safe distance and supported him and his followers with their donations. It is ironic that Francis should have garnered such respect for living a life that was, at face value, indistinguishable from the life of a leper, a life for which people in Francis's day would normally have felt nothing but repugnance. The secret to this is that Francis did not actually become a leper. He simply decided to act like one. More precisely, he dramatically and voluntarily appropriated the trappings of *physical* leprosy (by living on the edges of society, dressing in dirty clothes, and begging for his food) in order to make his rejection and criticism of *moral* leprosy more obvious and pointed. The simple fact that Francis *chose* to live as a leper, rather than being forced to live like one, made him as attractive to his guilty Christian audience as the leper that he kissed was repugnant. Ironically then, the power that ensued from Francis's voluntarily assumed leprosy was a power that ultimately owed its very existence to the prevailing image of the leper in that society,[35] yet it was a power to which no real leper, whose lifestyle was not a matter of personal choice, ever had access.[36]

Getting back to the question at hand—what did the leper get out of his contact with Francis?—the answer is: precious little, especially when one considers the enormous spiritual and social benefits that Francis took away from the encounter.[37] We can actually push this lack of reciprocity a bit further. For if we consider how popular Francis and his followers were to become as a focus of pious donations on the part of guilty burghers,[38] we might even begin to imagine some resentment brewing on the part of the leper. By letting himself be kissed by Francis, the leper was, in effect, participating in the creation of a "superleper" with whom he would henceforth have a very difficult time competing for the limited resources available to the collective beggars of Assisi.[39] For if giving food to a normal leper was considered spiritually beneficial on the grounds that God had a special place in his heart for the downtrodden, giving food to Francis the "superleper" amounted to an investment in the making of a saint who could potentially exercise great powers of intercession on behalf of his benefactors.

The idea that Francis and the Franciscan order that he created diverted charitable resources from actual victims of physical leprosy to the well-born sons of Italian merchants who *chose* to live like lepers is not well represented in the vast literature that the saint has inspired. Somehow the image of Francis giving up his life of privilege and embracing the life of a social outcast has never lost its romantic appeal. But there is a dark side to this kind of religiosity. For when Francis and his imitators interacted with lepers they did so primarily for the spiritual benefits to which they could lay claim for having voluntarily abandoned the world. They did not do so to relieve the pain and suffering, whether here or in the next world, of people who had no choice but to live the very life that Francis voluntarily assumed.

St. Francis and His Tunic

Francis was born the son of a cloth merchant. This is reflected clearly in Thomas of Celano's life of the saint, the first part of which is interwoven, one might say, with references to cloth and clothing. I have already mentioned how the young Francis strove to outdo his peers in "soft and flowing garments."[1] There are many other such examples to choose from. When Francis, on the eve of joining a military expedition to Apulia, experienced a vision in which his house seemed to be full of weapons, it struck him as odd precisely because "he was not accustomed to see such things in his house, but rather stacks of cloth to be sold."[2] Later when he began to realize that he could no longer in good conscience follow the career path his father, Pietro Bernardone, had laid out for him, the first thing Francis did was to sell cloth in Foligno and try to get a poor priest of the church of San Damiano to accept the money as a donation.[3] And finally, when his father disowned him, demanding that he "renounce . . . all rights of inheritance and return everything that he had," Francis complied by dramatically stripping off his clothes and giving them back to him.[4]

The role of cloth and clothing in Francis's conversion is multilayered. For one thing, cloth, then as now, represented status: the "soft and flowing garments" that Francis wore as a young man distinguished him as a member of the dominant merchant class. It even, as Thomas suggests, provided him with a means of distinguishing himself *within* his peer group, as long as his clothes were *more* soft and *more* flowing than those of his neighbors.[5] But for Francis cloth also represented his patrimony: he was expected to follow in his father's footsteps and engage in the trade of cloth as his life's work. So when Francis stripped himself, he was not only removing the clothes that set him apart as a man "of the world" but also cutting his ties to his father and abandoning the economic niche that was being prepared for him.

Francis's intimate relationship with cloth and clothing did not end with his conversion. Despite the fact that "he who once enjoyed wearing scarlet robes now traveled about half-clothed," Francis remained highly self-conscious about his attire.[6] Thanks to Thomas of Celano's attentiveness to every detail of Francis's extended conversion process, we actually have a better idea of what Francis wore after leaving the world than we do of his previous wardrobe. So we read in the *Life of St. Francis* that while the saint worked as a servant in a monastery he was "covered with only a cheap shirt."[7] Later he made his way north to Gubbio, "where he obtained a cheap tunic from an old friend."[8]

Just as the fancy clothes that Francis had worn in his previous life symbolized his elevated position in the social hierarchy of Assisi, so the poor, hand-me-down clothes that he donned after his conversion made a clear statement about his identification with the lowest social strata. As Thomas put it, "the father of the poor, the poor Francis, conformed himself to the poor in all things."[9] And that conformity to the poor expressed itself most obviously in his choice of attire. Many were initially confused by Francis's new look: "When all those who knew him saw him, they compared his latest circumstances with his former and they began to reproach him harshly. Shouting that he was insane and out of his mind, they threw mud from the streets and stones at him."[10] But, according to Thomas, their attitudes soon changed, and Francis was accorded the respect due to someone who with sound mind had voluntarily left this world to seek entrance into the other one.

Francis did not settle on one particular type of costume for his new life until he began restoring the ramshackle church at the Portiuncula. At that time, according to Thomas, Francis "wore a sort of hermit's habit with a leather belt. He carried a staff in his hands and wore shoes."[11] But one day in church, while Francis was listening to the gospel lesson for the day, he realized that Christ had specifically instructed his disciples to "take no gold, or silver, or copper in your belts, no bag for your journey, or two tunics, or sandals, or a staff."[12] Propelled by his feverish quest to imitate Christ and the apostles—as Thomas put it, "his highest aim, foremost desire, and greatest intention was to pay heed to the holy gospel in all things and through all things"[13]—Francis "immediately took off the shoes from his feet, put down the staff from his hands, and, satisfied with one tunic, exchanged his leather belt for a cord."[14] But, oddly enough, Francis did not stop there. Instead he set out to fashion for himself a special kind of robe. In the words of Thomas of Celano, Francis "made for himself a tunic in the shape of the cross, so that in it he would drive off every fantasy of the demons. He made it very rough, so that in it he might crucify the flesh with its vices and sins. He made it very poor and plain, a thing that the world would never covet."[15]

The level of self-consciousness and deliberation that the spiritually regenerated Francis came to exercise in his choice of clothing is striking. Initially it was enough for him simply to cast off the fine garments that he, as a merchant's son, had been expected to wear. But as his amorphous conversion began to coalesce and take its distinctive shape, he became as attentive to the

"style" of his new outfit as he had been to the old one that he had relinquished
to his father. In his effort to fashion a deliberately unattractive, uncomfortable,
cross-shaped tunic, Francis drew on his experience as a cloth merchant. After
all, Francis knew fabric. Just as he knew which materials to choose in order
to make garments that were "soft and flowing," so he knew which ones would
"crucify the flesh" with their roughness.[16] Just as he knew which fabrics would
allow him to "advance beyond all his peers in vanities,"[17] so he knew which
ones "the world would never covet."[18]

If by producing this "custom-made" tunic, Francis distinguished himself
from the apostles who had received no specific instructions as to how their
tunics were to be constructed, he also distinguished himself from the poor
people around him. For though it was Francis's expressed intention, in his
effort to distance himself from the lifestyle that had once been his own, to
"conform himself to the poor in all things,"[19] his decision to design a tunic
that would "out-rough" and "out-humble" every tunic in Assisi set his poverty
apart from the poverty around him.[20] For we must imagine that most poor
people, then as now, regularly wore the best of the poor clothes that they could
find. If they did exchange one garment for another, they did so with an eye to
maximizing warmth or comfort. The competitive "downscaling" of Francis's
wardrobe would have struck a chord only with those beggars who deliberately
paraded their worst rags in the hopes of attracting more sympathy from would-
be almsgivers. It was this subset of "the poor"—that is, those who exaggerated
and publicized their poverty in order to maximize their personal gain—that
Francis actually "conformed" himself to. Accustomed as Francis had been as
a young man to "surpass others" in his choice of wardrobe, he seems to have
taken to this new form of sartorial competition quite naturally.[21]

The ultimate irony in all of this is that every effort on Francis's part to create
a tunic "that the world would never covet" was doomed to failure. For the
more unattractive the garment was from an aesthetic standpoint, the more
attractive it became from a religious standpoint. Thomas is very clear about
this. When Francis preached, his listeners, "driven by great faith, often tore
his habit until sometimes he was left almost naked."[22] What did they do with
the pieces that they tore off of his ugly tunic? They kept them as precious
relics.[23] Certainly the "soft and flowing garments" of Francis's youth had never
been coveted more.

3

St. Francis and His Poverty

As the son of a prosperous merchant, Francis, *il Poverello*,[1] grew up surrounded not only by "stacks of cloth to be sold" but by all the amenities that
people of his rank enjoyed. Knowing this, it comes as no surprise that at the
heart of Francis's conversion we find a complete renunciation of the trappings
and values associated with the merchant class, a renunciation that Thomas,
in the *Life of St. Francis*, chose to frame in terms of a bitter struggle between
a father who was motivated by greed and a son who was not. So when Francis,
on the eve of his conversion, sold some cloth at nearby Foligno and then tried
to give the money to the poor priest at San Damiano, his father "raged" against
him in an effort to get his money back. His "thirsty greed" was quenched only
by the discovery that his money had never been spent.[2] In stark contrast,
Francis is depicted as "one who did not love money."[3] In fact, the moment
that he sold the cloth, Francis began to feel "the heavy weight of carrying
that money even for an hour." For him it simply had no value: it was like
sand or dust or dung.[4]

Francis, Thomas informs us, was searching for a different kind of wealth.
Faithful to Proverbs 16:16, "he wanted to possess that wisdom that is better
than gold and to acquire that prudence that is more precious than silver."[5] In
order to gain access to this spiritual treasure, Francis rejected the worldly riches
that constituted his patrimony and deliberately embraced poverty. He
encouraged his followers to do the same. The *Life of St. Francis* describes
how, on the way back from his famous audience with Pope Innocent III,
Francis and his brothers stopped for a time in a deserted part of the Spoleto
Valley, where, as Thomas put it, they "began to have commerce with holy
poverty."

> Greatly consoled in their lack of all things of the world, they resolved to ad-
> here to the way they were in that place always and everywhere. Only divine

consolation delighted them, having put aside all their cares about earthly things. They decided and resolved that even if buffeted by tribulations and driven by temptations, they would not withdraw from its embrace.[6]

The poverty with which Francis and his followers "began to have commerce" certainly looked a lot like the poverty that afflicted the less-than-fortunate inhabitants of Assisi. This was no accident. For, as the *Life of St. Francis* informs us in no uncertain terms, Francis "conformed himself to the poor in all things."[7] Modeling his new life on the lives of the destitute, Francis made certain that he owned nothing, wore only the simplest of clothes, and begged for his food. Some of the deliberation of this process is captured in the *Legend of the Three Companions*. According to this source, while Francis was repairing the church of San Damiano, he began to reflect on the fact that he was relying on a local priest to provide him with his food. "This is not the life of the poor that you have chosen," he told himself. "Like a beggar, going from door to door, you should carry a bowl in your hand and, driven by necessity, you should collect the scraps they give you." As in the case of his first close encounter with a leper, this proved easier said than done: "When he tried to eat the mixed food offered him, he felt revulsion because he was unaccustomed not only to eating such things, but even to looking at them. At last overcoming himself, he began to eat, and it seemed to him that no delicacy had ever tasted so delicious."[8]

Francis seems to have been satisfied that his poverty was authentic— authentic enough to make him and his followers eligible for alms, "a legacy and a justice due to the poor that our Lord Jesus Christ acquired for us."[9] Similarities in appearance, however, could never fully mask the fundamental differences that set Francis's poverty apart from the poverty of the poor.[10] For one thing, Francis had assumed his poverty *voluntarily* in an effort to protect himself from the corruption that he felt certain came with wealth. The same can be said about his earliest disciples. Brother Bernard of Quintavalle, the wealthiest of Francis's original followers, signaled his own conversion by selling all that he had and giving it to the poor, thus fulfilling the "counsel of the holy Gospel: 'If you wish to be perfect, go and sell all that you own, and give to the poor.'"[11] Thomas went on to observe that Bernard's "conversion to God stood out as a model for those being converted in the way he sold his possessions and distributed them to the poor." Indeed the *Earlier Rule* would mandate that all prospective friars do just that.[12] Yet for this kind of voluntary renunciation of one's property to have become obligatory, the typical follower would have had to have been a person of at least some means; someone, in other words, who was in a position to *choose* to live a life of poverty. As peculiar as it may seem, it is not at all clear whether someone who was already poor, who had nothing to sacrifice in order to become poor, would have been able to meet the minimum requirements for entrance into the new order.

Francis's poverty was distinctive in other ways. The willfulness of his desire to live the poorest possible life led Francis to deliberately push his poverty to extremes that no ordinary poor person would ever have entertained. I have already shown how Francis went out of his way to design a tunic that would be less comfortable and less attractive than any garment worn by any other poor person. He applied the same principle to his eating habits. In the *Life of St. Francis* we learn that Francis rarely allowed himself the pleasure of eating cooked foods, and when he did "he would sprinkle them with ashes or dampen the flavor of the spices with cold water."[13] One day when Francis was feeling ill, he allowed himself the luxury of eating a bit of chicken, only to feel so guilty that he ordered a brother "to tie a cord around his neck and drag him through the whole city as if he were a thief, loudly crying out: 'Look! See this glutton who grew fat on the flesh of chickens that he ate without your knowledge.'"[14]

Moreover, Francis's poverty is depicted as a poverty without the cares or concerns that one would normally associate with authentic destitution. For one thing, Francis and his followers found that their physical needs were always met as long as they avoided the temptation to be distracted by any *concern* about their physical needs. Hence the numerous instances in which a hungry or thirsty Francis suddenly found himself to be the beneficiary of some unexpected, timely act of charity.[15] Second, the early Franciscans were so focused on their quest for spiritual satisfaction that any physical deprivation that they might suffer in the process seemed insignificant by comparison. "As followers of most holy poverty, since they had nothing, they loved nothing; so they feared losing nothing. . . . So they were safe wherever they went. Disturbed by no fears, distracted by no cares, they awaited the next day without any worry."[16] This was so because "only divine consolation delighted them, having put aside all their cares about earthly things."[17] Francis's ability to see the connection between self-denial in this life and salvation in the next was the key. It made it possible for him not only to accept poverty but to embrace it. When asked how he could survive the cold of winter wearing nothing but a thin tunic, he responded: "touched within by the flame of desire for our heavenly home, we easily endure that exterior cold."[18] "The "care-less-ness" of this kind of poverty only makes sense when juxtaposed to the "care-full-ness" of the lives of wealth and influence that the original Franciscans left behind. Again Francis's poverty comes across as a spiritually therapeutic exercise designed for men of means. Poor people, born as they were into their poverty, were simply incapable of imagining the spiritual "hardships" that came from having possessions and thus were not in a position to appreciate the relief that ensued from shedding them.

Finally the poverty of Francis and his followers was a poverty that they had to work hard to maintain.[19] During their stay in the Spoleto Valley they "resolved [that] . . . they would not withdraw from [poverty's] embrace." Why was this resolution necessary? For one thing, these original Franciscans were accustomed to a very different lifestyle, a lifestyle to which any one of them might decide to return at any moment.[20] For even though they had been obliged to renounce their personal property when they joined Francis, they presumably still had their families and their social networks to help get them back on their feet, should they ever decide to resume the roles in the world that they had left behind. Moreover, the growing popularity of Francis and his followers meant that they soon became a preferred focus for charitable giving on the part of their former peer group. The more such attention they attracted, the more they had to resist the temptation to accept more than they really needed to get by for another day. Hence the resolutions to fortify their collective intention to remain poor.

The wording of the *Rule* itself reflects a form of poverty in need of protection from the ever-present threat of compromise. "The rule and life of these brothers is this," legislated the version promulgated in 1221: "to live in obedience, in chastity and without anything of their own."[21] "Let all the brothers wear poor clothes and, with the blessing of God, they can patch them with sackcloth and other pieces."[22] "Let all the brothers strive to follow the humility and poverty of our Lord Jesus Christ and let them remember that we should have nothing else in the whole world except, as the Apostle says: 'having food and clothing, we are content with these.' They must rejoice when they live among people considered of little value and looked down upon, among the poor and powerless, the sick and the lepers, and the beggars by the wayside."[23] That the brothers had to be told to wear poor clothes, avoid possessions, and relish the opportunity to interact with social outcasts testifies to the challenges that they faced in staying poor.

The difficulties that the earliest followers of Francis encountered in their attempts to maintain their poverty and humility as an order were nothing, however, compared to the challenges that Francis himself faced as someone who, long before his death, had already been recognized as a saint. Francis was the focus of immense popularity in his own lifetime. Thomas of Celano tells us that "men and women ran, clerics hurried, and the religious rushed to see and hear the holy one of God, who seemed to everyone a person of another age."[24] "When he entered a city, clergy rejoiced, bells rang, men exulted, women rejoiced, and children clapped."[25] This level of public adulation was not, we are told, something that Francis welcomed.[26] On the contrary, he regularly shrank from it, fearful of the pride that such attention could engender. "He strove to hide the good things of the Lord in the secrecy of his heart, not wanting to display for his own glory what could be the cause of ruin."[27] Hence Francis's attempts to maintain his holy equilibrium by constantly reminding himself how unworthy he really was. While "he was honored by all and merited high marks from everyone," observed Thomas, "he alone considered himself vile and was the only one to despise himself fervently."[28] "Since he was the most perfect among the perfect, he refused to think he was perfect and thought himself wholly imperfect."[29] "I must believe," said the Francis of the *Assisi Compilation*, "that if the Lord had granted a thief and even a non-believer as many gifts as he has given me, they would be more faithful to the Lord than I."[30] On more than one occasion, Francis publicly abased himself for having relaxed his harsh regimen, even when his own poor health demanded it. "You come to me with great devotion and believe me to be a holy man," he once told his audience, "but I confess to you that during Lent in that hermitage, I ate food flavored with lard."[31] Francis's logic is transparent in the *Assisi Compilation*: "I want to live before God, in hermitages and other places where I stay, just as the people see and know me. If they believe that I am a holy man and I do not lead a life becoming a holy man, I am a hypocrite."[32] In the same spirit of studied humility, Francis went out of his way to conceal his stigmata by wearing heavy socks and by rarely washing his hands and feet, thus "inflicting everlasting anathema on human favor."[33] Indeed, in his desire to insulate himself from pride, Francis went so far as to seek out—even to fabricate—the kind of abuse that he had "enjoyed" when he first made his decision to leave the world.[34] Thomas tells us that Francis

> would call one of his brothers to him, saying, "I command you under obedience to insult me harshly and speak the truth against their lies." When the brother, though unwilling, called him a boor and a useless hired hand, Francis would smile and clap loudly, saying: "May the Lord bless you, for you are really telling the truth; that is what the son of Pietro Bernardone needs to hear."[35]

In short, it required a considerable amount of effort on Francis's part to maintain the kind of poverty and humility that he had set out to embrace. Only for a brief time, when the people of Assisi thought he was crazy and greeted him with mud and stones, did Francis's poverty come even close to resembling the poverty of the poor in this regard. In no time he was reduced to manufacturing the kind of popular disdain that, for him, was a key ingredient of his rejection of the world.[36] Needless to say, no truly poor person ever had to work this hard to earn the disdain of his community.[37]

What, then, aside from a superficial similarity in appearance, did Francis's holy poverty have to do with regular, everyday, garden-variety poverty? Did the *poor* poor of Assisi benefit in any way from this voluntary assumption of poverty on the part of Francis and the other *rich* poor who followed his lead? In some ways they did. The *Life of St. Francis* tells us that part of Francis's conversion experience involved shedding his deep-rooted, merchant-class disdain for the poor: "One day, contrary to his custom (since he was very polite), he rebuked a poor person seeking alms from him [in the name of God], and he was immediately led to penance. He began to say to himself that to refuse what was asked of him by someone begging in the name of such a great King would be a shame and a disgrace."[38] Henceforth, as Thomas observed, Francis became most diligent about giving to the needy; at least, that is, until his conversion was complete. For after Francis left the world, he had nothing left to give to the poor; nothing, that is, except his own weak shoulders, which he would offer from time to time when he saw a poor person "burdened with wood or other heavy loads."[39] From Thomas's perspective, it was the thought that counted: "Francis's soul melted for the poor," he explained, "and to those to whom he could not extend a hand, he extended his affection."[40]

According to Thomas, that "most wealthy poor man"[41] Francis was himself aware of this dilemma and tried to remedy it by asking the "rich people of this world . . . to loan him their cloaks or furs" so that he could in turn give them to the poor people whom he met.[42] But these poor people, as fortunate as they might have been to run into Francis right after Francis had run into a rich person, must have wondered what it was about Francis's poverty that commanded this level of charitable response when their own plight so often went ignored by the rich people whom they encountered. So even when Francis *was* in a position to give alms to the poor, he could only do so after he had inadvertently *competed* with the same poor for the charity of the rich, charity that he had more of a claim to, from the perspective of the donors, because his poverty was more "holy" than the poverty of ordinary beggars.[43]

But there is more to the irony of Francis's poverty than this. His personal commitment to protecting his poverty at all cost not only meant that he had nothing of his own to give to the poor. It also meant that any act of charity on the part of a friar, regardless of its success in alleviating the poverty of its beneficiary, could potentially be seen as a dangerous compromise of his personal commitment to perfection through self-deprivation.[44] We see a hint of this attitude early on in Thomas's account of the saint's conversion, in reference to the money that Francis made on the sale of his father's cloth in Foligno. His first thought was to use the money to feed the poor and repair the dilapidated church of San Damiano, "but he who did not love money could not be deceived even by the appearance of good."[45] Two anecdotes from the *Remembrance* make this same point more directly. The first describes a friar, "deceived by false piety," who picked up a coin in the road and gave it to some lepers, only to be struck dumb, unable to speak until he had repented for this violation of the Franciscan *Rule*.[46] The second recounts what happened when Francis and a brother found a money belt lying on a road near Bari. The brother felt strongly that they should remove the money from the purse and donate it to the poor. But Francis "flatly refused to do it," saying "it was a trick of the devil." The brother reached down to pick up the purse anyway, but when he opened it, he found that it contained not money but a serpent. Francis gently admonished him: "Brother, to God's servants money is nothing but a devil and a poisonous snake."[47] Attitudes of this type theoretically prevented the Franciscans from involving themselves to any significant degree in poor relief, at least when it involved money. The *Earlier Rule* made this very clear:

> Let the brothers in no way receive, arrange to receive, seek, or arrange to seek money for leper colonies or coins for any house or place, and let them not accompany anyone begging money or coins for such places. However, the brothers can perform for those places other services not contrary to our life with the blessing of God. The brothers can beg alms for a manifest need of the lepers. But let them beware of money.[48]

In short, Francis would not let any form of material accumulation interfere with his pursuit of holy poverty, even if the goal of such accumulation was poor relief.

Nor was it, for Francis, simply a matter of staying away from money. He was equally wary of the potentially dangerous feelings of self-satisfaction that acts of charity often generated.[49] Once he met a poor old woman in Assisi and, for lack of anything else to give her, parted with his mantle. "But then," according to Thomas, Francis "felt an impulse of empty congratulations, and at once he confessed before everyone that he felt vainglory."[50] "Ah," lamented Thomas, "vanity inspires us more than charity; and the world's approval prevails over the love of Christ."[51]

Indeed Francis's frenetic concern with perfecting his own poverty and humility meant that as often as not his first reaction upon seeing a poor person was not so much one of compassion as one of comparison, or even competition. For "though he had laid aside all envy, he could not be without envy of poverty. If indeed he saw someone poorer than himself, he was immediately envious.[52] In the struggle for complete poverty he was afraid to be outdone by anyone else."[53] In the *Remembrance* Thomas relates how one day Francis, en route to a sermon, happened upon an extremely poor man. "Seeing the man's nakedness, he was deeply moved," not by the plight of this unfortunate man but by the fact that he had found a man poorer than himself! As the saint explained to his companion:

> "This man's need brings great shame on us. It passes a harsh judgement on our poverty." "How so, brother?" his companion replied. The saint answered in a sad voice: "I chose poverty for my riches and for my Lady, but look: She shines brighter in this man. Don't you know that the whole world has heard that we are the poorest of all for Christ? But this poor man proves us otherwise!"[54]

In short, the poverty that Francis encountered in the world around him was not something that he chose to combat. Instead it was something he chose to emulate and even to exaggerate for the sake of the spiritual benefits that it offered to him and to other people who were not born poor.

The point is not that Francis and his friars were never charitable toward the poor. The point is that charitable distribution was clearly ancillary to the Franciscan spiritual program, a program that put much more emphasis on the virtue that followed from *acting* poor than on the virtue that came from relieving the poverty of others.[55] It comes as no surprise, then, to find the spiritually mature Francis more concerned with seeking alms than with distributing them. From the perspective of the typical burgher, begging for food would have been one of the most humiliating experiences imaginable, making it, from the Franciscan point of view, a natural first step toward spiritual regeneration.[56] The Francis of the *Remembrance* urged his brothers to overcome their bashfulness in this regard, convinced that "being ashamed to beg was an enemy of salvation."[57] As far as Francis was concerned, it was precisely the humiliation of begging door-to-door that invested alms with their spiritual, as opposed to their material, significance. Donations that were given to the brothers spontaneously without them ever having to ask could not have the same therapeutic effect.[58] Whenever Francis felt that the friars were letting their pride get in the way of their begging, he would remind them about Jesus: "the Son of God was more noble than we are, and yet for our sake he made himself poor in this world. For love of him we have chosen the way of poverty. So we should not be ashamed to go for alms."[59] Francis would sometimes appeal to their mercantile minds by suggesting that when they begged, they were not so much asking for handouts as offering to exchange powerful blessings in return for bits of food. "You ought to go begging more willingly and with more joyful hearts than someone who is offering a hundred silver pieces in exchange for a single penny, since you are offering the love of God to those from whom you seek alms."[60] On other occasions he would point out that begging on the part of the friars served an important function as a test for prospective benefactors to see whether, in accordance with Matthew 25, they would be counted among the sheep on Judgment Day: "as you did it to the least of these my brothers, you did it to me."[61] Here Thomas of Celano goes so far as to equate the *fratres minimi* ("least brothers") of Matthew 25 with the *fratres minores* ("lesser brothers" or "friars minor") themselves. Thus Francis exhorts the friars: "Go, for in this last hour the Lesser Brothers have been given to the world so that the elect might carry out for them what the divine Judge will praise: What you did for one of my lesser brothers, you did for me."[62] The original Franciscans, then, were encouraged to seek alms as an exercise in their own humiliation, while people of means were encouraged to give alms to the Franciscans to make certain that they pass the test on Judgment Day. Where—getting back to my main point—did the involuntary poor figure into this self-contained spiritual economy? The earliest biographers of Francis did not say.

If Francis and his followers, concerned as they were about their own poverty, had little to offer the other poor in the way of material assistance, did they at least hold out some hope to them in the spiritual realm?[63] It might seem so, given the fact that Francis placed such a high premium on poverty as the first step toward spiritual regeneration. Seeing Francis dressed in a coarse and soiled tunic, begging for his food, the poor might have been led to believe that they were doing something right, spiritually speaking, at least insofar as they were living lives unburdened by the kinds of material attachments that made salvation so difficult for the rich. But once again it is important to emphasize that the kind of poverty that Francis endorsed was very different from the kind that afflicted the urban poor in thirteenth-century Assisi. Francis's poverty required deliberate renunciation of all material ties, because only such a willful divestment from this world could serve to verify the quality of one's commitment to the next world. People who were poor because of circumstances beyond their own control were not in a position to demonstrate that they held the world in proper disdain, because they had nothing to give up to prove it. The logical conclusion of this kind of reasoning, a reasoning that gave great status to those whose poverty was self-induced, was to disenfranchise, spiritually speaking, the poor who had not chosen to be poor— who were, in fact, prevented from choosing to be poor by the simple fact that they already were poor. To distinguish between ordinary poverty and holy poverty in this way was effectively to translate the class distinctions that separated the rich from the poor in this world to the other world.[64] "The Lord is pleased by poverty," noted Francis in the *Remembrance*, "and especially when one *freely chooses* to go begging."[65]

The early Franciscan sources never actually come out and say that the involuntary poor have little to hope for in the way of otherworldly rewards. But there are a number of instances in which it is implied that the ordinary poor are too preoccupied with the satisfaction of their physical needs to be sufficiently attentive to their spiritual ones. In the *Legend of the Three Companions* we find a poor man making his way to the Portiuncula asking for alms and being given "a cloak . . . that a brother had worn while in the world."[66] The practitioner of Francis's brand of poverty, in other words, rejected the cloak as an obstruction to the attainment of his spiritual goals, while the other kind of poor man accepted it in fulfillment of his material desires. In the *Assisi Compilation* we find Francis donating his mantle to a poor man. "I'm giving you this cloak," said Francis, "for the love of the Son of God, but on the condition that you do not hand it over to anyone unless they pay well for it."[67] In effect, Francis's single-minded concern that the poor man benefit materially from the gift of the cloak effectively precluded the poor man reaping the spiritual rewards that would come from donating the mantle to an even needier person.

Other anecdotes in the earliest lives of Francis subtly underscore the separation between holy poverty and the other kind of poverty, simply by illustrating that ordinary poor people are more than capable of being bad people.[68] In the *Remembrance* Thomas of Celano recounts how Francis, obliged to comply with a wealthy host's request to join him at a fine banquet, shared his sumptuous meal with a beggar, only to have the beggar denounce him the next day as a hypocrite. But the moment that the man produced— as evidence of Francis's culinary hypocrisy—the piece of a capon that the saint had given him, the meat miraculously turned into a fish, testifying to the purity of Francis's intentions, if not his palate.[69] Despite the fact, then, that the scene opens with Francis alleviating the poverty of a poor man, the effect of the story is to contrast Francis's brand of poverty with its "unholy" counterpart.

In the *Assisi Compilation* Francis comes across a poor man and feels pity for him, only to have a brother point out that while it may be true "that he is poor . . . perhaps there is no one in the whole province who *desires* riches more."[70] Francis immediately rebuked the brother, but not, interestingly enough, because he disagreed with this evaluation of the poor man. Francis was well aware that this kind of poverty, a poverty of circumstance rather than choice, was no guarantee of spiritual merit. Francis's point was simply that the proper Franciscan attitude toward a poor person was to see in his face the image of Christ and to act accordingly, without inquiring about the state of the poor man's soul. Again the anecdote does not explicitly deride the poverty of the poor, but by focusing attention on the attitude of the friar rather than on the moral status of the poor man, the idea that poor people are *worthy* of the pity that they should elicit from any true Franciscan is effectively eroded.[71]

In an episode recounted in the *Remembrance*, Francis retired to a cell on a cliff near Greccio, a town that he particularly appreciated, insofar as it was "rich in poverty."[72] Over the course of his time there, he discovered that Greccio was being afflicted by devastating hail storms and attacks by wolves. So he instructed the citizens to confess their sins, and once they had done so the storms and attacks suddenly stopped. But unfortunately the newfound physical security of the people of Greccio spawned more serious spiritual threats to the community. "Prosperity had its usual effect," observed Thomas. "They fell back to ways worse than before, forgetting the God who had saved them."[73] So on the one hand we find Francis attracted to the town in the first place because its poverty served to inspire his own poverty, but on the other hand, Greccio's poverty turns out to be entirely circumstantial, evaporating as soon as the factors that created it had been removed. In the end the involuntary poverty of Greccio could not compare in purity and durability to the voluntary poverty of Francis.

The *Legend of the Three Companions* recounts another episode in which Bernard and another friar found the doors of Florence shut in their faces as they searched for a place to spend the night.[74] The problem was that no one in Florence knew their story, nor was there anything about their appearance that distinguished them from the "scoundrels" and "thieves" who often requested similar favors. But the next day at church, a woman who had refused to help the friars the night before saw them actually turn down the alms that were being distributed to the other poor people who had gathered there. "Since you are poor, why don't you accept the coins like the others?" asked the almsgiver. Bernard responded: "While it is true that we are poor, poverty is not burdensome for us as it is for other poor people. For, by the grace of God, we have willingly made ourselves poor." He went on to explain that "they had indeed possessed much [but] for the love of God, they had given everything to the poor." Overhearing this interchange, the woman approached and immediately invited the two friars to be her guests. Knowing that these poor men had once been rich and that they had chosen their present poverty made all the difference in the world to her. Far from criticizing the woman for her selective charity, Bernard blessed her: "May the Lord reward you for your good will."

Finally, we read in the *Life of St. Francis* how the saint once "severely rebuked" a brother who had "insulted a poor man begging alms." In fact Francis made the brother "strip naked in front of the poor man and kiss his feet, to beg his forgiveness." What had the thoughtless brother said to the beggar to evoke such an uncharacteristically harsh response from Francis? He had simply asked: "Are you sure that you are not really rich and just pretending to be poor?" Francis let the brother know that such a comment was an affront to the Lord: "Anyone who curses the poor insults Christ whose noble banner the poor carry, since Christ made himself poor for us in this world."[75] In other words, Christ's decision to enter the world of flesh as a poor man in some way sanctified the state of poverty, and thus a poor person deserved some respect, at least insofar as he resembled the incarnate Christ.[76] But

Francis, so intent on correcting his brother, missed the irony of the situation. For if anyone could have been accused of being a rich man pretending to be poor, it was Francis and, for that matter, the brother who had posed the question in the first place.[77]

Looked at hypothetically from the perspective of the people of Francis's day who were born into poverty, the idea of *holy* poverty might well have seemed like a cruel trick. For it meant that just as no truly poor person had the means to climb out of his or her poverty in this world, so no truly poor person had the means to secure a place for himself in the next world by demonstrating his disdain for the things of this world. To be successful either in this life or in the next one, a Christian needed the one thing that poor people by definition did not have: money, either to be used to buy fine clothes and food, so as to get the most out of this life, or to be renounced, so as to "purchase" a comfortable place in the next life. Ironically, then, Francis's elevation of poverty—that is, holy poverty—to the status of spiritual virtue par excellence cannot really be seen, in the words of Isaiah, as "good news" for the poor. It was good news for the rich, for they were the only ones with the capital to invest in this kind of spiritual economy.

4

St. Francis and Lady Poverty

Thomas of Celano tells us that at one point before his conversion, Francis decided to join a military expedition bound for Apulia. This would have taken place in early 1205, a few months before the death of Walter of Brienne, who had been successfully championing the cause of Pope Innocent III in Apulia for the last three years.[1] According to Thomas, Francis so "seethed with desire" in this fleeting quest for military glory that one night he actually dreamed that his house, usually piled high with bolts of cloth, "was filled with soldiers' arms: saddles, shields, spears, and other equipment."[2] Thomas went on to chide Francis gently for taking this dream at face value, imagining, as he did, that it boded well for his future as a soldier. Thomas's hindsight allowed him to see that the "war" Francis was about to fight had nothing to do with southern Italian politics. It was a war against the spiritual complacency of his contemporaries, against those who, "displaying nothing of the Christian religion in their own lives and conduct," were content to be Christians in name only.[3] "Like a second David," Thomas explained, Francis was destined to "liberate Israel . . . from the long-standing abuse of its enemies" by showing the way to a new, more intimate relationship with God.[4]

Francis's naïve dreams of glory on the battlefield remind the reader of the *Life of St. Francis* that despite the mercantile basis of the northern Italian economy, burgher culture in cities like Assisi was still dominated by patterns and tastes that had been cultivated in the European countryside.[5] The heroes of Francis's youth were not rich merchants but brave knights, especially the "knights of old" whose tales dominated the repertoire of the troubadours from one end of Europe to the other: Alexander, Arthur, and Charlemagne, not to mention the more recent heroes spawned by the Crusades, such as Godfrey of Bouillon and Richard the Lion-Hearted. Collective nostalgia for what was already becoming a bygone era did not keep the troubadours of Francis's day from sing-

ing about the exploits of less obvious contemporary "worthies." Even someone like Walter of Brienne—whose career was embellished by the jongleurs of
Italy almost as it was unfolding—could capture the burgher imagination all over
the peninsula.[6] According to the *Legend of the Three Companions*, Francis
"yearned . . . to be knighted" in Apulia, "the promise of great chivalry and
nobility [being] so strong in him."[7] It should come as no surprise, then, that the
earliest Franciscan literature contains its share of military metaphors amid those
drawn from the mercantile world. Hence the references in Thomas's *Life* to
Francis as a "new soldier of Christ," as one "carrying the shield of faith for the
Lord."[8] Bonaventure even combined the two metaphoric realms when he observed that "a spiritual merchant must begin with contempt for the world and a
knight of Christ with victory over one's self."[9]

Consistent with the language of knighthood, the early Franciscan sources
also make use of courtly love motifs. According to Thomas of Celano,
Francis's second thoughts about fighting in Apulia fueled speculation among
his friends that he was contemplating marriage. When asked about this, he
responded: "I will take a bride more noble and beautiful than you have ever
seen, and she will surpass the rest in beauty and excel all others in wisdom."
Leaving nothing to the reader's imagination, Thomas identified the "bride"
of Francis's dreams as the "true religion" that he was about to embrace.[10]
Though it would remain undeveloped in the *Life of St. Francis*, this symbolic
identification between the conversion of Francis and his betrothal to a woman
would blossom, within a few years after Thomas finished his biography, into
a full-blown allegory known as the *Sacred Commerce of St. Francis with Lady
Poverty*. In it, Francis is presented to the reader as a suitor, successfully woo-
ing none other than "Lady Poverty" herself.[11]

The allegorization of poverty as a woman can be traced back to Plato's
Symposium, where the reader is told that "Love" is a child of "Poverty," who
gave herself to the drunken "Plenty."[12] But the character of Lady Poverty in
the *Sacred Commerce* has far more in common with the personficiation of
wisdom found in the biblical books of Proverbs and Wisdom.[13] Just as
Sapientia describes herself as a primordial force "set up at the first, before
the beginning of the earth," assisting the Lord "like a master workman," so
Paupertas traces her own history back to the Garden of Eden, where she was
a happy companion of Adam and Eve.[14] Moreover, Poverty, like Wisdom, is
depicted as the font of all human virtue.[15] The author of the *Sacred Commerce*
justified this lofty claim on the simple grounds that the poor were the very
first to receive Christ's blessing at the beginning of his Sermon on the Mount:
"Blessed are the poor in spirit for theirs is the kingdom of heaven."[16] In other
words, if poverty was the first condition to be acknowledged and rewarded
by Christ, it made sense that all other virtues followed from it.[17] Furthermore,
the author pointed to the use of the present tense in the first beatitude—"theirs
is the kingdom of heaven"—as opposed to the future tense ("shall"), which
is found in all the rest. His grammatically based conclusion: "While the other
virtues receive the kingdom of heaven only by way of [future] promise from
[Christ], poverty is invested with it by him without delay."[18] As the allegory

unfolds, Lady Poverty is consistently portrayed as a mentor, the "queen of virtues,"[19] a source of great wisdom. "Come, let us climb the mountain of the Lord and the dwelling of Lady Poverty," says Francis, "that she might teach us her ways and we might walk in her paths."[20]

While the author of the *Sacred Commerce* may have had *Sapientia* in mind when he conceived of Lady Poverty, this did not stop him from taking considerable liberties with the image. First and foremost, the "riches and honor" and "enduring wealth and prosperity" that Wisdom promised her devotees had no place in an allegory focused on poverty.[21] Beyond this, the reader is also confronted with a more overtly sexualized figure in the *Sacred Commerce* than in either Proverbs or Wisdom.[22] The frame story depicts a "lovelorn" Francis in search of his Lady Poverty as if she were the fairest of maids in some courtly romance or, perhaps more aptly, the bride in the *Song of Songs*. Christian exegetes had long interpreted the burning love that consumed the bridegroom in this Old Testament allegory to be symbolic of the relationship between God and his chosen people (i.e., the church) or between God and the soul of the individual believer.[23] The author of the *Sacred Commerce* simply recast the players in this biblical romance as Francis and his beloved Lady Poverty. So we see Francis, like the bridegroom in the Song of Songs, "going about the streets and squares of the city, as a curious explorer, diligently looking for her whom his soul loved."[24] At one point we even find Francis quoting the Song of Songs as he asks for directions from two old men: "Tell me, I beg you, where does Lady Poverty dwell, where does she eat, where does she rest at noon, for I languish with love of her?"[25] In short, Song of Songs, and the exegetical tradition it inspired, provided the author of the *Sacred Commerce* with the license he needed to employ sexual imagery to convey the unusual intensity and urgency of Francis's desire to embrace a life of poverty. That Lady Poverty should be presented to the reader as a *naked* woman—Francis found her at the top of a mountain "resting on a throne in her nakedness"[26]—only underscores the author's appreciation of this interpretative tradition.

The allegorization of Poverty as a desirable woman insisting that her suitors disengage completely from the world before enjoying her embrace is perfectly consistent with the glorification of voluntary poverty that I have described in the lives of Francis. Lady Poverty is simply the personification of that kind of poverty that Francis and his followers cultivated: a poverty without cares, a poverty that served as a source of comfort, a poverty that required great effort to achieve and to maintain. Not surprisingly, then, the lessons Lady Poverty gives to her new suitor Francis, lessons that take the form of a discourse on the history of holy poverty, epitomize the spiritualization and appropriation of poverty that I have been exploring in the earliest Franciscan biographies.

The history lesson begins in the perfect innocence of the Garden of Eden, where, Lady Poverty nostalgically recalled, "I was in man and walking with naked man through that entire splendid paradise."[27] As far as she was concerned, man's nakedness in the Garden constituted the purest form of poverty, the kind of poverty that came from the absence of all desire for earthly things coupled with a complete trust in God to provide all that was essential for day-to-day living. In that blissful era, Lady Poverty thought that she would be Adam's honored companion forever. But the primordial act of disobedience that led to his expulsion from the Garden also marked the end of his perfect poverty. For one thing, Adam's first impulse was to cover his nakedness with clothes, which, from Lady Poverty's perspective, constituted mankind's earliest material possessions.[28] Second, the "multiplication of labors" with which the Lord punished Adam heralded the beginning of a new work ethic that could only lead to the acquisition of more worldly possessions. Thus Lady Poverty lamented: "Seeing my companion clothed in the skins of the dead, I drew completely away from him because he had thrown himself into increasing his work to become rich."[29]

As clever and useful as this reinterpretation of Genesis 3 might have been for making poverty the keystone of human virtue, it did not turn out to be a particularly serviceable tool for understanding the remainder of the Old Testament. The problem, from Lady Poverty's exegetical perspective anyway, was that the God of the Jews did not typically regard poverty as a virtue. On the contrary, he regularly promised his chosen people "riches and a land flowing with milk and honey" if only they would live faithfully in accordance with his divine law.[30] So Lady Poverty had little choice but to wait for the Incarnation—which involved Christ choosing the life of a poor man as the vehicle for his redemption of mankind—before being restored to her rightful place as the foundation of all virtue. Consistent with Philippians 2:5–8, she treated Christ's divinity as a kind of wealth and interpreted his decision to leave "the great abundance of heaven" to trudge the earth in the form of a human being as a voluntary assumption of poverty. Having chosen this path, of course, Jesus earned the love and eternal devotion of his Lady Poverty, who remained his companion throughout the agony of his passion. As the Francis of the *Sacred Commerce* observes, in reference to Lady Poverty,

> you were with [Jesus] in the mockery of the Judeans, in the insults of the Pharisees, in the curses of the chief priests. You were with him in the slapping of his face, in the spitting, in the scourging. He who should have been respected by everyone was mocked by everyone, and you alone comforted him. You did not abandon him even to death, death on a cross. And on that cross, his body stripped, his arms outstretched, his hands and feet pierced, you suffered with him, so that nothing would appear more glorious in him than you.[31]

Here we see poverty being effectively identified with the central mystery of Christianity and in the process transformed into an implicit sine qua non of any true *imitatio Christi*. "For who is so dull, so ignorant," continued Francis, "as not to love, with a full heart, you [Lady Poverty], who have been chosen by the Most High and prepared from eternity? Who would not revere and honor you when he, whom all the powers of heaven adore, has adorned you with such honor?"[32] By extension, Francis's own quest for Lady Poverty is presented as a perfect imitation of Christ the king, who "left behind all the ranks of angels and the immense powers—of which there is a great abundance in heaven—when he came to look for you [Lady Poverty] in the lowest regions of the earth."[33]

Getting back to her history lesson, Lady Poverty regarded her relationship with the young church that Jesus left behind as an intimate one up through the period of the Roman persecutions.[34] But once the empire decided to embrace the church, even seemingly conscientious Christians found themselves lured away from their courtship of Lady Poverty by the enticements of the world around them. As Lady Poverty herself put it, "peace was made and that peace was worse than any war." For since that time, "everyone flees from me, drives me away, does not heed me, and abandons me."[35] Rather than attempt to recount every frustrating episode in the long history of Christian compromise, Lady Poverty confined herself to painting a generic portrait of the many generations of Christians who, despite their intentions to embrace her, found themselves lured away by her seductive rival, Greed.[36] The author probably had in mind the challenges faced by the many different orders of monks, hermits, and canons that had emerged over the course of the nine hundred years since the Edict of Milan. But it is highly likely that he intended to use this generic image of corruption to draw attention to the specific problems that faced the Franciscan order in the wake of its founder's death.

Her historical narrative complete, Lady Poverty proceeded to brief Francis about her rival, Greed, and to teach him how to recognize her wily ways despite her uncanny ability to disguise herself. For my purposes, one of the most interesting—and surprising—of Greed's strategies for seducing devotees of poverty was to assume the guise of Charity. As Lady Poverty explained, religious orders have at times been tempted "to provide for the needy and to give something to the poor,"[37] despite their resolve to leave behind the things of this world. While admitting that this was a noble enough goal, Lady Poverty was quick to point out that it simply could not be achieved without acquiring property—if only for the purpose of redistribution—thus inevitably opening the door to Greed. Lady Poverty took this opportunity to warn Francis lest he fall prey to the same temptation: "Consider your calling. Do not look back. Do not come down from the housetop to take something from the house. Do not turn back from the field to put on clothing. Do not become involved in the business world. Do not become entangled in the world's initiatives and in the corruption you have fled through knowledge of the Savior."[38] In short, in the pursuit of perfect poverty, the accumulation of material possessions was to be avoided at all cost, even if these resources were destined to be used to alleviate the suffering of the poor.

The end result of Greed's subtle yet determined campaign against holy poverty was, according to Lady Poverty's view of sacred history, the complete subversion of poverty as a Christian virtue. Those who succumbed to Greed, lamented Lady Poverty, "grew weak under the burden and were hardly able to breathe for want of spirit."[39] Before long they were taking shameless

advantage of the clout that they had come to wield in the world precisely for
having publicly rejected it.

> They began to fawn upon those of the world and to enter into marriage with
> them that they might drain their purses, enlarge their buildings, and multiply
> what they had thoroughly renounced. They sold their words to the rich, their
> greetings to matrons, and frequented the courts of kings and princes with all-
> out zeal so that they might join house to house and unite field to field.[40] Now
> they are magnificent and rich, the powerful of the earth, because they have gone
> from evil to evil, and have not known the Lord.[41]

Yet despite all this, they still insisted to Lady Poverty: "We are your friends!"[42]

Lady Poverty had little choice, over the course of this period, but to be
patient and wait for a new, more determined suitor, someone who would give
her the respect that she deserved—someone, in fact, like Francis. When it was
clear to Lady Poverty that Francis was different than the others and that she
could safely place her trust in him, she let him and his followers prepare an
appropriately "poor" wedding feast. They washed her hands with water from
a broken jar, led her to a place of honor on the bare ground, and served her
"crusts of barley or bran bread" dipped in water and wild herbs.[43] No cooked
foods, no wine, no tables, no plates, no eating utensils. "When they were satisfied more by the glory of such want than by an abundance of things," they
led Lady Poverty to a place where "she lay down naked upon the naked earth"
and slept "a most quiet and healthy sleep," content that there was hope for
poverty as a holy way of life after all.[44]

Lady Poverty's history of poverty is a history of *holy* poverty, that is, the
voluntary poverty of the rich. As such its sole concern is to illustrate the never-
ending battle on the part of formerly affluent Christians to resist the temptation to immerse themselves again in the things of this world. The author of
the *Sacred Commerce* understood well the social dynamics of sanctity: the
more the conscientious Christian of means left wealth and influence behind,
the more wealth and influence seemed to follow him. Hence the gentle and
ironic critique that God offered Lady Poverty as she watched her disciples
turning from her: "you have taught them against your own interest and have
instructed them against your own good. If they hadn't accepted you, they
would never have become so rich. They pretended to love you that they would
depart enriched."[45] And hence her advice for Francis: "Do not believe all of
the impressions you now have, because human senses are more prone to doing
evil than good and the spirit easily returns to what it is accustomed, even
though it may have been considerably distanced from it."[46]

Despite this focus on holy poverty, there are a couple of references in the
Sacred Commerce to the other kind of poverty, references in which the author expressed what we might consider to be more "normal" attitudes toward
poverty as a way of underscoring the uniqueness of Francis's love of it. In
his frenzied search for Lady Poverty, for instance, Francis found it difficult
to get directions from the materially minded people around him who "hated
[poverty] with a vengeance."[47] They greeted his entreaties with nothing but

reproach: "May the poverty you seek always be with you, your children, and your seed after you! As for us, however, let it be our good fortune to enjoy delights and to abound in riches, for 'the duration of our lives is tedious and demanding, and there is no remedy at one's final hour.'[48] We haven't learned anything better than to rejoice, eat, and drink while we live."[49] The closest that the author ever came to recreating the attitudes toward poverty of poor people themselves was to consider the case of those who had inadvertently fallen into financial ruin. "All living beings held you in great contempt," Francis reminds Lady Poverty, "All people ran from you and, as far as they could, cast you aside. Even though there were some who couldn't escape from you, you were no less contemptible and despicable to them."[50] Here we see poverty being despised not only by those who had managed to avoid it but by people who had fallen victim to it. Note how the involuntary poor are effectively lumped with the unregenerate rich, both facing the same obstacle to salvation since neither is capable of the one thing necessary to get into heaven: voluntarily embracing poverty.

As the author of the *Sacred Commerce* wrote unambiguously in his prologue, "the kingdom of heaven truly belongs to those who, of their own will, with a spiritual intention and a desire for eternal goods, possess nothing of this earth."[51] Only those poor people, in other words, whose poverty, motivated by spiritual concerns, was a matter of choice were in a position to "adorn [Lady Poverty] as a bride with a crown."[52] In marked contrast, the multitudes of poor people throughout history whose economic circumstances were beyond their control had a hard time catching the eye of Lady Poverty. Their poverty won them no more affection from her than the wealth of the rich. Both were hopelessly alienated from Lady Poverty: the rich by virtue of the fact that they *did not choose* to be poor, and the poor by virtue of the fact that they *had not chosen* to be poor.

ST. FRANCIS AND HOLY
POVERTY IN CONTEXT

My goal up to this point has been simply to identify the ironies in the relationship between Francis's brand of holy poverty and the poverty of the poor. In the first three chapters, I considered the earliest lives of the saint for what they had to say about his self-inflicted form of poverty as well as for what they revealed about his interactions with poor people. In chapter 4, I explored the curious figure of Lady Poverty in an attempt to illustrate the extremes to which this totemization of holy poverty could go in the minds of early Franciscans. The effect of this *nec nova sed nove* reading of these familiar sources has been to problematize the idea of holy poverty, an idea that has rarely been scrutinized for what we might call its social theological implications. Casual readers of the Francis corpus have all too easily assumed that his decision to become poor signaled a new era of appreciation for the spiritual advantages of poverty in general. But in fact Francis embodied and endorsed a very specific kind of poverty that only Christians of means could effectively embrace. Considered from this angle, Francis, whom we are accustomed to imagining as a "friend to the poor," comes across more like a Robin Hood in reverse, stealing the one spiritual advantage that the poor seemed to have—that is, their poverty—and giving it to the rich.

If the goal of this study were to criticize Francis for his part in the Christian appropriation of poverty as a spiritual virtue by the nonpoor, my readers would have good reason to accuse me of anachronism. I readily admit that the questions that I have been posing about Francis and the idea of holy poverty are questions shaped by modern liberal notions that would have been quite alien to Christians living in early thirteenth-century Italy. But as dubious as this approach might be as the basis for criticizing Francis, it is nevertheless a perfectly valid—indeed, I would argue, indispensable—method for heightening our sensitivity to the distance between his world and our own. Put differently, the more Francis and his followers come across to modern readers as rich men pretending to be poor for the sake of spiritual and social status, the clearer it becomes that the thirteenth-century authors of these accounts—in whose interest it was to leave behind as unambiguously positive a portrait of Francis as possible—were operating under a very different set of expectations than our own. As strange and self-incriminating as the Franciscan anecdotes and allegories may appear to sensitive readers today, we have to assume, based on the immense popularity of St. Francis, that he resonated in a profound and unproblematic way with the people of early thirteenth-century Italy—at least with a significant subset of these people. So if we are to appreciate Francis and the concept of holy poverty, we need to understand the contours of the world within which he and his biographers operated.

The remainder of this book will be dedicated precisely to reconstructing the historicocultural context within which the saint's "holy poverty" would have made such unambiguous sense to thirteenth-century Christians. This will be a two-part process occupying four chapters. First, I will consider Francis's poverty in terms of his explicit desire to model his life on that of Jesus and then show how his particular form of *imitatio Christi* compared to those of earlier saints. Second, I will assess the idea of holy poverty from more of a socioeconomic perspective, in an effort to appreciate Francis's conversion and mission in light of other contemporary experiments in urban sanctity, on the one hand, and in light of his close ties to the more affluent sectors of urban society, on the other. Taken together, these contextual frameworks will help us to appreciate the conceptual lineage of Francis's experiment in poverty, as well as the contours of the socioeconomic forces that contributed to its distinctive shape.

St. Francis and Jesus

If living a life in *imitatio Christi* is the single most important criterion for Christian sanctity, Francis has a legitimate claim to being considered the medieval saint par excellence.[1] The most consistent theme uniting all of the earliest literature about Francis is precisely his identification with Jesus. Thomas of Celano considered Francis to be "the holiest mirror of the holiness of the Lord, the image of his perfection"[2] and noted how he "used to recall with regular meditation the words of Christ and recollect his deeds with most attentive perception."[3] His fellow friars could attest to the fact that "talk of Jesus was always on his lips, sweet and pleasant conversations about him, kind words full of love."[4] Francis was, in short, "always with Jesus." He had "Jesus in his heart, Jesus in his mouth, Jesus in his ears, Jesus in his eyes, Jesus in his hands."[5] Even the name "Jesus" evoked a profound, emotional response from Francis: whenever he said it, "he was moved in a way beyond human understanding."[6]

This deep fascination with Jesus meant that Francis was naturally drawn to anything "in which he found an allegorical likeness to the Son of God";[7] hence his predilection for lambs, "since in sacred scripture the humility of our Lord Jesus Christ is frequently and rightly compared to the lamb."[8] One of the many lambs that Francis went out of his way to liberate ended up at the nunnery of San Severino, where its wool was crafted by the sisters into a tunic and sent back to Francis, a singularly appropriate costume for this new *agnus dei*.[9] The same quest for symbolic proximity to Christ accounts for Francis's unusual devotion to the Eucharist, which he regarded as an unparalleled opportunity to experience his Savior empirically. "In this world," wrote Francis himself, "I see nothing corporally of the most high Son of God except his most holy body and blood, which [priests] receive and which they alone administer to others."[10]

Francis was well known for his ability to conjure up vivid images of the human Christ that were practically palpable for him. According to Thomas, Francis used to bleat like a sheep whenever he said the word "Bethlehem" and would "lick his lips whenever he used the expressions 'Jesus' or 'babe from Bethlehem,' tasting the words on his happy palate and savoring their sweetness."[11] The same sweet affection for the baby Jesus led him to build, in Greccio, the first known nativity scene, for he wished "to enact the memory of that babe who was born in Bethlehem."[12] Christmas was a particularly emotional time for Francis; he was known to break down and cry, "groaning with sobs of pain," whenever he reflected on the "poverty of the blessed Virgin" or "the want of Christ her son" on that day.[13] On the other hand, his joy at the thought of God assuming flesh was so irrepressible that he felt obliged to admonish a brother who had asked him whether one should fast on Christmas Day when it fell on a Friday: "I want even the walls to eat meat on that day," Francis exclaimed, "and if they cannot, at least they should be rubbed with grease on the outside."[14]

As captivated as Francis was by the birth of Jesus, it was nothing compared to his fascination with Christ's passion and death. Having unsuccessfully sought his own martyrdom at the hands of the Muslims,[15] Francis spent the rest of his life essentially martyring himself with self-imposed austerities that were inevitably performed with vivid images of the crucified Savior in mind. From the time that he first heard the crucifix in the church of San Damiano speak to him, Francis "could not hold back his tears, weeping loudly over the passion of Christ, as if it were constantly before his eyes."[16] "His heart was wounded and it melted when remembering the Lord's passion. While he lived, he always carried the wounds of the Lord Jesus in his heart."[17] Once a man stopped the visibly troubled Francis on the road, thinking that the saint was sick or in pain. "I am crying," said Francis, "because of the passion of my Lord, for whom I should not be ashamed to go throughout the world crying in a loud voice."[18] In fact Francis was so completely absorbed by the image of the crucified Jesus that ultimately he came to be "stamped with Christ's brilliant seal,"[19] the stigmata, whereby his

> hands and feet seemed to be pierced through the middle by nails, with the heads of the nails appearing in the inner part of his hands and on the upper part of his feet, and their points protruding on opposite sides. Those marks on the inside of his hands were round but rather oblong on the outside; and small pieces of flesh were visible like the points of nails, bent over and flattened, extending beyond the flesh around them. On his feet, the marks of nails were stamped in the same way and raised above the surrounding flesh. His right side was marked with an oblong scar, as if pierced with a lance, and this often dripped blood, so that his tunic and undergarments were frequently stained with his holy blood.[20]

The appearance of these most distinctive wounds bore witness to the utter totality of Francis's *imitatio Christi*.[21] As Bonaventure put it, Francis was "truly the most Christian of men, who strove by perfect imitation to be conformed while living to Christ living, dying to Christ dying, and dead to Christ dead; he deserved to be adorned with an expressed likeness."[22] In all the previous history of Christian sanctity, the line between imitation of Christ and actual identification with Christ had never been so thin.

The biographers stopped short of claiming that Francis actually *was* a new Jesus, but not very far short. Francis "seemed to everyone a person of another age," wrote Thomas. "At that time, through the presence of St. Francis and through his reputation, it surely seemed that a new light had been sent from heaven to earth, driving away all the darkness that had so nearly covered that whole region that hardly anyone knew where to turn."[23] Just as Jesus, all man and yet all God, had shown mankind the way to salvation, so Francis, all man but perfectly inspired by his love of Jesus, reminded mankind how to get there. "Every order, sex, and age finds in him a clear pattern of the teaching of salvation and an outstanding example of holy deeds."[24]

Given the apparent totality of Francis's identification with Christ, it behooves us, in our effort to contextualize Francis's "holy poverty," to consider precisely how the saint conceived of the role of poverty in the life and teachings of Jesus. For, as Thomas tells us, Francis "was no deaf hearer of the gospel; rather he committed everything he heard to his excellent memory and was careful to carry it out to the letter."[25] And in the words of the *Assisi Compilation*, he "loved and followed the poverty of His beloved Son with much fervor and love in life and death."[26] Let us then turn to the books of the New Testament and consider what they would have suggested to someone like Francis about poverty and its role in the life of Jesus.

The Jesus that Francis knew from the Gospels lived a life apart from the things of the world, having "nowhere to lay his head,"[27] and advised his followers to do the same. When he sent his disciples out to preach, Jesus admonished them to leave behind everything they owned.[28] "Do not be anxious about your life," he counseled them, "what you shall eat or what you shall drink, nor about your body, what you shall put on. Is not life more than food, and the body more than clothing?"[29] The reasoning behind all of this was simple enough: material concerns could only divert attention from the spiritual ones that were the core of Jesus' program. The goal was to nurture a sense of complete dependency on God. "No one can serve two masters," Jesus put it succinctly. "You cannot serve God and Mammon."[30]

The Gospels are very clear about the role of volition in the poverty of Jesus and the apostles. In the desert, Jesus had a chance to rule over all the kingdoms of the world but chose instead to remain poor.[31] The disciples faced similar, if more prosaic, choices when Jesus asked each one of them in turn to give up his trade and to follow him. Peter, Andrew, James, and John opted to leave their nets and boats behind.[32] Likewise Matthew, a tax collector, "left everything and rose and followed him."[33] Of course not everyone that Jesus met was ready for this kind of sacrifice. The man who asked Jesus what he might do to "inherit eternal life," was told: "Sell all that you have and distribute to the poor, and you will have treasure in heaven; and come, follow me." He did not like this answer, "for he was very rich"[34] and preferred to stay that way.

Paul took the gospel emphasis on voluntary poverty to another dimension. In his second letter to the Christian community in Corinth, he wrote: "For you know the grace of our Lord Jesus Christ, that though he was rich, yet for your sake he became poor, so that by his poverty you might become rich."[35] Paul elaborated on this point when he wrote to the Christians of Philippi, noting that Jesus, prior to his Incarnation, enjoyed his own celestial form of "riches" as an all-powerful God. But

> though [Jesus Christ] was in the form of God, [he] did not regard equality with God as something to be exploited, but emptied himself, taking the form of a slave, being born in human likeness. And being found in human form, he humbled himself and became obedient to the point of death—even death on a cross. Therefore God also highly exalted him and gave him the name that is above every name.[36]

In these two important passages, Paul described Christ's divinity as a kind of wealth that Jesus had voluntarily shed when he took up the "poverty" of the human condition. Just as in the case of the disciples, who chose to leave their livelihoods behind, Jesus is depicted as *choosing* to sacrifice his divinity, a sacrifice of such colossal proportions, in fact, that it allowed him to redeem all of mankind from its collective sin.[37] By suggesting parallels between the Incarnation and voluntary poverty, Paul underscored the importance of willful renunciation of this world as a prerequisite for any true *imitatio christi*.[38]

Francis knew and appreciated these scriptural passages and referred to them directly in support of his own decision to live a life of voluntary poverty.[39] I have already mentioned how personally Francis took Jesus' instructions to the apostles as to what they should (or should not) take with them when they went out to preach.[40] But it was Paul's interpretation of the Incarnation as the ultimate act of self-impoverishment that seems to have left the deepest impression on the saint, surfacing as it did repeatedly in the saint's own writings.[41] In the second version of Francis's *Letter to the Faithful*, he underscored the Pauline connection between the Incarnation and voluntary poverty: "Though he was rich, he wished, together with the most Blessed Virgin, his mother, to choose poverty in the world beyond all else."[42] In his *Admonitions*, Francis explained how the Eucharist itself should serve as a daily reminder of this voluntary "humiliation" of God. "Each day [Jesus Christ] humbles himself as when he came from the heavenly throne into the Virgin's womb; each day he himself comes to us, appearing humbly; each day he comes down from the bosom of the father upon the altar in the hands of a priest."[43] For their part, Francis's biographers reinforced this notion. Thomas of Celano noted that whenever Francis's brothers shrank from the humiliation of begging, the saint would remind them that "the Son of God was more noble than we are, and yet for our sake he made himself poor in this world."[44] Thomas also recounted how Francis once embarrassed his host Ugolino—the future Pope Gregory IX—by opting to eat the bread crusts for which he had begged rather than the fine food that the bishop offered him at his own table. His rationale: "I consider it a royal dignity and an outstanding nobility to follow that Lord who, 'though he was rich, became poor for our sake.'"[45] In short, Francis, the son of a rich cloth merchant who left it all behind so that he could beg on the street corners of Assisi, seems to have felt a particular kinship with the God who gave up heaven itself to live the life of a man. His *imitatio Christi* was, more specifically, an *imitatio Incarnationis*.[46]

This is an extremely important point to keep in mind when trying to come to terms with the ironies inherent in Francis's relationship with poverty. As I have mentioned, it was well within Francis's power as a rich man to give away all that he had and, at least prima facie, to "conform himself to the poor in all things."[47] But it was nowhere nearly as easy for him to dispense with his status as a formerly rich man. There was nothing he could do to keep his divestment from this world from becoming an investment in the next world, an investment that would yield tremendously rich dividends in both worlds.[48] While this dynamic may have complicated Francis's effort to conform to the poverty of the poor, it facilitated his conformity to the "poverty" of the incarnate Christ. For the miracle of the Incarnation was itself grounded in the idea that no matter how much Jesus Christ may have "emptied himself . . . taking the form of a slave, being born in human likeness," he nonetheless remained God. Just as no one would have ever expected Christ to have relinquished his divinity once and for all upon assuming flesh, so Francis could hardly be blamed if his poverty retained some of the distinctive features of his former life as a rich man.[49] Beyond immediate appearances, then, Francis's poverty really had little to do with the poor per se. For him it was simply the most direct means of achieving a personal identification with Jesus, the practitioner of voluntary poverty par excellence.[50]

As much as Francis seems to have identified with Jesus and as intent as he was on expressing his *imitatio Christi* first and foremost in terms of poverty, there are two significant ways that the saint diverged from his gospel-based model. First of all, the mendicancy that played such a key role in Francis's conception of holy poverty is not scripturally based. There is nothing in the Gospels that suggests that Jesus and the apostles ever begged for their food.[51] This is significant because it reminds us that however focused Francis was on Jesus as a model for his own poverty, his sense of what poverty actually looked like was shaped more by his own personal experience with the poor people whom he met on the streets of Assisi. It may, in other words, have been a gospel reading that inspired Francis to become poor, taking "no gold, nor silver, nor copper"in his belt, but it was his own empirical observations of the activities of the Umbrian poor that taught him *how* to become poor.

Second, though the idea of voluntary poverty plays an important role in Christian scripture, it is not the only kind of poverty mentioned in the New Testament. Beyond advocating a life of voluntary poverty for those who wanted to "inherit eternal life," the Gospels also contain explicit references to the plight of the involuntary poor and to its alleviation, both as an eschatological promise and as a moral duty.[52] In the Book of Luke, for example, Jesus made public his intention to fulfill Isaiah's prophecies when he proclaimed in the synagogue of Nazareth that he had been anointed "to preach good news to the poor."[53] Paraphrasing Hosea 6:6, Jesus reminded his audience that God was more interested in mercy than in sacrifice.[54] Consistent

with Isaiah 61:1–2, Jesus linked his announcement of the coming new kingdom to promises of justice for the downtrodden: "Blessed are you poor, for
yours is the kingdom of God. Blessed are you that hunger now, for you shall
be satisfied. Blessed are you that weep now, for you shall laugh."[55] In a similar vein, the "woes" that counterbalance the blessings in Luke are meted out
on the explicit grounds that the rich, the full, and the laughing have already
enjoyed their "consolation."[56] Hence, observed Jesus in each of the synoptic
Gospels, "it is easier for a camel to pass through the eye of a needle than for
a rich man to go to heaven."[57] The story of Lazarus and the rich man illustrates this dual principle well. Upon his death the leprous beggar is given the
honor of residing "in the bosom of Abraham," from which vantage point he
can actually see the wealthy man, who had refused to share his feasts with
him, being punished for his lack of compassion.[58] Similarly Mary, in the
Magnificat, revels in her own exaltation, having begun her life as a "handmaid"
of "low estate,"[59] using the same language of social inversion found in the
Beatitudes: "He has put down the mighty from their thrones, and exalted those
of low degree; he has filled the hungry with good things, and the rich he has
sent away empty."

Related to but distinct from this idea that in the "age to come" the downtrodden would be uplifted and the rich humbled is the concept that acts of
charity toward the poor would be rewarded and that their neglect would be
punished. In Matthew 25 we find Jesus sanctioning assistance to the poor and
helpless in a dramatic way, by making it the one criterion that would be applied on Judgment Day to "separate the sheep from the goats." "For I was
hungry and you gave me food, I was thirsty and you gave me drink, I was a
stranger and you welcomed me, I was naked and you clothed me, I was sick
and you visited me, I was in prison and you came to me."[60] The passage effectively equates the hungry, thirsty, naked, and sick Jesus—the voluntarily poor
man par excellence—with the hungry, thirsty, naked, and sick involuntarily
poor person: for "as you did it to one of the least of these my brothers, you
did it to me." And in the process, it transforms an act of charity toward the
involuntarily poor into an act of faith directed at a voluntarily poor God, an
act that entitled the charitable to being counted among the sheep on Judgment Day; that is, to be saved.

These two aspects of New Testament poverty—that the involuntary poor
would be favored in the "age to come" and that in the meantime the rich would
be expected to help them in the "here and now"—do not have the same direct
implications for a life lived in *imitatio Christi* as does the idea of voluntary
poverty. To affirm that the poor will one day benefit from justice or that people
of means will be judged in accordance with their response to the needs of the
poor does not necessarily imply anything about how Jesus lived his life. Yet
if one considers the ideal Christian life not so much in terms of *imitating* Christ
as in *living up to* his explicit behavioral prescriptions, the vivid depiction of
poor relief as the sine qua non of divine mercy in Matthew 25 is hard to ig-
nore. Considering the full range of poverty images in the Gospels, then, we
find ourselves faced with what amounts to two distinct paths to Christian

salvation, each with its own take on the role of poverty. On the one hand, there is Christ's call to the apostles ("follow me") and the expectation that this would mean leaving behind the world of possessions and family ties once and for all. On the other hand, there is Christ's message to the people who gathered to hear him preach, which involved a charge to prepare for the coming Judgment by deepening their commitment to the Law and, specifically, by addressing the needs of the downtrodden.[61] That both of these paths could be expected to lead to salvation seems clear from the famous exchange between Jesus and the rich man. When Jesus was asked "What good deed must I do to have eternal life?" he answered: "Keep the commandments." Yet when the rich man pressed him as to what he might do *beyond* this, Jesus responded: "If you would be perfect, go, sell what you possess and give to the poor, and you will have treasure in heaven; and come, follow me."[62] Faced with the challenge of upgrading his commitment beyond simply keeping the commandments, the rich man ultimately decided against it. By so doing he opted to stay on the wide, well-worn path, designed for the rank and file, leaving the narrow and steep path of "perfection" for those few virtuosi followers—the apostles—who were intent on "working methodically at their own salvation."[63] When faced with the same choice, the apostles had accepted Christ's challenge and committed themselves to the perfection of following Christ's example rather than simply following his advice to live in accordance with the Law and assist the poor. Of course, since their sacrifices were greater, they could expect more in the way of recompense. When Peter asked what he and the other apostles would get for leaving everything behind and following Jesus, he was promised one of twelve thrones from which he would assist Jesus in judging all of Israel.[64] But, again, if the whole point of such judging was to separate the sheep from the goats, then clearly the apostolic path was not the only road to heaven.

Consideration of these dual, gospel-based approaches to "eternal life" helps us to appreciate the stages of Francis's own conversion as if he were himself the rich man in the Gospels struggling to decide which path to follow. His biographers tell us that Francis's first response to his own spiritual stirrings was precisely to follow the "low road" to salvation, not by imitating Christ but by responding to his call to relieve the sufferings of the poor and downtrodden. Each of the early accounts confirms this, although each one illustrates the point differently. The *Life of St. Francis* reports that "while staying in the world and following its ways, [Francis] was also a helper of the poor. He extended a hand of mercy to those who had nothing and he poured out his compassion for the afflicted."[65] According to the *Remembrance*, Francis's first inclination after kissing the leper was to seek out other lepers so that he could embrace them and give them money.[66] For its part, the *Legend of the Three Companions* claims that the young Francis would pile up bread on his family's dining-room table— presumably when his father was away on business—"as alms for the poor, since he had resolved to give to anyone begging alms for God's sake."[67] Indeed, explained the authors of the *Legend*, "his whole heart was intent on seeing the poor, listening to them, and giving them alms."

But when Francis finally settled on a particular way of life that made the most sense to him, it did not revolve around helping the poor, giving alms to lepers, or feeding the needy. Instead Francis opted for the "high road," imitating the self-imposed poverty of Jesus by disposing of his own possessions and living, as he saw it, anyway, in complete and total dependence on God. As noted in an earlier chapter, Francis embraced poverty with such determination that he could no longer really tend to the needs of the involuntary poor. His desire to perfect his own destitution meant that he had very little in the way of possessions to give away and even less inclination to do so, given the potential risk that such charity might pose to his own poverty and humility. Moreover Francis's fascination with the spiritual benefits promised to the *voluntarily* poor—those who had divested from this world in order to invest in the next one—meant that the gospel promises of justice for the *involuntarily* poor could be of no more than peripheral concern to the saint. Once his conversion was complete, Matthew 25 did not figure into Francis's holy life, except in a rather roundabout way that allowed him to substitute, as I have already mentioned, the "lesser brothers," that is, the Friars Minor, for the "least of these my brothers" as appropriate recipients of charity.[68] The role of the friars, in other words, was not to succor the poor of Matthew 25, but to *be* the poor of Matthew 25 and to let the rich succor them. From the moment that he decided to "follow" Jesus instead of simply following his advice, the poverty that rightfully concerned him was no longer the poverty of the poor and its alleviation, but the poverty of Christ and its imitation.[69]

It should be noted that neither Francis nor his biographers drew such a clear distinction between the imitation of poverty and its alleviation as two separate paths in the pursuit of Christian perfection, even though, as I have shown, the distinction is implicit in the Franciscan corpus. As far as Francis was concerned, it was simply a matter of living "according to the pattern of the holy gospel."[70] Paraphrasing Francis, Thomas of Celano once wrote that the saint's "highest aim, foremost desire, and greatest intention was to pay heed to the holy gospel in all things and through all things."[71] On this occasion, Thomas actually specified what he meant by "paying heed to the holy gospel," that is, "to follow the teaching of our Lord Jesus Christ and to retrace his footsteps completely with all vigilance and zeal, all the desire of his soul, and all the fervor of his heart."[72] In other words, Francis's fidelity to the Gospel was based both on following the teachings of Jesus *and* retracing his footsteps. Yet, as I have shown again and again in this study, the evidence that Thomas actually mustered in the *Life of St. Francis* is weighted decidedly in the direction of the latter.

St. Francis and Early Christian Sanctity

Francis was not the first saint to whom imitating Christ's poverty appealed more than alleviating the poverty of the poor. In fact, when we consider the history of Christian sanctity as a whole, Francis's fascination with becoming poor, as opposed to assisting the poor, turns out to be consistent with the vast majority of saints who came before him. Almost invariably, the *Lives* of these saints revolve around some form of radical, voluntary detachment from the "things of the world." Though their hagiographers often noted examples of their service to people within the world, it was their willful withdrawal from the normal course of life that typically set the saints apart from ordinary Christians. Using the terminology of the church, the *vita passiva* (or *vita contemplativa*), with its focus on detachment from all ties to this world in the interests of nurturing the ties between one's soul and God, dominated late antique and medieval interpretations of *imitatio Christi*. The *vita activa*, which involved working in the world to serve the spiritual or physical needs of others less capable of helping themselves, typically came up short by comparison.[1] Some understanding of the historically uneven competition between these two modes of *imitatio Christi* is essential for appreciating Francis's complex relationship with poverty.

The reasons for the dominance of the "passive" form of *imitatio Christi* in the history of Christian sanctity are not at all obvious when one considers the portrait of Jesus that has come down to us in the Gospels. There the reader finds the *vita passiva* and the *vita activa* in relative balance, often interpenetrating one another. On the one hand the scriptures depict a Jesus who has fully and deliberately separated himself from the things of this world by renouncing all material possessions and social ties. On the other hand, aside from his forty days alone in the desert and his occasional retreats to avoid the crowds, Jesus is most often found wandering from town to town, dividing his time quite "actively" between healing the physically infirm and preaching to the spiritually infirm.

But in the wake of Jesus' death, the "active" and "passive" paths began to diverge. As highly valued as the missionaries and bishops were for their efforts to expand and consolidate the church, the earliest Christian communities also placed a high premium on personal detachment from the surrounding world of Roman society. Not surprisingly, virginity emerged from the beginning as an effective and admired "distancing strategy," since it, by definition, precluded so many of the social bonds that potentially compromised otherworldly allegiance.[2] Paul's first letter to the Corinthians (c. 52–55) is the *locus classicus* for this early preoccupation with chastity, as well as the concomitant need to defend marriage as a reasonable choice for the salvation-minded.[3] This turned out to be an uphill battle. As early as the first decade of the second century, we find Ignatius of Antioch (d. 107) venting his frustration with virgins who regarded themselves, by virtue of their purity alone, as the *crème de la crème* of the Christian community. "If anyone can live in chastity for the honor of the Lord's flesh," Ignatius sniped in a letter to his fellow bishop, Polycarp of Smyrna, "let him do so without ever boasting. If he boasts of it, he is lost; and *if he is more highly honored than the bishop*, his chastity is as good as forfeited."[4]

Though virginity would always occupy an honored place as a sign of passive disengagement from the world, its primacy in this regard was soon eclipsed by martyrdom. The persecutions, launched by an empire concerned about the rapid growth of a potentially subversive sect, created a context within which individual Christians, at least in theory, had to define their primary allegiance. Those Christians who felt that they could not participate in "idolatrous" tests of imperial allegiance without compromising their ties to the "Kingdom of God" found themselves subject to arrest and execution. The bishops, to whom the beleaguered Christian communities looked for leadership, responded to the challenge of persecution by symbolically recasting the conflict in such a way as to make noncompliance with the Roman authorities seem like the only right thing to do.[5] In place of a powerful empire suppressing a politically suspect sect, they saw the diabolical forces of the world lined up to do battle against those of the elect. In the process they transformed the victims of the imperial judicial system into Christian heroes, more than willing to sacrifice everything in this world so that they could participate more fully in the benefits of the next one. Not surprisingly, given these very specific historical circumstances, the form of *imitatio Christi* that came to dominate the early church was an imitation of the *death* of Christ, who had himself voluntarily suffered persecution at the hands of a suspicious empire. The identification between the crucifixion of Jesus and the execution of individual Christians who failed their tests of imperial allegiance was in fact so close that it was difficult for members of the cult to imagine a form of Christian life that could compare in holiness to a martyr's death.[6] Even those Christians who managed to avoid arrest and execution were encouraged, in light of the political climate and their spiritual goals, to hold the world at arm's length and live out their lives in "exile," patiently awaiting the arrival of the only "Kingdom" that really mattered.

No sooner had the young church gotten used to the idea of living a form of exile in the midst of a hostile empire than Constantine rescinded the persecution edicts (312–13) and ushered in a radically new era of cooperation between Rome and the church. As relieved as most Christians must have been to see the threat of persecution evaporate, many must have wondered what it would mean for the church, which was to be transformed over the course of the fourth century from an exclusive, sectarian cult into an inclusive, imperial one. As a persecuted body, it had been easy for the communities of Christians to identify "the world" that they were supposed to reject. But now that the empire had embraced the church, how were conscientious Christians to recreate the perfect martyrial experience of resistance to the enticements of the world?[7] A significant number of them, troubled by Eusebius's (d. 339) conception of "one empire, one church," sought to recapture this distance in a very literal way by leaving the newly Christianized cities behind and living as hermits and monks in the desert. There they pursued lives of studied physical and social deprivation and imagined themselves to be experiencing, in a bloodless but no less authentic way, the ultimate sacrifice of the martyrs. The only difference, as far as they were concerned, was that their "martyrdom" was, for lack of the stroke of a sword, a "daily martyrdom," one that would have to be relived each day for the rest of their lives. St. Antony (d. 356) was paradigmatic in this regard. According to Athanasius, he had originally longed to be a real martyr but was forced by circumstances beyond his control to become a "daily martyr to his conscience, ever fighting the battles of the faith."[8]

With the rise of this new monastic form of "death" by means of self-denial, the idea that radically distancing oneself from the world was the sine qua non of a holy life became increasingly dominant as a criterion for Christian perfection. One of the so-called *Sayings of the Desert Fathers* compared the spiritual fortunes of three friends who had each decided to follow a different path in his effort to achieve holiness in *imitatio Christi*. The first "chose to make peace between men engaged in controversy, as it is written, 'Blessed are the peacemakers'; the second chose to visit the sick; and the third chose to be quiet in solitude." When the first two realized that they were making no spiritual progress, they went to visit the third to see how he was faring. "He was silent for awhile, and then poured water into a cup. And he said: 'Look at the water.' And it was cloudy. And after a little while he said: 'Now look, see how clear the water has become. . . . So it is with the man who lives among men. He does not see his own sins because of the turmoil. But when he is at rest, especially in the desert, then he sees his sins.'"[9] From the perspective of the new imperial church, with its gaze fixed firmly on the new "martyrs" in the desert, the prospects for living a holy life in the world, even when the goal was to recreate Christ's well-documented concern for the sick and the victims of strife, were comparatively bleak.[10]

The widespread nature of this tendency to equate a holy life with a life of distance from the affairs of the world is further evidenced by the fact that ordinary Christians in the cities felt compelled to come to the desert from time to time to bask in the glow of these holy men. It is ironic that those who lived lives of voluntary exile to this world should come to be so attractive to those who did not. Guilt was a major factor. Just as lapsed Christians in prior generations had rushed to seek the pardon of their coreligionists who had been sentenced to death for their refusal to sacrifice,[11] so the spiritually anxious citizens of newly Christianized Rome sought vicarious satisfaction from the virtuoso Christian exiles in the desert. Athanasius was full of praise for Antony's ability to handle the kinds of problems that the Christians from the city laid before him:

> For who came to him in grief and did not return in joy? Who came weeping for his dead and did not immediately put away his mourning? Who came in anger and was not transformed into friendliness? What down-and-out pauper met him, and seeing him and hearing him did not despise wealth and feel consoled in his poverty? What monk grown careless did not gain new fervor from a visit with him? What young man coming to the mountain, and seeing Antony, did not promptly renounce pleasure and love chastity? Who came to him plagued by a demon and was not freed? Who came with tortured mind and did not find peace of mind?[12]

One of the best examples of a hermit catering to the needs of his visitors is Daniel "the Stylite" (d. 493), whose particular form of "desert" was a column on the outskirts of Constantinople. Over the course of the many years that he spent living on top of his column, suspended between heaven and earth,[13] Daniel played host to innumerable visitors, ranging from ordinary people asking him to exorcise their demons or cure their diseases to emperors consulting him about their political fortunes. Daniel's hagiographers regarded this as "par for the course" for a man of such holiness. Occasionally they depicted him blushing from all the attention, but for the most part it seemed perfectly natural to them that such a relationship should develop between the people of this world and a holy man living in voluntary exile from this world. In the *Life of Daniel the Stylite* the line between the *vita passiva* that the holy man sought by removing himself from Christian society and the *vita activa* that his visitors expected him to exercise on their behalf is a thin one.[14]

But such a sanguine attitude about serving the needs of visitors is not typical of the lives of the desert saints as a whole. One of the principal leitmotifs of this literature is precisely the difficulty of maintaining a proper distance from the world while tending to the needs of visitors, and the importance of prioritizing the passive life even if it meant excluding the active. The best of the Egyptian hermits, as depicted in such sources, treated their guests from the world as intruders, threats to their perfect exile experience. Consider, for example, Arsenius, who flatly refused to see a woman who had come all the way from Rome to meet him and secure his blessing. When she presented herself to him anyway, Arsenius angrily rebuked her. "Why have you dared to come all this way across the sea? . . . Have you done it to go back to Rome and say to the other women: 'I have seen Arsenius?' Do you wish to turn the sea into a highroad for women coming to see me?" Embarrassed, but undaunted in her quest for his blessing, the woman asked him to pray for her. He curtly responded that he would most certainly pray; he would pray for God to "blot the memory" of her from his heart. But all was not lost for the well-meaning, if misguided, woman. The archbishop, whom she had approached to arrange the meeting in the first place, consoled her, reminding her that the men in the desert pray for the souls of all Christians all the time. He advised her in the future simply to leave them alone, lest she inadvertently compromise their solitude and cripple their ability to intercede on behalf of others.[15]

Antony, whom Athanasius described as a "physician . . . given by God to Egypt,"[16] falls somewhere in between Daniel and Arsenius in terms of his response to public adulation. Despite his impressive talents as an intercessor, we find Antony perennially "grieving," in the words of his hagiographer, "that so many disturbed him."[17] Over the course of his life he moved frequently, each time a bit further into the desert and away from civilization. But he never managed to achieve complete inaccessibility, even when, in the end, he had chosen a distant and formidable mountain retreat. On one occasion, some judges came to him there "begging him to come down from the mountain, since it was impossible for them to go there." At first Antony refused, but ultimately he agreed to meet his petitioners halfway, at the "outer mountain," where he deftly advised them on the administration of true justice.[18] Once, when a visitor asked Antony to stay with him a bit longer, the saint replied: "Just as fish exposed for any length of time on dry land die, so monks go to pieces when they loiter among you and spend too much time with you. Therefore we must be off to the mountain, as fish to the sea. Otherwise, if we tarry, we may lose sight of the inner life."[19] On one occasion, some visitors, who sensed that Antony was becoming annoyed with the crowds that were hounding him, began to tell others to leave the holy man alone. But Antony, resigned to his fate, would not turn them away. After all, he observed wryly, "these people are no more numerous than those demons we wrestle with on the mountain."[20]

It may seem strange that so many Christians in need of spiritual or physical assistance should have sought it at the hands of practitioners of the *vita passiva*, when the institutional church in the cities was designed to offer precisely this "active" kind of service. Traditionally it was the responsibility of the bishop to tend to the spiritual needs of his flock by preaching, just as it had long been the task of the deacon to administer physical relief to the needy. But if we keep in mind the importance of martyrdom as the original foundation of sanctity in *imitatio Christi*, the bishops and deacons stood at a real disadvantage when compared to the practitioners of "daily martyrdom" in the deserts. As indispensable as their services might be, secular clerics were, by definition, immersed in the world and thus lacked the aura of sanctity that the visitors to the desert could feel emanating from the hermits. This discrepancy was the source of no little tension during the heyday of eremitic monasticism in the fourth and fifth centuries. Many of the hermits felt strongly that, by living in their self-imposed exile, they had found the real church that had eluded them in the cities. In the words of Athanasius, the desert seemed to them like "a land of piety and justice, a land apart" from the urban Christian world that the monks had left behind.[21] Though the bishops appreciated the spiritual heroism of the holy men in the desert and regularly referred to them in their sermons as examples of a pure Christian life, many found themselves wondering whether the hermits might have gone too far in rejecting the world to which the bishops ministered. As early as 345, the bishops gathered at Gangra in Asia Minor felt obliged to rebuke hermits who had wondered aloud whether Christians living in the cities could reasonably expect to be saved! One of the principal themes of the vast corpus of desert literature produced in this period is the distinction between good hermits, who showed great respect for the institutional church and did their best to protect themselves from the "vainglory" of public adulation, and bad hermits, who disparaged the church of the cities and paraded their virtues in front of their visitors at the expense of the secular clergy.

Despite the prevailing sense that the most obvious road to heaven was the one leading out of town, there were members of the secular clergy who managed to earn a place for themselves in the canon of saints strictly by virtue of their extraordinary dedication to one or more aspects of the *vita activa*. One such saint was John "the Almsgiver" (d. 619), a widower from Cyprus who was chosen late in life to be the patriarch of Alexandria. From the moment John took charge of his see, he actively "spread the gospel" of his Catholic teachings in this heavily Monophysite city, increasing the number of orthodox churches from seven to seventy in less than a decade.[22] But John's real forte, from the perspective of his biographer Leontius of Cyprus,[23] was his dedication to poor relief. The first thing that he did after being ordained was to send his clergy throughout the city to register all of the poor people or, as he put it, to "make a list of all my masters down to the last." For, as he explained, "those whom you call poor and beggars, these I proclaim my masters and helpers. For they, and they only, are really able to help us and bestow upon us the kingdom of heaven."[24] Leontius went on to describe how John, an "imitator of Christ," ordered his private treasurer to "apportion a daily sum" to each of the seven and a half thousand names on the list.[25] Over the course of his term as patriarch, John became famous for the timely and generous assistance that he directed toward victims of local disasters. In the midst of a famine, John ordered seven forty-bed hospitals built specifically for undernourished women, weak from childbirth.[26] When Christian refugees began to pour into Egypt as a result of the Persian conquest of Syria, John not only built poorhouses and hostels but allocated church revenues to pay for rations of bread.[27] He also sent money and supplies to Christians after the sacking of Jerusalem and used church money to ransom Christians prisoners.[28] John's overriding concern for the poor and the uprooted meant that he was hard on his stewards whenever he suspected that they were holding back out of fear of depleting the episcopal treasury. He wanted them to give without any thought to tomorrow, under the principle that God's resources would never run out as long as they were being used for charitable purposes.[29]

But Leontius's effort to base John's claim to sanctity almost entirely on his extraordinary compassion and generosity turns out to be unusual when we consider it within the context of early episcopal hagiography as a whole. The vast majority of the early bishop saints were known more for their efforts as preachers and missionaries, working either to extend the boundaries of the church or to protect it from heresy and schism. Augustine, bishop of Hippo Regius (d. 430) and "father" of the Latin church, is a case in point. Possidius's account of Augustine's thirty-five-year career as bishop bears witness to an endless stream of sermons, letters, council addresses, and public debates all aimed at leading dissident African churches and their bishops back to the Catholic fold.

> He opposed with the fullest confidence the African heresies and especially the Donatists, the Manichaeans, and the pagans, in carefully finished books and in extempore sermons. . . . In fact, by God's good gift, the Catholic church in Africa began to lift its head again after a long period during which it had lain prostrate—led astray, overpowered and oppressed, while the heretics grew strong.[30]

Intent as he was on illustrating Augustine's role as a defender of the faith, Possidius had little to report about the bishop's efforts in the area of poor relief. In the event of a shortfall in church revenues, Augustine was known to break up and melt down church vessels "for the benefit of captives and of as many of the poor as possible." And the bishop also made a point of visiting "widows and orphans in their affliction."[31] But his legacy was not to be one of catering to the physical needs of the poor. In fact, in his lifelong effort to "free" his mind "from all mundane anxieties," he preferred to delegate all aspects of the administration of the diocese to his priests and stewards.[32] As far as Possidius was concerned, Augustine was "appointed by the Lord" specifically to serve "as a 'watchman for the house of Israel,' as one appointed to 'preach the word, to be urgent in season and out of season, to convince, rebuke, and exhort, and to be unfailing in patience and teaching.'"[33] In short, Augustine's strength, as a holy exponent of the *vita activa*, was tending to the spiritual rather than the physical needs of his flock.

It should be noted that despite the praise lavished on John and Augustine for their respective interpretations of the *vita activa*, neither Leontius nor Possidius seems to have been entirely comfortable basing a case for sanctity on exclusively "active" grounds. It was as if they could actually hear their readers wondering how these episcopal candidates for sanctity could be compared to the practitioners of the *vita passiva* in the desert. At one point in his account, Leontius observed:

> Now the really remarkable thing in the life of the saintly patriarch [John] was this: although he had not practiced the discipline of the monk, though he had not spent his time in churches among the clergy, but had lived in lawful wedlock with his wife; despite the fact that he remained a layman until the hour

when he was consecrated as patriarch, yet he so mastered the ordering of the church and he attained to such a height of virtue that he excelled many of those who had distinguished themselves in the asceticism of the desert.[34]

The audience that Leontius had in mind when he was writing the *Life* was used to thinking of sanctity in conjunction with the eremitic lifestyle. For that matter, John himself is depicted as having the utmost respect for monks. In his futile desire "to be numbered among those who lived the monastic life," he contented himself with endowing two monasteries of his own, to be "supplied from the lands belonging to him in his native city." When the preparations were complete, John "spoke to the monks, beloved of God, and said: 'I myself—after God—will take thought for your bodily needs, but you must make the salvation of my soul your care, so that your evening and night vigils may be set to my credit with God.'"[35] In other words, despite John's herculean relief efforts and his unparalleled openhandedness with regard to church revenues, he still feared that he would come up short in terms of heavenly "credit." Prevented by his patriarchal responsibilities from pursuing the *vita passiva*, he did the next best thing by providing material support for other monks, thus reaping for himself some vicarious satisfaction.[36]

For his part, Augustine's biographer Possidius seems to have been even more certain that the *vita passiva* was the preferred path to perfection. We are told that Augustine, after being duped into entering the priesthood of Hippo Regius, openly wept, "bemoaning the great dangers to his way of life that he anticipated would be crowding in on him if he had to govern and direct the church."[37] Consistent with this sentiment, Augustine lost no time in "establishing a monastery within the precincts of the church and entered upon a life with the servants of God in accordance with the method and rule established under the holy apostles."[38]

The works of Leontius and Possidius are by no means the only lives of late antique bishops that betray a sense of the superiority of the *vita passiva* even as they extol the virtues of the *vita activa*. The early fifth-century writings of Sulpicius Severus, who went to extraordinary lengths to promote the cult of Bishop Martin of Tours (d. 397), provide the *locus classicus* for this kind of hagiographic tension in the Latin West. One of the works that Sulpicius dedicated to Martin's memory was the *Dialogues*, a long conversation between one Postumianus, who had just returned to Gaul after visiting hermits in the Egyptian desert, and a small group of enthusiastic listeners that included Sulpicius himself. At one point, in the middle of this holy travelogue, Sulpicius interrupted the speaker.

When I was listening just now with the greatest interest to what you were telling us about the miracles of these holy men [in the desert], my mind kept going back to my Martin, though I said nothing; and I could not help noticing that whereas each of your Egyptians performed one kind of miracle, this one man of ours did more than all that they did between them. You certainly told us some very remarkable things but—if I may say so without offense to these holy men—there was absolutely nothing that I heard from you in which Martin was not their equal.[39]

But more impressive than the number of Martin's miracles, argued Sulpicius, was the fact that he had performed them as a man operating fully within the world. Sulpicius went so far as to claim, on these grounds, that

in comparison with the hermits . . . [Martin] was unfairly handicapped. For when they perform those undoubtedly marvelous feats we hear of, they are free from all entanglements and have only heaven and the angels looking on. Martin, on the other hand, moved among crowds and in the haunts of men, amidst quarreling clergy and raging bishops, and harassed by almost daily scandals on every side. Nevertheless, he stood unmoved amid all of these things upon a foundation of unshakeable spiritual power and worked wonders un-equalled even by those dwellers in the desert of our own day and other days, of whom we have been hearing. And even if their achievements had been equal to his, would any judge be so unjust as not to see good reason for holding that Martin was the mightier?[40]

The point that Sulpicius was trying to make was simply this: that as impressive as the desert saints were, they had, by comparison to Martin, taken the "easy" road to sanctity. They had left the world and all of its distractions behind so as to concentrate all of their energies on nurturing their ties to God. Martin, on the other hand, did not permit himself this luxury. He had to earn his sanctity the hard way, while "moving among crowds and in the haunts of men."

Despite the fact that Sulpicius Severus—along with a number of other Latin hagiographers who had accepted the challenge of promoting the sanctity of particular bishops—can be credited with broadening the spectrum of Chris-tian holiness to include people who did not flee from the world, his arguments actually reinforced the longstanding identification between sanctity and the *vita passiva*. For one thing, in his effort to accentuate Martin's holiness, Sulpicius felt obliged to make the most of every hermitlike aspect of Martin's life as a bishop.

What Martin was like, and his greatness, after entering the episcopate, it is beyond my powers to describe. For with unswerving constancy he remained the same man as before. There was the same humble heart and the same pov-erty-stricken clothing; and, amply endowed with authority and tact, he fully sustained the dignity of the episcopate without forsaking the life or the virtues of a monk. For a time he occupied a cell next to the cathedral. Then, when he could no longer endure the disturbance from his many visitors, he made him-self a hermitage about two miles from the city. The place was so secluded and remote that it had all the solitude of the desert.[41]

Though this emphasis on Martin's eremitic inclinations no doubt contributed to his perceived saintliness, it could not help but leave the distinct impres-sion that Martin was a saint in spite of his episcopal status, not because of it.

Sulpicius indirectly promoted the *vita passiva* in other ways as well, par-ticularly by contrasting Martin so sharply with other bishops of the day whom Sulpicius invariably depicted as proud and worldly. According to the *Life of*

St. Martin, when the local bishops were asked to approve Martin as the new bishop of Tours, many thought him unworthy, on the basis of his "insignificant appearance" and his "sordid garments."[42] On a later occasion, when the emperor summoned the bishops to his court, Martin was the only one who did not engage in "foul fawning" and was not afraid to challenge the ruler on the violence that accompanied his rise to power.[43] Finally, and not surprisingly, given Martin's distinctive approach to his episcopal responsibilities, "nearly all his calumniators" who opposed his elevation to the ranks of sainthood "were bishops."[44] Again, as useful as this strategy may have been for highlighting Martin's holiness, it could only have added to the reader's suspicions that bishops on the whole made unlikely saints and that Martin was the rare exception that proved the rule.

At an even more subtle level, the *Life of St. Martin* undercut the notion of episcopal holiness by making much of Martin's spiritually risky decision to accept the office in the first place. According to Sulpicius, Martin had established a monastery for himself near Poitiers and would presumably have continued to seek self-perfection in the peace and quiet of the *vita passiva* had he not been duped into assuming the vacant see of Tours.[45] By accepting the position, Martin surrendered his chance to leave the world in pursuit of his own perfection. In other words, he sacrificed his own opportunity to sacrifice the world, an exponentially higher order of sacrifice that made Martin's holiness—in the eyes of his creative hagiographer, anyway—all the more impressive. Implicit in all of this is the notion that working within the world was so dangerous that only the most spiritually self-assured holy men could attempt it and expect to come out unscathed. Indeed even Martin stumbled once or twice. One of Sulpicius's three extant letters lambastes certain unnamed detractors who wondered how it was that Martin, to whom Sulpicius attributed such impressive miracles, had once been injured in a fire that had engulfed a building where he was sleeping.[46] Sulpicius did his best to explain away the incident—which he had conveniently neglected to mention in the *Life*—claiming that on this occasion the devil had simply caught Martin off guard. But it is hard to read the letter without getting the sense that Sulpicius's self-appointed task as apologist for this bishop-saint was a challenging one.

Sensitive to the fact that his Christian readers, fed on stories of heroic solitude and deprivation, would have a difficult time imagining a bishop occupying the same spiritual heights as a desert ascetic, Sulpicius locked himself into an apologetic strategy that sought, in large part, simply to recast Martin as a would-be monk forced to become a bishop. In the process, he, of course, indirectly endorsed the superiority of the *vita passiva*. The only way to avoid completely subsuming Martin's episcopal status to his suppressed monastic yearnings was to emphasize a different form of *imitatio Christi*, one that operated independently of the themes of "daily martyrdom" and "escape from this world" that characterized the desert ascetics. To this end, Sulpicius invoked the image of Christ and the apostles as preachers of the gospel, working within the world to spread their holy message.[47] This accounts for the portion of the *Life of St. Martin* that is dedicated to Martin's missions to the countryside around Tours, where he found rural villagers still dedicated to the pagan cults of pre-Christian times. Martin, the ex-soldier, took it upon himself to burn down temples and cut down holy trees, establishing Christian shrines and monasteries in their places.[48] This kind of activity was certainly not unknown in the accounts of the desert hermits, who on occasion went out of their way to make local villagers aware of their religious errors. But in the hands of Sulpicius, it became an important apologetic tool for elevating Martin's *vita activa* above the world-rejecting *vita passiva* of the hermits. Moreover, the fact that Jesus and the apostles, as missionaries, had managed to operate effectively within the world while holding it at arm's length, made it possible for Sulpicius to bridge some of the gap between the two *vitae* to which his own high opinions of the eastern hermits contributed.

Readers accustomed to the famous image of Martin dividing his cloak with the beggar[49] may be surprised to learn how little Sulpicius Severus had to say about Martin's charitable activity as a bishop. In fact, beyond this anecdote, which is intimately tied to Martin's conversion, the references to poor relief are nonexistent. Though Martin, like Jesus, did punctuate his missionary efforts with miraculous healings and exorcisms, there is no information about any efforts on his part to tend to the ordinary physical needs of his flock. This is particularly interesting when considering how self-conscious—and not a little defensive—Sulpicius was about his role as a promoter of Martin's claim to holiness. After all, it would have been Martin's responsibility, as bishop, to oversee some form of assistance to the poor in his diocese. Did Sulpicius consider Martin's missionary activity in the countryside around Tours to be the only part of his episcopal *vita activa* worth mentioning in his effort to stake Martin's claim to sanctity? Was the lack of attention to charity simply a function of Sulpicius's emphasis on those aspects of the *vita activa* (i.e., spreading the gospel) that suggested the most direct parallels between Martin and Christ? Might it have been counterproductive for Sulpicius to have enumerated Martin's efforts at poor relief, given that one of his strategies was to underscore the saintly bishop's distance from the things of this world? It is hard to say for sure. Whatever the reason, the immense popularity of the *Life of St. Martin* in the West and the influence that it wielded over later saints' lives certainly contributed to the fact that the role of poor relief as a criterion for episcopal sanctity was minimal, especially when the bishops in question had, like Martin, a reputation for propagating the faith.

Though Sulpicius Severus's *Dialogues* testify to the fact that the lives of the desert hermits were a source of fascination for Latin as well as Greek audiences, the eremitic form of monasticism itself never really caught on in the West to the extent that it did in the East. More typical of the Western monastic experience were communal, coenobitic forms of Christian retreat from the world. Though in the beginning the differences between solitary monks and those living in community were more quantitative than qualitative, before long these two forms of monasticism began to evolve in very different directions. Though both approaches sought to create a sense of "daily martyrdom," their methods were quite distinct. While the hermits in the desert were known for the competitively individual nature of their ascetic regimens, the monks in community tended to downplay individual expressions of self-denial in the interests of promoting a more even spiritual experience for the group as a whole. In place of virtuoso asceticism, the directors of the many coenobitic experiments focused on the less dramatic challenges posed by loss of individuality and self-determination through the total submission and obedience of the monk to the abbot.

One of the most influential endorsements of obedience as an alternative form of "daily martyrdom" is a letter that Augustine wrote in 423 to his sister and the community of nuns with whom she resided. Augustine was responding to reports that the nuns were chafing under the discipline imposed by their strict abbess. His advice:

> Let your superior be obeyed as a mother, with due respect, lest God be offended in her person. . . . It will be the particular responsibility of the superior to see to the observance of all these regulations; and if anything is not observed she is not to neglect or overlook the lapse, but to take pains to amend and correct it. . . . Let her rebuke the unquiet, comfort the feeble-minded, support the weak, be patient toward all; let her maintain her authority with good will, but impose it with fear. And, however necessary both may be, let her seek to be loved by you rather than feared, always bearing in mind that she will have to give an account of you to God. Thus, by your ready obedience you will show consideration not only for yourselves but also for her, because . . . the one who is in the higher position runs the greater risk.[50]

From Augustine's perspective, the abbess had no choice but to be strict because ultimately God was going to hold her responsible for the spiritual progress of every woman in her community. Far from criticizing their spiritual director, the nuns should be grateful to her—the way children ought to be grateful to their parents—for assuming the awesome burden of overseeing their spiritual growth. Such a system allowed each nun to commute her own self-denial into simple obedience to the abbess, thus offering spiritual security for the price of one's individuality and self-determination.

Because the coenobitic approach, with its emphasis on obedience, did not lend itself to the showy, ascetic experimentation of the desert saints, its proponents often felt obliged to offer their own *apologiae*, lest it seem that their form of monasticism was somehow inferior to the other. John Cassian (d. 435) was one of the first to do just that. Speaking through a former hermit who had ultimately chosen to live out the rest of his life in a monastery, Cassian observed that before the desert had become overcrowded with hermits on the one hand, and overrun with visitors on the other, an ascetic life alone in the desert could "only be compared to the bliss of the angels."[51] But once the "freedom of the vast wilderness" had become "cramped," monasteries began to look more attractive. "Even if that liberty and those spiritual ecstasies are denied me, yet as all care for the morrow is avoided, I may console myself by fulfilling the precept of the gospel, and what I lose in sublimity of contemplation, may be made up to me by submission and obedience." In short, though Cassian's hermit-turned-monk admitted that he did not expect the coenobitic option to yield the same ecstasies as the life of ascetic self-determination that he had known in the desert, he regarded the monastery's own version of self-abasement in the form of submission and obedience as no less legitimate and considerably safer.

A century later, the hermit-turned-abbot Benedict of Nursia (d. c. 550) endorsed and institutionalized this coenobitic focus on obedience in his famous *Rule*. "Readily accept and faithfully follow the advice of a loving father," he told his monks, "so that through the labor of obedience you may return to Him from whom you have withdrawn because of the laziness of disobedience. My words are meant for you, whoever you are, who laying aside your own will, take up the all-powerful and righteous arms of obedience to fight under the true King, the Lord Jesus Christ."[52] Here obedience is actually elevated above all other virtues as a perfect remedy for that primordial act of disobedience on the part of Adam and Eve that had opened the door to original sin in the first place. Influenced by his own experiences as well as by his reading of Cassian, Benedict developed a healthy appreciation for the potential dangers of the hermit's life, advocating it only for those who "have spent much time in the monastery testing themselves and learning to fight against the devil."[53] As far as he was concerned, the risks of trying to pursue the *vita passiva* on one's own were so great that the coenobitic option of "living in a monastery waging war under a rule and an abbot" was, for all intents and purposes, the "best" option.[54]

Although this type of monasticism, with its emphasis on obedience rather than heroic asceticism, did not elicit the level of public enthusiasm that surrounded the desert fathers, it still benefited immensely from the longstanding, martyrially inspired bias in favor of the *vita passiva*. The writings of Gregory "the Great," bishop of Rome (d. 604), are the most telling in this regard. Influenced directly by the works of Sulpicius Severus, Gregory's corpus is infused with his own defense of the episcopacy in the face of an audience accustomed to associating holiness with a life of coenobitic monastic withdrawal. Like Martin, Gregory began his religious life in a monastery, in this case one that he established on family lands in Sicily. But before long Gregory was summoned to Rome to serve as deacon, a position he filled for twelve years before finally being elected pope.[55] That very year, he wrote his *Pastoral Rule*, a handbook of episcopal duty that was inspired, significantly enough, by the "rules" that traditionally governed monastic life. One of the points of the book was precisely the justification of the *vita activa*. Building on Sulpicius's notion that a bishop, forced to perform his duties in the midst of a corrupt world, deserved special credit, Gregory went so far as to criticize talented individuals who, "in their eagerness for the pursuit of contemplation only, decline to be of service to their neighbors by preaching; they love to withdraw in quietude and desire to be left alone for meditation. Now, if they are judged strictly on their conduct, they are certainly guilty in proportion to the public service which they are able to afford."[56]

Three years into a singularly turbulent pontificate, Gregory published his own version of the *Dialogues*, the preface to which would suggest that he had come to lament his decision to leave the monastery in the first place: "At times I find myself reflecting with even greater regret on the life that others lead who have totally abandoned the present world. Seeing the heights that these men have reached only makes me realize the lowly state of my own soul."[57] His interlocutor's request for examples of miracle-working, in illustration of the claim that such holy men in fact still existed, provoked the long string of miracle stories that make up the bulk of the work. What is interesting about the *Dialogues*, in light of this inquiry, is that Gregory did not really live up to his expressed intention. The prologue specifically acknowledges the spiritual heights achieved by those who had "totally abandoned the present world," implying that the subsequent narratives would involve exclusively monastic agents. And indeed his *Dialogues* open with miracles performed by abbots, priors, and monks. But by the end of the first book, two bishops have joined the ranks of the miracle workers. And after a lengthy section devoted entirely to Benedict in the second book, the third opens with a string of miracles worked by more than a dozen different bishops and popes. In fact, when the final score is tallied, miracle workers from the ranks of the *vita activa* actually outnumber those pursuing the *vita passiva*. By quietly elevating bishops to the miracle-working heights usually reserved for the monk, Gregory did his part to relieve some of the tension between the high spiritual status that he was claiming for the *vita activa* and the lack of miracles traditionally associated with it.

The comparison between Martin and Gregory would not be complete without considering the importance of missionary activity to the bishop of Rome as the crowning glory of his *vita activa*. Just as Sulpicius made much of the apostlelike missions that Martin undertook in the area around Tours, so Gregory's biographers emphasized the famous missionary work that he sponsored among the Anglo-Saxon kings of England. The monastic author of the earliest life of Gregory, conscious of the lack of miracles associated with Gregory, actually devoted the bulk of his brief *vita* to the English mission and to his literary production.[58] For his part, Bede, whose *Ecclesiastical History of the English People* contains a biographical encomium to the pontiff who "transformed our still idolatrous nation into a church of Christ," felt justified in "regarding him by the term apostle."[59] Aware of Gregory's own misgivings about the sacrifice he had made when he left his monastery, Bede concluded: "We cannot but believe that he lost none of his monastic perfection through his pastoral cares, and indeed made greater spiritual progress by his labors for the conversion of souls than in his former peaceful life, especially since, even when he became pope, he ordered his house as a monastery."[60] Again it is important to note, in light of this study, that neither of these sources mentioned anything about Gregory's execution of his episcopal responsibilities toward the poor. As far as Gregory's first biographer was concerned, the proof of the pope's sanctity lay in the "innumerable people throughout the world . . . revived by the refreshing shower of [his] words."[61]

The struggle for respectability on the part of the *vita activa* in a cultural milieu dominated by the idea that the most reliable path to Christian perfection was one of withdrawal from secular involvement did not get any easier with the Benedictine reform movement inaugurated at Cluny (910). The phenomenal growth of the Cluniac order, from its humble beginnings in the early tenth century to its zenith in the late eleventh, itself testifies to the pervasiveness of the idea that monasteries provided the only sure escape from an early medieval world beset by external raids and internal dissension. The immunity from outside jurisdiction that Duke William of Aquitaine bestowed on the new community at Cluny became paradigmatic for every subsequent monastery that submitted to the authority of the abbot of Cluny, creating a sense that this particular order represented the most detached and therefore the purest form of the *vita passiva*. But at the same time, noblemen like William, who donated the land and resources necessary to sustain the community, expected some kind of spiritual benefit for their efforts. In William's case, the foundation charter is quite explicit: he made the donation with the expectation that "there shall be prayers, beseechings and exhortations sedulously directed to God" on behalf of William's soul as well as the souls of his wife, his king, and his parents.[62] As more monasteries submitted themselves to the jurisdiction of Cluny, this symbiotic relationship between the landed elite, who were fully involved in the world, and the Benedictine monks, who were considered to be fully involved in the other world,[63] developed to the point where the monks, like some of their eremitic counterparts in the fifth century, found themselves working more for the benefit of their "visitors" than for themselves. In a sense, the monks, with their endless liturgical celebrations on behalf of their benefactors, were being forced to compromise their *vita passiva* with a peculiarly monastic kind of *vita activa*.[64] When, in the late eleventh century, monastic reform movements began to sprout up at places like Chartreuse, Cîteaux, Grandmont, and Camaldoli, the driving force behind them was the desire to restore the original goal of monasticism—the perfection of the monk's soul—by deliberately cutting away the ties of expectation that bound the Cluniac monasteries too closely to their benefactors.[65] Again, as in the case of the desert literature with its focus on the sin of vainglory, the goal was to preserve the *vita passiva* through a renewed commitment to detachment from the surrounding world, even at the expense of serving the spiritual needs of the laity.[66]

Eleventh-century practitioners of the *vita passiva* were not alone in their reform-minded efforts to extricate themselves from the demands of the world around them. Influenced by what was happening in the monasteries, cathedral priests—known as canons—began to experiment with their own modified forms of the monastic, regular life.[67] Historically the canons had supported themselves on prebends, portions of diocesan properties and revenues, which often fell under the direct responsibility of the canons to oversee. This inevitably involved the canons in a relationship with "the world" that seemed to their critics to narrow the sphere of their *vita activa* to dangerously selfish concerns regarding the productivity and defense of their prebends. The mid–eleventh century witnessed the beginnings of a widespread effort to create a communal, propertyless type of canon who could claim to be a true heir to the apostles, who, according to Acts 2:44, "had all things in common." Though apologists for the canons made much of their supposed *imitatio apostolorum*, it was inevitably to the practitioners of the *vita passiva* that the canons turned for ideas on how to live a communal life. It is telling in this regard that the sixth-century "Rule of St. Augustine"—the heart of which was the letter (emphasizing obedience) that Augustine had written to his sister and her fellow nuns—should have become so popular as the basis for organizing reformed canonries.[68] Equally indicative of this general push toward the "monastification" of the canons is the fact that some of the "holiest" of the eleventh- and twelfth-century canonries came to be almost indistinguishable from monasteries in terms of their daily regimen and their collective retreat from the outside world.[69] Despite the fact, then, that some apologists argued for the precedence of the reformed canons over monks on the theoretical grounds that they imitated Christ and the apostles more closely "in preaching, baptizing, and administering the other sacraments of the church,"[70] in practice, the energy that came with reform seems to have been expended in the attempt not so much to make the canons better priests as to make them more like monks. This is reflected clearly in an encomium that Pope Urban II (d. 1099), who had spent time as a canon as well as a monk, directed toward the canons regular.

> Those who by divine favor abandon the things of the world are in their turn divided into two groups the religious purpose of which is almost identical, that of the canons and that of the monks. The latter way of life greatly aided by divine mercy flourishes in the entire universe; the former, on the contrary, because the fervor of the faithful grows cool, has declined almost everywhere. Yet this is the way of life that was instituted by Pope Urban the Martyr;[71] that Augustine organized by his rules; that Jerome molded by his letters;[72] that Gregory commissioned Augustine, the bishop of the English, to institute. Thus it should not seem any less praiseworthy to revive this earliest life of the church with the inspiration and help of the spirit of the Lord than to maintain the prosperous religion of the monks through continuing steadfastly in the same spirit.[73]

Here we find the distinction between the reformed canons and the monks all but disappearing in their mutual determination to "abandon the things of the world." Indeed Urban's admiration of the canons regular is couched entirely in terms of their withdrawal from the world, to the point where he regarded their "religious purpose as almost identical" to that of the monks. There is no mention of how the reform affected their efforts to minister to the Christians in their diocese; that is, no reference to their pursuit of the *vita activa*, which was, after all, the very raison d'être of the canons.

Given all of this, it should come as no surprise to learn that Ivo of Chartres (d. 1115), an important early codifier and interpreter of ecclesiastical law, should actually have had to defend the idea that canons living in community according to a rule should be free to exercise their traditional pastoral role! "We firmly maintain," countered Ivo, "that those who say that the regular canons ought to be barred from the care of the souls because they have renounced the world should not be listened to." His reasoning followed the same logic that Sulpicius Severus had used seven centuries earlier to explain why the monks at Martin's monastery were so sought-after as bishops:[74] "On the contrary, they are all the more suited to assume [the care of souls] because they have rejected the pleasures and pretensions of the world."[75] For my purposes, Ivo's response is less interesting than the original query that prompted it. For lurking behind it is the familiar, centuries-old assumption that the pursuit of the *vita passiva* and the pursuit of the *vita activa* were antithetical and that the former was to be preferred over the latter as a more certain path toward spiritual perfection. Despite the effort on the part of their apologists to give the canons regular a respectable pedigree by linking them to the apostles, reform was defined in terms of monastic standards of detachment from the world. It was, in short, the "regular" in "canons regular" that left the deepest impression on eleventh- and twelfth-century Christendom.

Although this survey of the relationship between the *vita passiva* and the *vita activa* as the two dominant forms of *imitatio Christi* is far from exhaustive, it is sufficient to illustrate at least one important fact: that the *vita passiva*, with its roots firmly planted in the martyrial tradition, consistently exercised greater clout in defining early Christian sanctity than did the *vita activa*. Simply put, it was the hermits and monks who captured the collective imagination of late antique and early medieval Christendom as worthy heirs of the martyrs, living their own forms of "daily death" in relative isolation from the rest of the world. Somehow the bishops and priests, serving the needs of Christians who lived in the world, seemed tainted by comparison. Advocates of the *vita activa* did what they could to redress this imbalance by proclaiming its own gospel roots and occasionally even going on the offensive to criticize the monastic approach as a socially irresponsible, "easy" way to heaven. But it was a losing battle. Even as they were decrying the "selfishness" of those saints who had physically removed themselves from Christian society, they were forced by the expectations of their imagined audiences to emphasize how detached their own candidates were from the world to which they were ministering, thus inadvertently endorsing disengagement as the key to sanctity.

A consideration of the relative merits of the *vita passiva* and the *vita activa* in historical context is an important part of any attempt to appreciate the significance of Francis's own *imitatio Christi*. Considering the *Lives* of Francis through the lens of a thousand years of accumulated hagiographical literature, the first thing one notices is how well they fit into the long tradition of hagiographic apologetic on behalf of the *vita activa*. Consistent with the strategies pioneered by Sulpicius and Gregory, the earliest biographers of Francis underscored the saint's radical disdain for the secular world while at the same time highlighting his indefatigable determination to convert it.

Thomas of Celano and the other biographers of Francis were of one mind when it came to the emphasis they placed on Francis's deliberate and total rejection of the things of this world, a rejection that expressed itself in his quest for a "perfect" lack of property. Practically everything that I observed in the first three chapters about Francis's identification with the lepers and the other poor people around him is relevant in this regard. But if we broaden our scope beyond poverty per se, the sources show how consistent Francis's own brand of urban asceticism was with the "martyr-monk" model that provided the theoretical basis for the *vita passiva*. For one thing, Francis's biographers made much of the saint's longing for persecution and physical abuse.[76] As Thomas observed, Francis and his followers

> sought to be where they would suffer persecution of their bodies rather than where their holiness would be known and praised, lifting them up with worldly favor. Often mocked, objects of insult, stripped naked, beaten, bound, jailed, and not defending themselves with anyone's protection, they endured all of these abuses so bravely that from their mouths came only the sound of praise and thanksgiving.[77]

Francis's quest for perfect self-denial actually led him, like Antony, to "burn with desire for holy martyrdom." Indeed he repeatedly sought passage to Egypt and Morocco, so that he might "preach the Christian faith and repentance to the Saracens and other unbelievers" and invite his own execution.[78] On one such occasion Francis actually managed to reach the Nile delta city of Damietta while it was being held by the Christian armies of the Fifth Crusade (1219–21) and from there set out for the sultan's camp, fully prepared to suffer martyrdom in his effort to spread the gospel. Indeed "before Francis even reached the Sultan, he was captured by soldiers, insulted and beaten, but was not afraid. He did not flinch at threats of torture nor was he shaken by death threats."[79] As it turned out, Francis's hopes of "reaching the summit of perfection"[80] at the sharp end of a sword were dashed by the unexpected hospitality of the sultan.[81] So Francis, again like Antony, had to be content with a kind of daily martyrdom. Thomas reveals that once, when Francis was seeking advice on how best to achieve spiritual perfection, he "took the [Bible] from the altar, and opened it with reverence and fear. When he opened the book, the first passage that met his eye was the passion of our lord Jesus Christ that tells of the suffering he was to endure." Finding similar passages each time he opened the book, "this man, filled with the spirit of God, understood that he would have to enter the kingdom of God through many trials, difficulties and struggles."[82] The miracle of the stigmata, through which Francis experienced the ultimate form of Christian martyrdom without ever having actually been martyred, followed in due course. As Bonaventure put it: "O truly blessed man, whose flesh, although not cut down by a tyrant's steel, was yet not deprived of bearing a likeness of the lamb that was slain!"[83]

It is also significant in this regard that the painful disease of the eyes that ultimately left Francis blind is treated in the biographies as an analogue to martyrdom. Seeing Francis so afflicted,

> one of the brothers asked him what he would prefer to endure: this long-lasting illness or suffering a martyr's cruel death at the hands of an executioner. "My son," he replied, "whatever is more pleasing to the Lord my God to do with me and in me has always been and still is dearer, sweeter, and more agreeable to me. . . . But to suffer this illness, even for three days, would be harder

for me than any martyrdom. I am not speaking about its reward but only of the pain and suffering it causes."[84]

Thomas could only marvel at Francis's appetite for pain: "O martyr, martyr laughing and rejoicing, who endured so gladly what was bitter and painful for others even to see!"

In addition to the martyrial imagery, Francis's biographers also made much of the more monklike aspects of the saint's life, drawing attention to his periodic retreats to out-of-the-way places for the purposes of meditation.[85] It was inevitably "in remote places," such as a "cave near the city" or a "pit" in his house that we find the young Francis trying to sort out his earliest spiritual stirrings.[86] The leprosaria, where he tended to the sick during the early stages of his conversion process, were inevitably located outside the city walls. It is indicative of his desire to withdraw physically from the world that Francis's first "home" after his conversion should have been in the rural, roadside church of San Damiano a kilometer or so outside of town.[87] Later he and his brothers lived in an "abandoned hut" on the banks of the Rivo Torto[88] before moving to the Portiuncula, a "truly a holy place and the dwelling place of God," about three kilometers from Assisi.[89] Even when his desire to preach forced him to seek out an audience, the fact that he would sometimes visit four or five towns or villages a day meant that he was constantly traversing the Umbrian countryside, communing with nature in the process.[90] In between missions, he frequently retired to hermitages, like the one on the cliff outside of Greccio.[91] "In the clefts of the rock he would build his nest and in the hollow of the wall his dwelling. With blessed devotion he visited the heavenly mansions; and, totally emptying himself, he rested for a long time in the wounds of the Savior. That is why he often chose solitary places to focus his heart entirely on God."[92] As Francis approached the end of his life, and the effects of his own austerities had begun to take their toll, his desire for solitude only increased.

> At one time the blessed and venerable father Francis, with worldly crowds gathering eagerly every day to hear and see him, sought out a place of rest and secret solitude. He desired to free himself for God and shake off any dust that clung to him from the time spent with the crowds. It was his custom to divide the time given him to merit grace and, as seemed best, to spend some of it to benefit his neighbors and use the rest in the blessed solitude of contemplation. He took with him only a few companions—who knew his holy way of living better than others—so that they could shield him from the interruption and disturbance of people, respecting and protecting his silence in every way.[93]

La Verna for Francis was what the "outer mountain" had been for Antony: a world apart from the disruptive world of men.[94]

But Francis's desire to withdraw from the world—reflected in his futile quest for martyrdom on the one hand and his regular need to withdraw to hermitages on the other—is only part of the picture painted by his biographers. Francis's life may have been a constant struggle to hold the world at arm's length, but he never allowed himself the "luxury" of actually leaving it behind for any length of time. Thomas recounts how, during their initial "re-treat" to the Spoleto Valley, Francis and his brothers discussed "whether they should live among people or go off to solitary places." Seeking the answer in prayer, Francis came to realize that he had been sent by the Lord "to win for God the souls which the devil was trying to snatch away."[95] In the *Major Legend*, Bonaventure portrays Francis, at a later point in his career, mired in doubt and revisiting the issue: "What do you think, brothers, what do you judge better? That I should spend my time in prayer, or that I should travel about preaching?" Interestingly enough, in Francis's list of "pros and cons," the contemplative life of prayer seems to have held all the advantages:

> I am a poor little man, simple and unskilled in speech; I have received a greater grace of prayer than of speaking. Also in prayer there seems to be a profit and an accumulation of graces, but in preaching a distribution of gifts already received from heaven. In prayer there is a purification of interior affections and a uniting to the one, true and supreme good with an invigoration of virtue; in preaching, there is dust on our spiritual feet, distraction over many things and relaxation of discipline. Finally, in prayer we address God, listen to him, and, as if living an angelic life, we associate with the angels. In preaching it is necessary to practice great self-emptying for people and, by living humanly among them, to think, see, speak, and hear human things.

But despite the attractions of the *vita passiva*, there was one aspect of the *vita activa* that "seems to outweigh all these considerations before God": that "the only begotten Son of God, who is the highest wisdom, came down from the bosom of the Father for the salvation of souls." Given Francis's commitment to "doing everything according to the pattern shown to us in Him," it is no surprise that he opted to "interrupt [his] quiet and go out to labor."[96] No matter how much Francis may have longed for martyrdom or for a life of eremitic withdrawal, in other words, his fundamental raison d'être—his imitation of Christ—led him to stay within the world and tend to the souls of others who lived within the world.[97] The fact that Francis was not a bishop—indeed he was never even ordained as a priest—did not dissuade his hagiographers from making this connection.[98] For they knew that Francis had received an extraordinary authorization from the pope not only to live a life of poverty but to go about preaching penance. All that Thomas of Celano and the others had to do was to package Francis's penitential sermons as a form of mission aimed not so much at the conversion of pagans as at the spiritual awakening of complacent, spiritually tepid Christians.[99]

The many parallels between the *Life of St. Francis* and the *Life of St. Martin* testify to the self-consciousness of Thomas of Celano's reliance on the well-worn tools of episcopal hagiography. Readers of the two *Lives* find Martin and Francis both kissing lepers;[100] having "run-ins" with brigands;[101] showing great respect for the clergy;[102] "refusing to flatter kings and princes"[103] bravely withstanding the assaults of demons;[104] and wearing shabby clothes, the threads of which were imbued with thaumaturgical power.[105] At one point in the *Remembrance*, after recounting Francis's gift of clothing to a "poor, half-naked knight," Thomas explicitly compared this act of charity to Martin's famous division of his cloak with a beggar.

> Did [Francis] do any less than the great Saint Martin? They did the same thing, with the same purpose, though in different ways. Francis first gave away his clothes, then everything else; Martin gave away everything else and then gave away his clothes.[106] Both lived poor and humble in this world and both entered heaven rich. Martin was poor, but a knight, and clothed a poor man with part of his clothes. Francis was rich, but not a knight, and he clothed a poor knight with all his clothes. Both of them, having carried out Christ's command, deserved to be visited by Christ in a vision. Martin was praised for his perfection and Francis was graciously invited to what was still missing.[107]

Of greater significance, however, are the more subtle parallels between the two saints. Both Martin and Francis, for instance, began their lives fully ensconced in the most secular occupations of their respective worlds, Martin as a soldier and Francis as a merchant. Both came to realize how spiritually dangerous their worlds were and sought to leave them, only to realize that their true calling was to stay there and make other people aware of the same dangers. And both became missionaries, with Martin, the soldier, burning down temples and cutting down holy trees, while Francis, the merchant, "selling" his audiences on the idea of divesting from this world and investing in the next.[108]

All of this is highly suggestive as I return to consider the question that originally inspired this foray into the history of Christian sanctity and the uneven relationship between the *vita passiva* and the *vita activa*. Francis's decision to imitate Christ's poverty, rather than heeding his admonitions about assisting the poor, was a decision that the vast majority of Christian saints up to the time of Francis's conversion had already made. In their quest to live up to the example set by the martyrs, they gravitated toward forms of life that allowed them to experience the purest forms of self-abnegation on a daily basis. Even members of the secular clergy, whose responsibilities prevented them from fleeing the world in any literal sense, did everything possible to distance themselves from it in other ways. The only advantage that they enjoyed over monks, when it came to making their cases for sanctity, was the typological parallel between their defining activity and that of Jesus and the apostles: spreading the gospel outside of the community of Christians (the missionary role) and tending to physical and spiritual needs within the community of Christians (the pastoral role). That both of these aspects of the *vita activa* could be pursued to extraordinary, self-sanctifying degrees is apparent from the cases of St. Martin on the one hand and St. John the Almsgiver on the other. But as it turned out, the apologists for the episcopacy who were the most influential in constructing the idea of the "holy bishop" in the Latin West were those who highlighted missionary activity and the spread of the faith, as opposed to pastoral service to Christians in need.

Thus when Thomas confronted the daunting task of writing the life of a saint who, as a layman, was *ipso facto* even more enmeshed in the world than any bishop, the sheer weight of hagiographical expectation would have pushed Thomas in two predictable directions. First, he would have felt obliged to hyperbolize Francis's detachment from the world, a detachment that Thomas had no choice but to define in socioeconomic (as opposed to geographic) terms, since Francis never physically left the world for any length of time. This inevitably uphill battle to make a layman living in the world seem holy helps explains why the *Life of Francis* is so full of anecdotes that reiterate the saint's extreme asceticism. Second, insofar as Thomas had to make a virtue out of the more "active" parts of Francis's religiosity, he would have felt most comfortable taking a page from Sulpicius Severus and highlighting Francis's "missionary" work. The fact that his was an internal mission, directed at the souls of people who were already baptized, was not a problem, given Francis's special papal commission to preach. Moreover, this kind of internal proselytization could even double as a kind of pastoral work, insofar as it involved addressing the spiritual needs of the immediate community.

The piece that is missing from the profile of Francis as a practitioner of the *vita activa* is the other part of the pastoral picture: service to the physical needs of the poor. But, once again, this is a piece that was already missing from the traditional hagiographical patterns of episcopal sanctity to which Thomas turned in his search for a serviceable model for a lay saint like Francis. This is a point well worth keeping in mind. For, given Thomas's choice of models, he may well not have known what to do with Francis's contact with the poor and the sick without compromising his hagiographical task. In other words, with Sulpicius Severus as his principle guide, it may have been inevitable that Francis's interactions with lepers would end up reading like Martin's encounter with the beggar at the gates of Amiens; that is, as a symbolic moment to signal the world-rejecting conversion of a saint, not as a precedent for a life lived in the world in service to the poor and helpless.[109]

St. Francis and St. Raymond

Considered within the context of the long history of Christian sanctity, Francis's preference for imitating poverty over alleviating it was, as I have shown, consistent with the traditional bias that favored the *vita passiva* as opposed to the *vita activa*. That said, however, it is important to realize that Francis lived at a time when Italy—the focal point of the medieval "commercial revolution"[1]—witnessed a dramatic increase in the number and type of charitable efforts aimed precisely at addressing the problems of the urban underclass.[2] By considering some of these late twelfth and early thirteenth-century experiments in poor relief—in particular those that were spearheaded by laymen who aspired, no less than Francis, to their own *imitationes Christi*—we will be in a better position to appreciate how Francis's attitudes about and interactions with the poor compare to those of his saintly contemporaries.

The work of Jacques de Vitry (d. 1240), bishop of Acre and titular patriarch of Jerusalem, provides a convenient window into this increase in charitable activity directed at the poor. Jacques's *Historia Occidentalis*, written sometime between Francis's audience with the sultan in 1219 and his death in 1226, contains an invaluable survey of the many forms of religious life that were thriving in Latin Christendom at this time. One of these, in which Jacques seems to have taken a special interest, was a branch of the Augustinian canons that administered hospices on behalf of the poor and sick.[3] "In all the western regions," observed Jacques, "there are innumerable congregations of both men and women who, renouncing the world and living according to a rule in the homes of lepers and in the hospices of the poor, minister with humility and devotion to the poor and the sick."[4] "These ministers of Christ," Jacques continued, "so sober and frugal with regard to themselves and so strict and severe when it comes to their own bodies, overflow in their hearts with mercy toward the poor and sick and, with a ready spirit, administer the necessities to the extent that they are able." Jacques was particularly impressed with the heroism that these canons displayed as they went about their tasks, "putting up with so much in the way of sick people's filth and their practically intolerable stenches." Indeed he could not imagine any other "kind of penance comparable in the eyes of the Lord to this holy and precious martyrdom" and was convinced that these canons would be recompensed for exposing themselves to this horror on a daily basis. "The Lord will transform the dung of this filth—by which their minds are fertilized so that they might bear fruit—into precious stones, and a sweet odor will replace the fetid one." It is significant, given my earlier comparison of the relative merits of the *vita passiva* and the *vita activa*, that Jacques de Vitry should have depicted this kind of selfless service to the poor and the sick as a form of martyrdom, noting the potential "violence" to their own bodies that these canons faced every day as they tended to their patients. Since the majority of the religious options that he described in the *Historia Occidentalis* involved some form of monastic retreat from the world, he may have felt the need to defend the efforts of these canons, who, rather than turn their backs on the distractions of this world in pursuit of a life of contemplative penance, sought penitential purification through their total immersion in the most unsavory aspects of life in the world.[5]

As attentive as these canons were to the physical needs of the poor and the sick, they by no means neglected their spiritual needs. As part of their daily regimen, the *Historia Occidentalis* tells us, the canons "instructed the uneducated with divine preaching, consoled the weak in spirit, and encouraged them to be patient and to engage in acts of thanksgiving." Their attempts to help the unfortunate in this world find relief in the next are perfectly consistent with what we know about changes in the use and contents of sermons in the same period. Whereas the traditional goals of preaching within the Christian church had been to provide doctrinal instruction for the laity and to promote uniformity in belief and practice, by the end of the eleventh century we see signs of sermons being used more to promote and channel the spiritual anxiety of their Christian audiences.[6] By the late twelfth century, this kind of preaching was beginning to evolve into a new subgenre, the *sermones ad status*: sermons created to meet the specific needs of a particular subset of Christian society.[7] Jacques de Vitry, who was himself an early episcopal pioneer of this kind of preaching, began writing sermons for audiences all across the social spectrum, including ones aimed at the poor (*ad pauperes*) and lepers (*ad leprosos et alios infirmos*). In his sermons to lepers, Jacques reminded his afflicted listeners of the patience of Job and the quiet suffering of Lazarus, calling on them to accept their own afflictions as a God-given opportunity to purge themselves of sin and focus their attention fully on the next life.[8] The logic behind sermons such as these was, in fact, the same logic that informed the contemporary rise and spread of a new kind of leprosarium that was actually modeled on the monastery.[9] After all, whether the institution in question was a *congregatio leprosum* or a *congregatio monachorum*, the goal was much the same: to create an environment in which the members of the community would be best able to prepare for their deaths to this world and their rebirths into the next one.

Beyond the efforts of religious orders like the Augustinian Canons, the twelfth and thirteenth centuries also witnessed an impressive surge in the number of laypeople who dedicated their lives and resources to the needs of those urban dwellers who occupied the lowest rungs of the social ladder.[10] One of these so-called civic saints was Omobono of Cremona (d. 1197), who was elevated to the ranks of sainthood by papal decree in 1198.[11] According to Innocent III's bull *Quia pietas*, Omobono combined an extraordinarily intense devotion to the liturgy with selfless service to the poor. In the words of the bull, "he did as much for the poor—whom he kept with him, caring for and attending to them in his very own house—as he did for the other indigents, diligently carrying out acts of humanity on behalf of the living and devoutly offering burial for the dead." Though the document says nothing about Omobono's status or occupation, we know from the metrical choral office composed in the saint's honor later in the thirteenth century that he was a merchant or businessman of some sort.[12] The relevant verse reads: "Cutting himself off from the companionship of perverse business, he was summoned to the office of blessed contemplation; . . . deserting the commerce of worldly things, he was transformed into a merchant of the kingdom of heaven."[13]

The city of Monza was home to another such saint, Gerardo Tintori (d. 1207), who founded a "hospice for the poor" there in 1174 with money he had inherited from his father.[14] Gerardo "would go anywhere in the region of Monza where the poor and sick lay and would with his own hands—or sometimes with the help of a friend—carry them to his hospice and lay them down on clean beds.[15] He personally scrubbed lepers clean and received with the kiss of peace every sick person to whom he gave shelter. He ministered to them personally every hour as necessary and performed without indignation whatever service was required."[16] Gerardo was also a generous almsgiver, who had a reputation for never turning anyone away empty-handed. In fact when the region suffered a severe famine, Gerardo's compassion led him to open the storehouses of his hospice and distribute every bit of food and wine that they contained, trusting in the Lord to replenish his supplies.

Gualtiero of Lodi (d. 1224) also dedicated his life to ministering to the sick.[17] Upon the death of his parents, he distributed his inheritance among the poor and began to work in a hospice in Piacenza. After two years he returned to the city of his birth and worked in another hospice just outside the city gates until he decided to found his own, which he administered while living the life of an ascetic. In the words of his hagiographer, "he assailed his flesh with assiduous fasting and wept most frequently while he prayed. He went about barefoot, content with little food and the poorest of clothes." Indeed "the example of Gualtiero attracted many from both sexes to his eremitic lifestyle." By the time he died he had founded four other hospices in neighboring cities, each of which was overseen by one of his *confratres*.[18]

Andre Gallerani (d. 1251) of Siena was another saint of this type.[19] Despite his noble background, he chose to spend his life serving as an amateur physician to the poor. His hagiographer noted that Andre's compassion for the sick was so intense that "the sufferings of these wretches afflicted him more than they did those who actually experienced them." Thus Andre, like Gerardo Tintori, "diligently sought out the sick and the afflicted, visiting and consoling them, admonishing and exhorting them to be patient." Once he happened upon a man too poor to have his infected leg properly treated. Andre applied a make-shift dressing, and the leg healed. On another occasion he came across a solitary woman who was about to give birth. "Moved by pity, he assumed the role of midwife himself and performed the task perfectly." Andre's preoccupation with his medical mission met with considerable resistance from his family, who seemed to regard his activities (not to mention his patients) as beneath the dignity of his social standing. They expressed their disdain by tossing his vials of medicine out the window or by refusing to open the door for Andre when, "occupied with his service to the poor," he was late getting home.

Despite the fact that these four Italian laymen—all of whose lives overlapped Francis's—were eventually added to the canon of the saints in recognition of their efforts on behalf of the poor and sick, we know disappointingly little about them.[20] Their official *Lives* are short and the descriptions of their charitable activities unelaborated. One of the very few saints of this type and of this generation who has come down to us in more than a two-dimensional image is Raymond "Palmario" of Piacenza (d. 1200), his memory having been preserved by a singularly conscientious and detail-oriented hagiographer named Rufino.[21] Rufino's text allows us to delve much deeper into the urban-based religiosity of a saint dedicated to living a life of poverty while still helping the poor.

According to Rufino, Raymond's father was a shoemaker of some means, "neither rich nor poor."[22] By the time Raymond had turned twelve, he was spending most of his time in the workshop learning the craft for himself. But two years later, Raymond's father died, and the boy, less than excited about pursuing the family trade and already beginning to feel the stirrings of his own religious vocation, decided to go on a pilgrimage. Accompanied by his mother, Raymond made his way to Jerusalem and visited all of the significant sites in and around the city.[23] But no sooner had their ship brought them back to the shores of Italy than Raymond's mother became ill and died. Back in Piacenza, Raymond reluctantly returned to his work at the shoe shop and earned enough money to support a wife and a growing family. But "the pursuit of this craft was not pleasing to him," and Raymond found himself spending more and more time with religious men, who were impressed with his zeal and his knowledge. "He appeared to them to be most learned and not without the gift of divine wisdom even though he was unlettered."[24] At the same time Raymond made a point of distancing himself from the "lascivious conversations and vain amusements" of the other practitioners of his trade as he resolved to live a more deliberately religious life filled with fasting, prayer, and almsgiving.

Raymond's life took yet another tragic turn when, in the space of a single year, all of his five children died. This misfortune "extinguished in blessed Raymond all the desires associated with this life," leading him to ask his wife—

right after the birth of yet another child—to join him in a vow of perpetual chastity. But as it turned out, she herself died a few months later, and Raymond took this as a sign that it was time for him to leave behind the things of this world. So he handed his only remaining child over to the care of his parents-in-law and set out for Santiago de Compostela to inaugurate what he seems to have imagined would be a life of perpetual pilgrimage. After paying his respects to St. James, Raymond wandered through southern France and northern Italy visiting every notable shrine along the way. He proceeded in this manner until one day in Rome—in the midst of preparations for a second pilgrimage to Jerusalem—he received a vision that completely changed the course of his life. In his dream Jesus himself appeared before Raymond dressed as a pilgrim and said:

> You have already visited all of the most spiritually soothing holy sites. You have no vows left to fulfill except to return to my Holy Sepulcher. But I do not like this plan. There are other things that you could do that would please me more and be of greater use to you. I want you instead to occupy yourself with works of mercy. . . . I do not want you to wander throughout the entire world. I want you instead to return to your native Piacenza where there are many poor and sick people, weighed down with their various afflictions, imploring me for help. For there is no one there to give it to them. You will go, and I will be with you, and I will give you grace, so that you will be able to encourage rich men to give alms, guide disruptive factions toward peace, and direct erring and wayward women toward a virtuous way of life.[25]

Inspired by this vision, Raymond returned to Piacenza and sought the bishop's blessing for his new way of life, a way of life that he described most succinctly to his wife's parents: "I want to live the life of a poor man and be of service to the poor."[26] Acting on the specific instructions he had received in his vision, Raymond found, with the help of a community of sympathetic canons, a suitable place to establish a hospice. Then, dressed in a hoodless tunic "the color of the sky" and carrying a cross on his shoulder, Raymond set out, combing the poor neighborhoods of the city looking for people in need of his help. "I cannot say," wrote his biographer,

> how many unwanted infants he came upon, infants who had been abandoned. He took them to his hospice, often by binding two of them at a time to his chest, to nourish them with his concern so that they would not die in misery. How many sick people, oppressed with their illnesses, and pilgrims on the street without any means of supporting themselves, did he carry on his own shoulders?[27]

Raymond took to the streets searching not only for people who needed his help but also for the kind of funding required to keep his hospice going. Brandishing the cross that he always carried on his shoulder, he called out to would-be donors, paraphrasing Luke: "Blessed are the merciful, for they shall themselves receive mercy. Woe to you greedy and rich, for the harshest judgment will be pronounced upon you." The promise of rewards for the merciful combined with the threat of damnation for the stingy proved compelling. According to his hagiographer, "his words ignited the good and generous while at the same time terrified the avaricious and hard-hearted. He thus received a great deal of alms from both."[28]

Rufino tells us that Raymond took women as well as men into his hospice, installing "matrons" of spotless reputation to oversee the female quarters. In addition to poor women, Raymond also accepted women from "dens of iniquity," if they were finally ready to repent for their sins. Their rehabilitation required constant "exhortations to decency" on his part: "Consider, my daughters, how unhappy your way of life is. If you return to such filth, you will prostitute your honor and lose your souls. You will become the slaves of evil men and die in misery."[29] Once these women had been spiritually rejuvenated, Raymond arranged for them either to be married to "decent men" or to be admitted into convents.

Raymond's efforts were not, however, confined to ministering to the physical and spiritual needs of the guests at his hospice. He regularly made his way to the city jail, where he visited and consoled the condemned. Rufino's text actually provides a glimpse of the kinds of sermons that Raymond, cross in hand, would deliver on such occasions:

> My sons, the end of one's life is not the same for everyone. Some die in bed, some in war, some at sea, some in solitude. Here is one who dies a natural death, and over there is another who dies a violent one. Do not for this reason abandon your hope and your souls, thus becoming fearful of those things that can kill the body but then afterwards have no power to do anything. Instead fear that which is capable of sending you to hell after you die, just as my Savior—who sacrificed himself for you on this most cruel cross—once said.[30]

Raymond also took it upon himself to serve as an advocate for the politically powerless. When approached by a band of beggars who complained that their best efforts were not enough to melt the hearts of the rich, Raymond took to the streets with them, calling out: "Help me, oh help me, cruel and hard-hearted Christians, because I am dying of hunger while you have so much!" When the citizens heard this they called out specifically to Raymond: "Come and eat! Do not torture yourself so!" Raymond responded: "This mouth, which puts up with the vexations of poverty of its own free will, is not my only mouth. All of the mouths that you see before you dying of hunger are mine. I implore you, through this most holy cross: have mercy on the poor of Jesus Christ!"[31] The effect of this dramatic gesture, by which Raymond linked his own voluntary poverty to the involuntary poverty of the poor, was not only to increase the flow of alms but to attract the attention of other pious men who, leaving their homes, joined Raymond in his quest to serve the poor and the sick.

Raymond also spoke out publicly on behalf of justice for the poor and powerless. Once after being approached by a group of "poor widows and children" whose pleas had been ignored by corrupt judges, Raymond accompanied them to the courtroom. Waving his cross, he called out: "Take care to administer justice to the poor, O you judges who judge the land. . . . Remember that after this life you will no longer be judging, but will be judged."[32] Raymond made such an impression on the leaders of the city that, from that point on, they began to consult him, "as if he were a prophet," whenever they were faced with any difficulty. Indeed Raymond distinguished himself as an effective mediator—"Blessed are the peacemakers"—resolving conflicts between the various factions in Piacenza by reminding them that Christ had come to earth to reconcile man with God: "Why, then, do you want to make yourselves enemies, one against another?" Raymond applied his skills as a negotiator to external conflicts as well, in particular to the tensions that threatened to erupt into a war between Piacenza and Cremona. His intrusive efforts at mediation led to his arrest in Cremona, but he was freed as soon as the authorities realized that they were dealing with a holy man with formidable clout.[33]

In the end, the hagiographer Rufino rhetorically despaired of ever being able to recount all that this saint, "the common parent and protector of all the miserable,"[34] had accomplished in the way of charitable service to his community: "If I were to try to record one-by-one all of the virtues of blessed Raymond, all of his labors, and all of his works of piety, an entire year would not suffice for the task."[35] It was indeed a long, twenty-two-year career of service to the poor and the sick of Piacenza that ended only when Raymond himself contracted a fever and never recovered. His final act was to commend to his faithful companions the continued welfare of the poor.[36]

Given the fact that there were so many laymen living in Italy at the turn of the thirteenth century who sought entrance into the next world by alleviating the plight of the poor and the sick in this one, it is significant that Francis, a product of the same urban environment that produced Omobono, Gerardo, Gualtiero, Andre, and Raymond, should ultimately have decided to follow a different path. Though Francis began his holy career much the same way, by feeding the poor and by ministering to the sick, he soon shifted the focus of his regimen. Instead of continuing to fill his tables with bread for the poor or retiring to a leprosarium and tending to the needs of the sick, Francis opted to become a beggar and seek out charitable benefactors of his own. As consistent as this decision might have been with long-term trends in the history of sanctity, it nevertheless represented a decisive shift away from the new civic saint paradigm, where the goal was to tend to the needs of the urban underclass and where ascetic self-denial, though inevitably a part of the picture, had never been so extreme as to compromise that goal.

That Francis should have decided against this kind of service-oriented life is all the more interesting when one realizes that, like Francis, the civic saints took their cues directly from the Gospels. Rufino could not have been more explicit about locating Raymond's inspiration in his desire to live in *imitatio Christi*. Jesus himself appeared to Raymond telling him to stop wasting his time visiting shrines. Significantly enough, in light of my earlier discussion of gospel poverty, it was the Jesus of Matthew 25 who addressed him on that occasion:

> "Do you think that these pious pilgrimages will be held in particular regard by me at the time of judgment, when I say: 'Come, blessed of my Father, and take possession of the kingdom of heaven. I was hungry and you gave me something

to eat; I was thirsty and you gave me something to drink; I was naked and you clothed me; I was sick and you visited me; I was in jail and you ransomed me'?"[37]

From that point on, Raymond, "occupying [himself] with works of mercy," assumed for himself an explicit form of *imitatio Christi* that combined self-denial with service to the needy of Piacenza, addressing both their physical and spiritual concerns. With a cross propped on his shoulder, he preached sermons to rich men to encourage their almsgiving, to magistrates to curb their injustice, to urban factions to bring about their reconciliation, to prisoners to forestall their despair, and to prostitutes to effect their rehabilitation. And when he was not preaching, Raymond quietly went about his business tending to the patients in his hospice, preparing them either physically to go back out into this world or spiritually to move on to the next one.

What was it that led Francis to reject the civic saint model and embrace a different form of *imitatio Christi*, one that led him to identify with the poor without directly tending to their physical or spiritual needs? Unfortunately the sources do permit a satisfactory answer to this question from Francis's own perspective. But it may turn out that the circumstances that led Francis and Raymond to such different ideas about the role of poverty in *imitatio Christi* are not as significant as those that led to one of them being elevated to the status of a second Christ while the other languished in obscurity.[38] So let us consider what it was about Francis's brand of poverty that sparked such unprecedented interest among his contemporaries and what it was about Raymond's that did not.

St. Francis and His Audience

Francis's conversion played itself out within the urban world of early thirteenth-century Assisi. That being the case, it would not be unreasonable to expect the biographies to reflect the distinctive contours of this world; and to some extent they do. The reference to the "stacks of cloth" that lay about the Bernardone home waiting to be sold is one obvious example.[1] The caricature of Pietro Bernardone as the personification of avarice—the sin par excellence of the merchant class—is a more subtle one.[2] Francis's great aversion to touching coins and his decision to support himself by begging fall into the same category, given the close associations between urban life, money, and mendicancy.

Beyond these examples, however, easily identifiable references to the urban context that gave birth to St. Francis are harder to come by. This is, in large part, a function of the conservative nature of hagiography as a genre. The task that the author of a saint's life faced was first and foremost an apologetic one, aimed at convincing an imagined audience of Christian readers that the candidate in question had a legitimate claim to be included in the canon of saints. To this end, the hagiographer was charged with the responsibility of painting a portrait of a particular, historical holy person in such a way that it bore an unmistakable resemblance to the universal, idealized images of already recognized saints. In the process, much of the individuality of the saint would be sacrificed. Operating under these constraints, Thomas of Celano and the other early biographers predictably constructed their accounts of Francis's conversion as the story of a budding holy man trying to realize his spiritual aspirations in the midst of a world intent on subverting his holy purpose. The precise characteristics of the "world" that conspired against Francis did not really matter to them.

The opening lines of the *Life of St. Francis*, where Thomas of Celano indicts the Bernardones for corrupting their child, are a case in point. "From the earliest years of his life his parents reared him to arrogance in accordance with the vanity of the age. And by long imitating their worthless life and character he himself was made more vain and arrogant."[3] Before launching into his account of the saint's frivolous youth, Thomas took the opportunity to vent about the failings of contemporary Christian parenting in general.

> A most wicked custom has been so thoroughly ingrained among those regarded as Christians, and this pernicious teaching has been so universally affirmed and prescribed, as though by public law, that, as a result, they are eager to bring up their children from the very cradle too indulgently and carelessly. . . . Compelled by the anxiety of youth, [the children] are not bold enough to conduct themselves honorably, since in doing so they would be subject to harsh discipline. . . . Even when the children advance a little more in age, they always fall into more ruinous actions by their own choice. For a flawed tree grows from a flawed root; and what was once badly corrupted can only with difficulty be brought back to the norm of justice. But when they begin to enter the gates of adolescence, what sort of individuals do you imagine they become? Then, without question, flowing on the tide of every kind of debauchery, since they are permitted to fulfill everything they desire, they surrender themselves with all their energy to the service of outrageous conduct.[4]

"This is the wretched early training," observed Thomas, "in which that man whom we today venerate as a saint . . . passed his time from childhood and miserably wasted and squandered his life almost up to his twenty-fifth year. Maliciously advancing beyond all his peers in vanities, he proved himself a more excessive inciter of evil and a more zealous imitator of foolishness."[5] Had Francis not been "bridled" by the Lord, observed Thomas, he would have squandered his life "in his flamboyant display of vain accomplishments: wit, curiosity, practical jokes and foolish talk, songs and soft flowing garments."[6]

For all the passion and sting of Thomas's critique of the saint's upbringing, there is nothing in it that allows us to locate this form of corruption in a specifically urban, commercial context. But even if Thomas's description of the "world" against which Francis struggled is too generic for us to make out its distinctive shape, his hagiographic emphasis on the utter polarity between Francis, the saint, and his father, the man of the world, is still highly suggestive. When, in response to his father's demands that he renounce his patrimony, Francis obliged by removing all of his clothes,[7] he sent a strong signal to his father—and to the reader of Thomas's account—that it was his intention to live a life as different as possible from the worldly one that had been laid out for him. If his father was proud, Francis would be humble. If his father lived a life of excess, Francis would embrace a life of deprivation. If his father loved money, Francis would treat it like dung. As diametrically opposed as father and son were, it is of the utmost importance to recognize that Francis's new life, forged in reaction to the life for which his father had been preparing him, could not help but reflect the life that the saint was trying so hard to reject. The only "world" that Francis knew, hence the only world that he could have fled, was the world of the urban elite of Assisi. To flee such a life meant to embrace its opposite. But to embrace its opposite, was to embrace a life that, by its very nature, was defined by the life left behind. Put differently, the more Francis distanced himself from his father's world, the more his new life began to take on the shape of the old one—albeit inside out and upside down.

This simple but indispensable observation helps explain not only why Francis's spiritual regimen centered around poverty but why his poverty was so different from ordinary poverty. In his effort to distance himself from his peer group, to live a life as different from the life of a well-to-do burgher as possible, Francis naturally gravitated toward destitution. But the fact that Francis approached poverty as a rebellious member of the merchant class meant that his destitution would have to be constructed artificially, not out of the actual experience of the poor but out of a theoretical inversion of the experiences of the wealthy; hence the vast gulf between holy poverty and ordinary poverty that I discussed in chapter 3. For Francis's poverty to have no cares, for it to serve as a source of comfort, for it to require hard work to maintain, it had to be conceived of as a commodity that was precious and valuable and difficult to obtain.[8] Indeed Francis's pursuit of poverty was no less feverish than most men's pursuit of riches. "No one," according to Thomas, "coveted gold as avidly as [Francis] coveted poverty; no one was as careful to guard a treasure as he was to watch over this pearl of the gospel."[9] In short, Francis's poverty had much more in common with the wealth of his former peer group than with the destitution of the poor people of Assisi.

Such an appreciation of the conceptual continuity between Francis's new world and the world he left behind is equally essential for understanding why, despite the fact that Francis's life was absolutely antithetical to the life of his father, other burghers inevitably found themselves drawn to him and to the "wealth" of his poverty. Francis was not just any saint. He was a saint whose conversion and holy life had sprouted in the distinctive soil of early thirteenth-century Italian urban culture. His sanctity, which expressed itself specifically as an inversion of the values of the burgher culture that had spawned him, was precisely the kind of sanctity that would strike a chord in people who had imbibed this value system from birth.[10] This is not to imply that Francis was immediately hailed as a saint by his peer group. "Striking a chord" could just as easily lead to hostility as veneration, there being only a thin line between sanctity and insanity as far as social perception is concerned.[11] I have already noted that the citizens of Assisi first greeted Francis's new life with a shower of mud and stones. But soon their passionate rejection gave way to an equally passionate acceptance of Francis as a saint who had somehow managed to touch a nerve, who knew how to speak to their particular spiritual concerns.[12] Even those who did not appreciate Francis's inversion of their value system enough to want to restructure their own lives accordingly seemed to know exactly what he was doing and had a hard time not feeling guilty for their own continued participation in the dominant urban culture.[13]

Realizing that Francis, by the very nature of his background and his conversion, "spoke the language" of the burgher is fundamental if we are to appreciate his phenomenal success as a preacher.[14] We need to consider this in some detail not only because preaching was such a major part of Francis's spiritual regimen but because his sermons served as the medium through which his own personal inversion of the burgher ethos was packaged for consumption by other citizens. As all of Francis's biographers made eminently clear, Francis was not content with his own spiritual regeneration. He felt obliged to bring others along with him, to make them see the world through his own inverted eyes. "For he knew that he was sent for this: to win for God souls which the devil was trying to snatch away."[15]

It is unfortunate that no detailed accounts of any of Francis's sermons have survived. What we have instead are a few potentially firsthand accounts of how he preached and how profoundly he affected his audiences. "His word was like a blazing fire," observed Thomas of Celano, "reaching the deepest parts of the heart and filling the souls of all with wonder."[16] "He was a forthright preacher of truth," noted the author of the *Legend of the Three Companions*, "not using fawning words or seductive flattery, because he first convinced himself by action and then convinced others by word."[17] The *Anonymous of Perugia* reports that "the Lord placed in his mouth uncompromising, sweet words that flowed like honey, so that hardly anyone ever tired of listening to him."[18] In the *Remembrance*, Thomas quotes a physician as saying: "I remember the sermons of other preachers word for word; only what the saint, Francis, says eludes me. Even if I memorize some of the words, they don't seem to me like those that originally poured from his lips."[19] Another eyewitness, who attended one of Francis's sermons in Bologna in 1222, recalled, in greater detail:

> I saw Francis preaching in the square in front of the public palace, where practically the entire city had gathered. . . . He spoke so well and sensibly that this preaching of an unlettered man stirred the very enthusiastic admiration of even the especially erudite people who were there. He did not, however, hold to the classical manner of preaching but just shouted out practically whatever came into his mind. . . . His clothing was filthy, his whole appearance contemptible, and his face unattractive. But God put such force in his words that many factions of nobles, among whom the wild fury of old hatreds had caused much bloodshed, were in fact peacefully reconciled. So great was the respect and devotion of this audience that men and women crowded in on him, seeking to touch his hem or to carry off a piece of his ragged clothing.[20]

All who heard Francis seemed to agree that his skill as a preacher was not the kind of skill that could be taught.[21] From their perspective it was "Christ, true power and wisdom," that made Francis's voice "a voice of power."[22]

We know that the main subject of Francis's sermons was penance; penance in preparation for the New Age to come.[23] His inspiration for this kind of sermon came directly from the Gospels, where Francis discovered that from the moment Jesus began to preach, he was calling on his audiences to "repent, for the kingdom of heaven is at hand."[24] The official approval that the new order won from Innocent III included the charge to "go with the Lord, brothers, and as the Lord will see fit to inspire you, preach penance to all."[25] Francis complied by going "around the cities and villages, proclaiming the kingdom of God and preaching peace and penance for the remission of sins."[26] When he sent his brothers out two-by-two to preach, he instructed them to do the same.[27]

Francis seems to have had a real aptitude for this kind of hortative preaching, making his listeners feel the full weight of their guilt.[28] He understood, in particular, the persuasive power of his own example, thus allowing him, in a manner of speaking, to make "of his whole body a tongue."[29] Considering himself to be the greatest sinner of all, Francis "was not ashamed . . . when he did something wrong . . . to confess it in his preaching before all the people."[30] Once, as I have mentioned, Francis had a brother lead him through the streets on the end of a rope, publicly embarrassing him for eating a piece of chicken. Those who witnessed this pathetic scene went away in tears: "Woe to us! We are wretches and our whole life is steeped in blood! With excess and drunkenness we feed our hearts and bodies to overflowing!"[31] On another occasion, when invited to preach before the Poor Clares, Francis simply made a circle of ashes on the floor around him, recited the *Miserere mei Deus*, and left. "The handmaids of God were so filled with contrition by the power of this mime that they were flowing with tears, and could hardly restrain their hands from punishing themselves."[32] As Thomas succinctly put it, "a true scorner of himself, [Francis] taught others to despise themselves by word and example."[33]

It is hard to imagine Francis in the midst of one of these dramatic penitential sermons without being reminded of the jongleurs, the popular street-corner entertainers and storytellers who were a fixture in every medieval city of the time.[34] In fact the Francis whom we know from the earliest biographies was captivated by this particular form of popular entertainment. Thomas of Celano cited "practical jokes, foolish talk, and songs" among the litany of merchant class "frivolities" in which the young Francis had immersed himself before his conversion.[35] But even when he left the world he took with him the songs and dances that he had learned, reworking them for more holy purposes. According to the *Assisi Compilation*, Francis was known to "pick up a stick from the ground and put it over his left arm, while holding a bow bent in his right hand, drawing it over the stick as if it were a violin, performing all the right movements, and in French would sing about God."[36] The same source has Francis encouraging one of his musically inclined brothers—who had given up the lute when he had given up the things of the world—to take it up again "and play for me a decent song and with it we will say the words and praises of the Lord."[37] Singing and dancing would in fact become part and parcel of Francis's preaching technique. Again the *Assisi Compilation* describes how—in conjunction with Brother Pacifico, who had a reputation as "a very courtly master of singers" and who was known to his friends as the "king of verses"—Francis composed the *Canticle of the Sun* so that the friars could supplement their sermons with music and thus become "minstrels of the Lord."[38] Even in the midst of an audience with the pope, Francis "could not contain himself for joy. As he brought forth the words from his mouth, he moved his feet as if dancing."[39] According to Thomas, Cardinal Ugolino was worried at first that Innocent III might mistake Francis's behavior for that of a common entertainer or, as he put it, "despise the blessed man's simplicity." Hence Thomas's apologetic observation that Francis danced "not playfully but burning with the fire of divine love, not provoking laughter but moving them to tears of sorrow." Francis certainly did not learn to preach this way from bishops, like Ugolino, to whom the task of Christian instruction had traditionally been relegated. He learned it from the troubadours and jongleurs whom he had listened to all his life on the streets and in the squares of Umbria.

But the techniques used by the medieval troubadours were really not all that different from those employed by medieval merchants. Lester K. Little, who has done more than any other scholar of the mendicant orders to appreciate their distinctive religiosity in light of the socioeconomic context of thirteenth-century Italian cities, has drawn attention to Franciscan and Dominican preaching as a religious version of the "defining activities" of burgher culture.

> The dominant members of the urban sector of society were merchants, bankers, lawyers, notaries, school masters, and certain of the landlords who organized production on their lands for the market. They did not make their living by praying, or by fighting, or by "working," not, at least, by working with their hands. They talked; they argued; they negotiated, they wrote; they entertained; above all, they tried to persuade other people. Such were the defining or characteristic activities of those who prospered in the urban environment.[40]

It was thus no surprise, according to Little, that the same emphasis on verbal persuasion should come to characterize the mendicant orders, whose preaching techniques were never far removed from "street-corner or public-square hawking."[41] Francis is the *locus classicus* for Little's observations. As much as he may have tried to sever his ties to the family cloth business, he never seems to have lost his ability—honed, we would imagine, by years of experience in the markets of Assisi—to persuade potential customers to buy what he was selling.[42] The commodity was different: instead of peddling cloth, Francis peddled heaven. But the process was much the same. Like a merchant in his stall, Francis deliberately made a spectacle of himself in order to get the attention of his "customers." Once he had their ear, he filled it with vivid language about sin and redemption, trying to "sell" his listeners a different way of looking at their lives, one that would lead them to the kind of heartfelt contrition that he knew from personal experience was the first and most important step toward salvation.[43]

Not only the style of Francis's preaching but its content betrayed his basic merchant mentality. Little underscored the mendicant reliance on "a marketplace vocabulary" when preaching,[44] as well as a tendency to differentiate between good and bad uses of wealth.[45] But at a more fundamental level it is imperative to realize that the penitential challenge that Francis laid before his audiences was, in and of itself, an economic one: he advised them to "divest" from this world so that they could "invest" in the next one and by so doing enjoy incomparable returns. Francis's own writings are imbued with the language of investment, reflecting not only his own mentality as a product of the urban elite but his deep fascination with the Gospels, which contain many such economic metaphors and images.[46] The earliest form of the Franciscan *Rule* is a case in point. It required would-be brothers to sell everything they had and give it to the poor so that they would have "treasure in heaven."[47] It also cautioned the friars against wearing "expensive clothing in this world . . . so that they may have a garment in the kingdom of heaven."[48] And it proscribed the use of money on the grounds that "we who have left all things" ought to be careful not to "lose the kingdom of heaven for so little."[49] In his *Later Admonition and Exhortation*, Francis encouraged the auxiliary "brothers and sisters of penance" to give alms: "for although people lose everything they leave behind in this world, they nevertheless carry with them the rewards of charity and the alms they have given for which they will receive a reward and a fitting repayment from the Lord."[50]

The biographies of Francis are even more steeped in the imagery of economic exchange and investment as metaphors for conversion. Thomas compared the young Francis to "an experienced merchant" who, upon realizing that he had found a priceless "pearl," began selling all that he had so that he could buy it.[51] Later he identified Francis as "the greatest scorner of earthly things and the most outstanding seeker of heavenly riches," adding that "he wanted to own nothing so that he could possess everything more fully in the Lord."[52] In the *Remembrance*, Francis is "glad to exchange perishable treasure for the hundredfold," insofar as "poverty makes us heirs and kings of the kingdom of heaven."[53] According to Bonaventure, Francis was a "gospel merchant," intent on living a pure life so that he could "melt down all the present time into merit."[54] "You know," Bonaventure's Francis once instructed the brothers, "that poverty is the special way to salvation. . . . For this is the hidden treasure of the Gospel field; to buy it, everything must be sold."[55] In the *Anonymous of Perugia*, we find the Franciscans "filled with great joy, as if they had just acquired an immense treasure."[56] "They rejoiced in their poverty, for they desired no riches except those of eternity."[57] In the *Legend of the Three Companions*, the young Francis finally realized how silly it was to use his money to purchase his friends' approval rather than giving it to the poor "on account of God who repays most generously."[58] According to the *Assisi Compilation*, Francis coached his brothers to consider their begging to be an investment opportunity for the would-be donor: "Whoever will give me a penny, I will give him a hundred silver pieces, nay, a thousand times more."[59] Elsewhere in the *Assisi Compilation*, we find Christ himself consoling the saint, laid low by the pain in his diseased eyes, with vivid images of the compensation that awaited him in heaven.

> Tell me, brother, what if, in exchange for your illnesses and troubles, someone were to give you treasure? And it would be so great and precious that, even if the whole world were changed to pure gold, all stones to precious stones, and all water to balsam, you would still judge and hold all these things as nothing, as if they were earth, stones, and water, in comparison to the great and precious treasure which was given you. Wouldn't you greatly rejoice?[60]

That the style and content of Francis's preaching should reflect the "defining activities" of burgher culture was not simply a function of the saint's own upbringing. It also reflected the composition of his audience. The sources that I have been considering emphasize the universality of Francis's appeal. According to Thomas of Celano, for instance, when Francis preached, people of all stripes would gather around him and be moved by what they saw and heard.[61] "Many people, well-born and lowly, cleric and lay, began to cling to blessed Francis' footsteps."[62] "Rich or poor, noble or insignificant, wise or simple, cleric or illiterate"—all responded to Francis's words and "accepted the habit of holy religion."[63] The wide range of Francis's appeal meant that he had to be ready to adjust the content of his sermons depending on the educational level of his audience. "Although the evangelist Francis preached to the simple in simple, concrete terms," the *Remembrance* tells us, "still, when he was among spiritual people with greater abilities, he gave birth to life-giving and profound words."[64]

But there are two important caveats to consider when assessing the social breadth of Francis's appeal. The first has to do with language. Though Thomas's work has left the impression that everyone in Assisi was hanging on the saint's every word, it is important not to read more into the account than his own social terminology can actually support. The term "illiterate" was commonly used in this period simply as a way of distinguishing laymen from clerics. Even the designations "noble" and "well-born," as opposed to "insignificant" and "lowly," do not necessarily imply anything about relative wealth. They simply allowed Thomas to distinguish between those families in Assisi that could lay claim to knightly status and those that could not.[65] This is not to say that there were no poor people in Francis's audience. After all, we know that he was a spectacle, a sight to behold. We can safely assume that people of all types—including social outcasts of every description—gathered around him when he started singing and dancing. Captivated as they were by his unusual and charismatic presence, the poor and sick may not have cared much what Francis actually said.[66]

Second, and more fundamental, it is important to keep in mind the different obstacles that members of Francis's audience faced when considering his program for spiritual reform and how class-specific these obstacles could be.[67] It is true that from a theological perspective, Francis's message of repentance and detachment from the things of the world was a message that every conscientious Christian was expected to hear and take to heart. Whether rich or poor, individual Christians had to demonstrate to God that they valued their ties to the other world more than their ties to this one. Though a poor person may have had little to give up in the way of material attachments—so little, in fact, that it might not have been apparent to an outside observer that anything about the poor man's life had changed upon his conversion—God would still expect him to give up the little that he had and would know, in his omniscience, whether that sacrifice had indeed been made. If a person truly had nothing, then God would expect him to give up completely any *desire* for worldly things, so that if he ever did have access to such things in the future, he would reject them on principle.[68] Considering this moral challenge from the perspective of an all-knowing God, the poor were the equal of the rich, and both could benefit from Francis's words.

But if we consider sanctification from a sociological perspective, it was not God who scrutinized individual Christians to determine whether they had achieved a proper level of disdain for the things of the world but the community of believers acting in the name of God.[69] Lacking divine omniscience, the community had little choice but to rely on empirical evidence of material sacrifice in order to determine who had truly distanced himself from the world and who had not. From this perspective, the affluent Christian had a decided advantage over the poor one, for he was in a position to relinquish money, property, or social standing in such a way as to impress the community with the magnitude of his sacrifice. The analogous sacrifice of the poor man, regardless of its completeness and sincerity, was much less likely to win the approval and respect of the community, because this kind of sacrifice—which would have involved giving up little more than the *desire* for material things and patiently accepting what had never been a matter of choice in the first place—did not lend itself to any obvious form of empirical verification. Unable to offer such unambiguous signs of his regeneration, where was the poor person to look for the kind of social support and admiration that the man of means knew would be there waiting for him the moment he decided to relinquish his possessions? If pressed, thoughtful Christians in Francis's day would certainly have assented to the possibility of a poor person who was also "poor in spirit" entering the kingdom of heaven. After all, everyone knew the story of Lazarus and how, through his supposed patient resignation to his lot, he managed to turn his involuntary poverty into a form of voluntary poverty. But the same Christians would have been at a loss for how to distinguish (in the absence of the kind of scriptural verification that Lazarus enjoyed) this kind of holy poor man from the others who occupied the same socioeconomic niche but who despised their condition.[70] And even if they were able to make such distinctions, they probably would have had a difficult time placing this kind of a poor person, regardless of how poor his spirit might have been, on the same level as a Francis or a Bernard of Quintavalle, on the simple and pragmatic grounds that their sacrifices (as formerly affluent men) had been, in monetary terms, so much greater than his.[71]

Considering the idea of voluntary poverty from both a theological and a sociological perspective allows us to appreciate how Francis's message of penance and detachment from the things of this world could be both universal in its scope yet quite specific in its application. Though poor Christians were, technically speaking, under the very same obligations as Christians of means to cut their ties to things secular, they operated under a great disadvantage when it came to publicly verifying that they had actually taken this step.[72] So even if Francis as a preacher held out the prospect of spiritual regeneration through disengagement from the world to all Christians, the community around him, forced as it was to rely on some form of empirical evidence in order to determine which of its members were living up to these high

standards, naturally found it easier to identify and reward the penitential sacrifices of the man of means. The poor who came to listen to Francis's sermons were, in this sense, inevitably (even if inadvertently) shortchanged.

This assessment of Francis's audience parallels what can be ascertained
about the actual social composition of the early order. In a letter of 1216,
Jacques de Vitry categorized the Franciscans as "many well-to-do secular
people of both sexes" who, "having left all things for Christ, had fled the
world."[73] Lester Little's research led him to conclude that among the early
friars who can be identified and whose social circumstances can be ascertained
"there were no peasants or lower class workers of any kind."[74] More recently
C. H. Lawrence interpreted the same data this way:

> Voluntary poverty is not an ideal that has much meaning for those who are
> poor by birth or force of circumstance. The poor of this world dream of get-
> ting rich. Understandably, therefore, although the early Franciscans recruited
> their members from all social groups except the unfree, their chief attraction
> was for the young of the most affluent classes and the clerical intelligentsia,
> young people who had never experienced real want.[75]

The unusual case of brother John "the Simple," who was tilling a field when
he saw Francis and approached him about joining the order, is not as excep-
tional as it might seem. When Francis told him "you must rid yourself of all
your things that you can get without scandal, and give them to the poor," John
"went into the field where he had left the oxen and, untying them, brought
one of them back to blessed Francis. 'Brother,' he said to him, 'I have served
my father and everyone in my household for many years. Although my portion of the inheritance is small, I want to take this ox as my share and give it
to the poor."[76] John may have been "simple," but he was not particularly
poor.[77]

This interpretation also fits what we know about the early patrons of the
Franciscans. According to Little, "the friars seem . . . to have stepped in as
new beneficiaries to an ancient, solidly established tradition [of patronage by
princes and nobles]. . . . The new element in patronage . . . lay in the participation of the prospering and influential people of urban society."[78] The examples that he invokes, drawn from studies of Franciscan patronage patterns
over time, show a steady rise in burgher support, at the expense of the nobles
whose donations to the order dominated its early years.[79] Though the sources
do not allow for identifying many of Francis's original benefactors, that is,
those who offered him food or other assistance at the very beginning of his
religious experiment,[80] we can imagine that they represented every subset of
urban society but that of the urban poor themselves. In the words of Little,
"no evidence, and no logic either, would suggest that the urban poor, themselves so badly off that they sometimes had to beg, gave alms to the friars."[81]

Francis was not the first saint in history to participate in a symbiotic,
sociospiritual relationship with Christians of means. Though at its root Christian sanctity has always been conceived in terms of a life lived in *imitatio
Christi*, the actual interpretation of what constituted a legitimate imitation

depended on extrascriptural factors, prominent among which were the interests of the economically dominant classes and how they conceived of Christian perfection.[82] In an important article published almost thirty years ago,
Barbara Rosenwein and Lester Little specifically addressed this theme as it
pertained not only to Franciscan spirituality in thirteenth-century Italy but to
Benedictine spirituality in tenth-century France.[83] Just as Francis emerged
from the ranks of the burghers and relied on his former peer group for alms
to support his mission, so the monks of Cluny were inevitably products of
rich rural families, which provided the monasteries with the vast tracts of land
that they needed to support themselves and their liturgical activities. Just as
Francis described Christian perfection in terms that Italian merchants could
understand by offering them the opportunity to invest in the next world,[84] so
the monks of Cluny imagined the neighboring castellans as their natural al-
lies in a holy war waged against the legions of the devil, both visible and
invisible.

Rosenwein and Little did not stop to consider the impact of these elite
spiritualities on the truly poor, but their model is nonetheless suggestive.
Thirteenth-century burghers held Francis's "holy poverty" in higher esteem
than they did the poverty of the urban poor, in much the same way that tenth-
century castellans regarded the monks of Cluny as the only true *pauperes
Christi*. As a result, the bulk of almsgiving on the part of burghers and
castellans alike was directed toward maintaining the artificial poverty of the
mendicants and the monks rather than alleviating the very real poverty of
the involuntary urban and rural poor. Moreover, just as Francis's burgher-
focused spiritual economy for all intents and purposes excluded paupers,
so the symbiotic relationship between the "poor" monks and their rich benefactors constituted a closed system that offered no spiritually meaningful
role to the peasant.

The long-term effect of such patronage on the history of medieval sanctity
quite naturally highlighted the activities of those saints who spoke most directly to the needs of the dominant sectors of Christian society. Inevitably it
was *their* versions of Christianity and *their* renditions of *imitatio Christi*
that were endowed and immortalized. Looked at from this perspective, the
spirituality of St. Francis of Assisi is different from that of a holy abbot like
Odo of Cluny (d. 942), primarily insofar as Francis lived at a time when
Christendom's center of economic gravity had shifted from the countryside
to the city. The fact that Francis's religiosity relied more on merchant metaphors than military ones was, to use Aristotelian terminology, accidental, not
essential. His spirituality was still one that properly belonged to the affluent
sectors of Christendom and reflected their particular interests.

What is missing from Francis's repertoire as a preacher, especially as a
preacher who deliberately associated himself with the poor, is the kind of
sermon that would have specifically helped paupers make the most of their
involuntary poverty by treating it as a virtue rather than a vice. Nowhere in
the early sources is there any reference to any sermon of his that specifically
allowed for the possibility of poor people sanctifying themselves by recog-

nizing the spiritual riches that lay dormant in their economic or physical misfortune.[85] As understandable as the absence of such a sermon may be, given what I have said about the focus of Francis's mission, it is still a somewhat surprising omission, given his fascination with the Gospels and his affinity for lepers. For the story of Lazarus, the poor man covered with sores who was denied charity at the rich man's table only to find himself elevated to the bosom of Abraham after his death, provided a ready-made example of a poor and sick man who was actually saved for living a life of apparently patient resignation to the will of God.[86] It is an even more surprising omission when we see Francis using this very logic to console friars who suffered from some illness: "I beg the sick brother to thank God for everything and to desire to be whatever the Lord wills, whether sick or well, because God teaches all those he has destined for eternal life by the torments of punishments, sicknesses, and the spirit of sorrow."[87] Francis advised the sick among the Poor Clares in the same way: "Those weighed down by sickness and the others wearied because of them, all of you: bear it in peace. For you will sell this fatigue at a very high price and each one will be crowned queen in heaven with the Virgin Mary."[88] But if it ever occurred to Francis, in the course of his ministrations to the needy in and around Assisi, to apply this logic to their plight, thereby giving them some hope in the life to come, neither he nor his biographers made any mention of it.[89]

Getting back to the question that I posed at the end of the preceding chapter—what it was about Francis that inspired such intense adulation, well above and beyond the attention garnered by the civic saints—it is important to acknowledge, first of all, that they, no less than Francis, relied on the resources of affluent citizens to support their poverty-based missions. Again Rufino's *Life of Raymond* provides the most detailed case for comparison. Like Francis, Raymond benefited directly from a pervasive and deep-seated combination of guilt and mistrust on the part of such burghers vis-à-vis the urban underclass. Christians of means who experienced some compunction about the uneven distribution of wealth in Assisi or Piacenza, yet wondered whether the beggars who confronted them were truly deserving of alms, presumably welcomed the opportunity to donate to men like Francis or Raymond, whose lives of "holy poverty" were, as far as they were concerned, beyond reproach. This burgher skepticism toward the poor seeped into the hagiography of both saints. The Franciscan brother who wondered aloud if the beggar whom he met was not really a rich man in disguise and the citizens who singled out Raymond from a crowd of hungry beggars, inviting him alone to "come and eat," both reflect this discriminating attitude on the part of would-be almsgivers.

But while both saints provided affluent citizens with an opportunity to give alms with the security of knowing that the recipient was truly "worthy" in God's eyes, Francis offered them something more: a mission directed specifically at their spiritual needs. While Raymond sought "to live the life of a poor man and be of service to the poor," Francis sought to live the life of a poor man so as to induce others in his peer group to repent for their worldliness. While Raymond identified with the poor to make certain that they were not ignored by almsgivers and judges, Francis identified with the poor to dramatize his rejection of the values of his social class. While Raymond sought alms to support his hospice, Francis sought alms as an exercise in humility that would give him credibility as a preacher of penance. While Raymond's sermons offered spiritual consolation and hope to social outcasts, Francis's sermons offered spiritual consolation and hope to those who were in a position to enjoy life enough to feel guilty about it.[90] In short, Francis, unlike Raymond and his like, offered his burgher audience a form of religiosity that truly gave them the spiritual upper hand, the moral "inside track," in the race to heaven. It was not simply about affluent Christians counteracting the spiritually deleterious effects of wealth by engaging in acts of charity toward the poor. It was about redefining poverty altogether in such a way that only Christians of means could really appreciate it and aspire to it.

As the son of a prosperous cloth merchant who had radically reconsidered his own investment in the material world, Francis found himself in an ideal position to challenge his peers to do the same. While only a very small percentage of the burghers whom he invited to reinvest in heaven actually entered the ranks of the voluntarily poor, many more must have appreciated the way Francis, in a sense, sanitized poverty by underscoring the particular merits of *voluntary* poverty. Indeed one could argue that it was his success in taking poverty as a virtue away from the involuntary poor and giving it, in a newly spiritualized form, to the rich that secured for Francis the respect and veneration of guilty burghers who had the resources and the influence to transform him overnight into an *alter Christus* and his followers into a powerful order. This was a vein that neither Raymond nor any of the other civic saints ever managed to tap.

Comparing Francis to the other urban saints allows one to appreciate not only the range of religious experiments in the burgeoning cities of twelfth- and thirteenth-century Italy but also the power of wealthy patrons to shape the future of these experiments. It may be that Francis deliberately broke from the "civic saint" model when he realized that a whole sector of society—the burgher of means—was being overlooked by holy laymen focused on the needs of the urban poor. Or it may be that Francis was simply sucked into a vacuum of spiritual need, a void that the civic saints had done little to fill. Be that as it may, once Francis and his followers found themselves operating within this niche and speaking to the needs of the nonneedy, they managed to unleash tremendous economic forces. One is left to wonder what effect this colossal channeling of resources in support of Francis's mission had on the relief programs that were being run by holy men, like Raymond, who were comparatively less attractive to affluent urban benefactors. Would the revenues generated by the Franciscans have found their way to other more "poor-friendly" institutions and saints if Francis had remained a merchant? Or would they simply have stayed in the pockets of the burghers until someone like Francis finally came along and spoke to them about a kind of poverty that they could truly appreciate? In either case, the unprecedented speed with which

Francis was canonized and laid to rest in a monumental new basilica would seem to say more about the economic clout of his primary constituency than about the relative authenticity of his *imitatio Christi*. There were, after all, plenty of "second Christs" at work in early thirteenth-century Italy, but perhaps only one whose conception of poverty spoke so directly to the needs of the nonpoor.

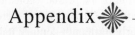

A Consideration of the Sources

The thirteenth-century sources on which this study relies were not written in a vacuum. As I noted at the outset, the authors all operated in the midst of an intense and often volatile controversy about the precise meaning of Franciscan poverty, a controversy that cannot but have affected the way they chose to depict Francis's life. The problem for historians has been how to identify and then to interpret the actual points in the texts where the controversy might have influenced the wording of the biographies. This dilemma will become clearer as I consider each of the sources in its historical context. Before doing that, however, it will be useful to consider in some detail the history of that portion of the Franciscan poverty controversy that overlapped the period within which the earliest biographers were writing.[1]

Even before Francis's death, differences of opinion with regard to the precise role of poverty had begun to surface among the architects of the order. For Francis the pursuit of poverty in *imitatio Christi* was, as I have shown, the keystone of his distinctive religiosity. But from the perspective of his papal supporters, poverty played an ancillary role to the primarily pastoral one that they envisioned for the new order. Francis's *Testament*, dictated only a few weeks before his death in 1226, bears witness to the saint's fear that his radical commitment to poverty would not survive him, given the growth and redirection of the Friars Minor. The specific warnings in the *Testament* testify to real changes that were already underway, specifically the proliferation of buildings in violation of the order's vow of poverty,[2] the reliance on papally endorsed privileges that allowed friars to preach with or without episcopal approval,[3] and the reinterpretation of the *Rule* that made these modifications possible.[4] Despite Francis's deep aversion to glossing, he felt compelled to insist that the *Testament* be read alongside the *Rule* at every chapter meeting, so that "we might observe the *Rule* we have promised in a more Catholic way."[5]

Francis's suspicions were confirmed only four years after his death, with the publication of Gregory IX's pivotal bull, *Quo elongati* (1230). The pope issued the bull in response to an appeal on the part of the friars for clarification of the *Rule*, which Gregory—in his previous capacity as Cardinal Bishop Ugolino, the protector of the Friars Minor—had helped to craft in the first place. He took the opportunity provided by this request to modify Franciscan poverty in three important ways. First of all, *Quo elongati* dismissed the *Testament*, with its powerful endorsement of poverty, as nonbinding on the friars on the grounds that it had been issued after Francis had relinquished his leadership of the order.[6] Second, the bull authorized the Friars Minor to use intermediaries to handle donations and supplies on their behalf so as not to violate the letter of their sworn commitment to poverty.[7] Third, it established a crucial distinction between *usus* and *dominium*, which allowed the Franciscans to "use" the things donated to them while the actual "dominion," or ownership, over those things remained in the hands of the benefactors.[8] While this distinction provided the Franciscans with a theoretical basis for claiming that their poverty went deeper than traditional monastic poverty, insofar as the friars disavowed not only individual but collective ownership, such a focus on poverty as a function of ownership rather than consumption did little to discourage levels of material use that went well beyond what Francis had intended. Under Gregory and his immediate successors, the gap between those Franciscans who were satisfied with the *dominium*-based interpretations of poverty (the so-called Conventual Franciscans) and those who advocated adherence to the level of *usus* modeled by Francis himself (the Spiritual Franciscans) widened. Innocent IV's *Ordinem vestrum* (1245) not only amplified the role of intermediaries but reinforced the Franciscan notion of complete "dominionlessness" by declaring papal ownership of everything donated to, and used by, the Franciscan order.

Disagreements over poverty from within the order opened the door to criticism of the Franciscans from without. Beginning in 1253, the secular masters of Paris, resentful of the papal privileges enjoyed by the mendicant orders in the university, began to question their role within the church.[9] One of the strategies that masters like William of St. Amour adopted with regard to the Franciscans was to challenge their claims to perfect, apostolic poverty on the grounds that Jesus and the apostles had, in fact, owned things. The "bag" mentioned twice in the Gospel of John provided all the scriptural evidence that William needed to posit communal ownership on the part of Jesus and the apostles, despite the fact that it was Judas who carried it.[10] The debate that ensued ultimately led Bonaventure, the most famous and prolific of the Franciscan ministers general, to compose an extended *Defense of the Poor* (1269),[11] which attempted to explain away the "bag" and uphold the idea that Jesus' poverty—and by extension, that of the Franciscans—was in fact a poverty based on the complete absence of ownership, both personal and communal. Ten years later, Nicholas III (1277–80) weighed in heavily on the side

of the Franciscans, confirming the Bonaventuran interpretation of their poverty with the bull *Exiit qui seminat* (1279).

Nicholas intended his word to be the final one on the subject of Franciscan
poverty. But the growing split between the Conventual and Spiritual Franciscans in the later thirteenth century opened the door to another even more ran-
corous debate over the level of appropriate "use" of material goods by the
order. As important as the so-called *usus pauper* controversy was for the history of the Franciscan order, it began too late to exercise any influence over
the sources with which I am concerned in this study, all of which date from
within thirty years of Francis's death.[12] At this point, it is time to introduce
each of these sources, consider what is known about its author, and, insofar
as is possible, correlate its depiction of Francis with the politics and chronology of the earliest phases of the Franciscan poverty controversies.

The first to write a life of Francis was Thomas of Celano, an early disciple
about whom unfortunately we know very little. The contemporary *Chronicle*
of Brother Jordan tells us that Thomas was one of twenty-five friars sent in
1221 to establish the Friars Minor in Germany.[13] Within a short time, Thomas
became *custos* for the nascent Rhineland communities of Mainz, Worms,
Speyer, and Cologne and was appointed vicar when Caesar of Speyer, the
first provincial minister of Germany, returned to Rome.[14] It is unclear why
and when Thomas returned to Italy, but he was there in the summer of 1228
when Gregory IX commissioned him to write an official life of Francis as part
of a canonization process that was, for all intents and purposes, already complete.[15] There were many friars who knew Francis better than Thomas did,
which suggests that the pope may have picked him precisely because he was
more removed from the fissures that were already beginning to divide the
young order.[16] In any case, Thomas composed the *Life of St. Francis* over
the next three years and submitted it to Gregory, who officially endorsed it in
February 1229.[17] The result of Thomas's efforts was an enthusiastic piece of
hagiography that aimed higher than simply justifying Francis's inclusion in
the canon of the saints. Thomas's Francis was to be nothing less than the saint
par excellence, "the most perfect among the perfect,"[18] whose unusually intense *imitatio Christi* was empirically verified by the miracle of the stigmata.[19]

Not surprisingly, given the fact that the *Life* had been papally commissioned, Thomas had nothing but good things to say about the popes whose
careers intersected Francis's. Innocent III, "a glorious man, prolific in learning, brilliant in speech, burning with zeal for justice," welcomed blessed
Francis and sent him off "to preach penance to all."[20] Any hesitation on
Innocent's part about this religious experiment is submerged in the ringing
endorsement he bestows on the young order.[21] But it was Gregory, who as
Cardinal Ugolino had overseen the order before his own papal election, whom
Thomas linked most closely to Francis.[22] As Thomas described it, Ugolino's
"soul was joined to the soul of the holy man" the moment he met him.[23] For
his part, "Francis clung to the bishop as a son does to his father and an only
child to his mother, safely resting and sleeping in the lap of his kindness."[24]
With this union of saint and pope in mind, Thomas reserved the third book of

his *Life of St. Francis* for the actual canonization ceremony. There we are presented with the dramatic spectacle of a grief-stricken pope raising his hands to heaven and decreeing that Francis's name be added to the catalogue of the saints.[25] In light of what the *Testament* reveals about Francis's concern over the relaxation of the *Rule*, and what *Quo elongati* reveals about Gregory IX's views on Franciscan poverty, it is hard not to see Thomas's heavy hand at work, smoothing over the substantial differences between saint and pope.

Such exaggeration of the like-mindedness of Francis and Gregory is consistent with Thomas's portrayal of harmonious relations between the friars and the episcopacy as a whole. He never mentioned the deep suspicions that bishops throughout Christendom harbored with regard to the friars who came into their dioceses expecting to preach. He offered only a generic indictment of all those who "tried to suffocate the chosen vineyard which the Lord's hand had so kindly planted anew in the world," applauding the fact that these "opponents" had been figuratively slain "with the sword of the venerable father and lord," Ugolino.[26] On the other hand, Thomas made a big point of highlighting the key role played by Bishop Guido II of Assisi. Faced with a standoff between the naked Francis and his angry father, the bishop did not hesitate to side with the former. "Observing [Francis's] frame of mind and admiring his fervor and determination, he got up and, gathering him in his own arms, covered him with the mantle he was wearing."[27] As far as Thomas was concerned, Guido's was the most appropriate episcopal response to Francis, even if it was by no means typical of subsequent encounters between bishops and friars.

Other aspects of the *Life* suggest subtle efforts on Thomas's part to defuse the potentially explosive issues that we know the order was facing at the time of its founder's death. For one thing, Thomas's references to the relaxation of Franciscan poverty are nebulous and hard to pin down. In the midst of Francis's prophecy about the future growth of the order, Thomas had him refer in an elliptical way to its growing pains. "In the beginning of our way of life together we will find fruit that is very sweet and pleasant. A little later, fruit that is less pleasant and sweet will be offered. Finally, fruit full of bitterness will be served which we will not be able to eat. Although displaying some outward beauty and fragrance, it will be too sour for anyone to eat."[28] Elsewhere Thomas recorded Francis's misgivings about brothers who "had abandoned their early deeds and, in the midst of new discoveries, had forgotten their original simplicity,"[29] but without further elaboration. Thomas had the dying Francis warn the brothers to "persevere in what we have begun," prophesying unspecified "scandals" that were to come.[30] But again, specific information about these scandals is not to be found in the *Life*.

Nor does Thomas reveal anything about the rift that we know was beginning to develop within the order. Individuals from both camps are given their share of positive attention in the *Life* without Thomas tipping his hand to reveal where his sympathies lie. On the one hand, Thomas described the four brothers who took care of Francis when he was too sick to take care of himself as the "four pillars" on which the saint rested.[31] Out of respect for their modesty, he would not name them, but it is likely that they included Leo, Angelo, and Rufino, all of whom were, at the time Thomas was writing, earning reputations as rigorists in their interpretation of the *Rule*. Thomas even identified Rufino as the only person who had ever actually touched the wounds of the stigmata while Francis was still alive.[32] On the other hand, Thomas singled out Elias, whom the saint had appointed as his vicar in 1221[33] and who, at the time Thomas was writing, was overseeing the construction of the colossal basilica that would soon house the saint's body. According to Thomas, Elias also "mothered" Francis when he was sick and prophesied his death two years before it happened. And it was Elias whom the dying Francis blessed and designated as a "father to the rest of the brothers."[34]

Two additional biographies of Francis came to light in the years immediately following the publication of the *Life of St. Francis*. The first was the work of a poet, Henri d'Avranches, who, sometime between the years 1232 and 1234, was commissioned by Rome to apply his literary talents to the life of the saint. The result was the *Versified Life of St. Francis*.[35] At the same time, the friar Julian of Speyer set his hand to writing a concise *Life* for the convenience of his Franciscan brothers.[36] Unfortunately neither Henri nor Julian felt inclined to add any information about the saint beyond what could be found in Thomas's official *Life of St. Francis*.

The mid-1230s also saw the publication of the *Sacred Commerce of St. Francis with Lady Poverty*. Although, as I have noted, this allegory contains no biographical information about Francis, it provides a particularly valuable window into the minds of the earliest Franciscans through which we can observe their thoughts on the subject of poverty. While some of the manuscripts explicitly assign the work to the year 1227, contextual considerations suggest that it was actually written the following decade. Such a potent endorsement of strict interpretations of Franciscan poverty makes more sense after the publication of *Quo elongati* in 1230, the election of Elias as minister general in 1232, and the construction of the new church at Assisi, which was largely completed by 1236. The manuscripts of the *Sacred Commerce* that name an author are inconsistent, some attributing it to Anthony of Padua and others to John of Parma. Current scholarship has been leaning more in the direction of a third candidate, Caesar of Speyer, known for his particularly "radical" stance on Franciscan poverty.[37] Regardless of its author's actual identity, though, it is clear from the content, tone, and early appearance of the *Sacred Commerce* that it was intended to affirm the order's dedication to absolute poverty at a time, in the immediate wake of Francis's death, when that commitment was first beginning to fade. In particular, the extended lesson that Lady Poverty gives to Francis about the wily ways of her nemesis "Greed" seem to have been directed, at least in part, toward those responsible for undermining Francis's original commitment to poverty after he had relinquished control of the order.[38]

Internal evidence suggests that the next of the biographies, known today as the *Anonymous of Perugia*, was composed sometime between the spring of 1240 and the summer of 1241.[39] Although the author deferred to Thomas of Celano more than modern historians of Francis would have liked, what he added in the way of information sheds important new light on the early years of the order. The work as a whole represents a significant shift in focus away from Francis's life per se to the formation and character of the Friars Minor. So while the account begins and ends the way Thomas's does, with Francis's conversion and his canonization, the intervening chapters are all dedicated to the experiences of "the brothers" as a whole. Indeed the original title of the work was actually *The Beginning or Founding of the Order and the Deeds of Those Lesser Brothers Who Were the First Companions of Blessed Francis in Religion.* Given the time frame within which the author was writing, roughly ten years after *Quo elongati*, such a corporate angle may well reflect an effort on the author's part to underscore the primacy of the order at a time when the memory of the founder, kept alive by his companions, as well as by the officially discounted *Testament*, loomed large as a potentially dissident source of authority.

The production of new biographical material about Francis received a real boost in 1244, when the recently appointed Franciscan minister general, Crescentius of Iesi, decided that the *Life of St. Francis*, for all its virtues, was incomplete, there being much in the way of additional information still circulating orally about the saint. With this in mind, he invited all who had actually known Francis to send him "whatever they could truly recall about the life, miracles, and prodigies of blessed Francis" so that these reminiscences might be edited as a supplement to the *Life of St. Francis*.[40] The single largest contribution seems to have come from three of Francis's closest companions, Leo, Angelo, and Rufino, who worked together for a year to record what they remembered about the saint. Unfortunately the text of their reminiscences has not survived in its original form. Instead we are left with a number of works that seem to have relied on it and reproduced it to varying degrees.

One of these is known as the *Legend of the Three Companions*. Textual comparisons reveal that a third of the information contained in the *Legend* can be traced to the *Life of St. Francis* and another third to the *Anonymous of Perugia*. What is left adds primarily to our knowledge of Francis's early life and conversion. Much ink has been spilled sorting out the *Legend*'s complicated manuscript tradition and determining the relationship between its introductory letter (which specifically claims that the *Legend* was written by Leo, Angelo, and Rufino in 1246 in response to Crescentius's call for information about Francis) and the contents of the *Legend* proper, which do not fulfill the promises made by the letter.[41] Even if, as many scholars suspect, the letter was added later to give the *Legend* more credibility, most accept the authenticity of the information provided by the text itself, assigning the bulk of it to the period between 1241 and 1247. Though there is not a great deal of new information in the *Legend* that speaks directly to contemporary concerns about poverty, the anecdote describing the inspiration behind Francis's decision to beg for food rather than simply rely on the support of patrons is at least suggestive of the radical Franciscan stance on property and revenues.[42]

The effects of the poverty dispute are easier to discern in the second of these composite biographical texts: the collection known as the *Assisi Compilation*, which, in contrast to the *Legend of the Three Companions*, has survived in only one manuscript.[43] At one point, for instance, we find the ministers pushing Francis to relax his stand on poverty, urging him "to allow the brothers to have something at least in common." After consulting Jesus in prayer, Francis specifically prohibits—in language that reflects Gregory's *Quo elongati*—"everything held individually or in common" on the grounds that Christ would provide for his family of friars "as long as it would put its hope in him."[44] In the same spirit, the *Assisi Compilation* repeatedly reiterates Francis's opposition to the acquisition of buildings to house the growing number of friars. It tells, for instance, of Francis's insistence on sending a basket of fish to the monastery that owned the Portiuncula, despite the fact that "the abbot and monks had freely granted that church to blessed Francis and his brothers without any payment or annual tax." The text explains: "[Francis] did this as a sign of greater humility and poverty, so that the brothers would not have any place of their own, and would not remain in any place that was not owned by others, and thus they in no way had the power to sell it or give it away."[45] Similarly, we find Francis poised to dismantle a building that was erected adjacent to the Portiuncula in his absence, until he learns that it belongs to the commune of Assisi.[46] In short, Francis "did not want the brothers to live in any place unless it had a definite owner who held the property rights."[47]

The problem of books was another major sticking point for the Francis of the *Assisi Compilation*.[48] "When a minister asked Francis for permission to keep some elegant and very expensive books, he got this reply: 'I refuse to lose the book of the gospel . . . for these books of yours! Do as you please, but don't use my permission for a trap.'"[49] After he had relinquished control of the order, Francis told a novice who requested a psalter, "Do as your minister tells you." But after thinking about it, Francis called the novice back to him, apologized for his hesitation, and simply told him: "Whoever wishes to be a Lesser Brother must have nothing but the tunics, the cord, and the short trousers that the *Rule* allows him."[50] This attitude toward books explains why the Francis of the *Assisi Compilation* did not hesitate for a moment to part with the only copy of the scriptures that he and the brothers had, when they found that they had nothing else to give a poor beggar.[51]

Beyond the problems associated with the ownership of books, the *Assisi Compilation* depicts a Francis concerned about the deleterious effects of "owning" even the information that comes from books. Francis's ideal minister general was, among other things, not a "book collector," nor was he "too intent on reading."[52] "Those brothers of mine who are led by curiosity for knowledge," Francis warned, "will find themselves empty-handed on the day of reckoning."[53] To drive home the point, the saint once gave a brother a handful of ashes in response to his request for a psalter.[54] But it was an uphill fight. The Francis of the *Assisi Compilation* "could smell in the air that a time was coming, and not too far away, when learning would be an occasion of ruin."[55] "He knew through the Holy Spirit and even repeated it many times to the brothers, that many, under the pretext of edifying others, would abandon their vocation, that is, pure and holy simplicity, prayer, and our Lady Poverty."[56]

The *Assisi Compilation* pulls no punches when it comes to criticizing the order for compromises with regard to poverty. The text openly accuses the ministers of removing "the chapter in the *Rule* where it says 'take nothing for your journey, etc.'"[57] This was, from Francis's perspective, tantamount to deceiving God, for although the ministers might well amend the *Rule*, they had no authority to change the wording of the Gospels, on which Franciscan poverty was ultimately based. As Christ made clear to Francis in a vision recorded elsewhere in the *Assisi Compilation*: "Nothing of yours is in the *Rule*. Whatever is there is all mine. And I want the *Rule* observed in this way: to the letter, to the letter, to the letter, and without a gloss, without a gloss, without a gloss."[58]

The *Assisi Compilation* contains a number of other direct testimonies to the relaxation of the *Rule* under pressure from the less rigorous friars.

> We who were with him when he wrote the *Rule* and almost all his other writings bear witness that he had many things written . . . to which certain brothers, especially prelates, were opposed. . . . Because he greatly feared scandal, he gave in, although unwillingly, to the wishes of the brothers. But he often repeated this saying: "Woe to those brothers who are opposed to what I know to be the will of God for the greatest good of the religion, even if I unwillingly give in to their wishes."[59]

Once Francis had abdicated responsibility for the order, the movement toward relaxation of the *Rule* only gathered momentum. When asked by a friar why he "renounced the care of all the brothers and turned them over into the hands of others," Francis responded:

> Son, I love the brothers to the extent that I am able, but if they would follow my footsteps, I would surely love them more, and would not make myself a stranger to them. For there are some among the prelates who draw them in a different direction, placing before them the examples of the ancients and paying little attention to my warnings. But what they are doing will be seen in the end.[60]

In a less sober moment, the Francis of the *Assisi Compilation* lashed out: "Who are these people? They have snatched out of my hands my religion and that of the brothers. If I go to the general chapter, then I'll show them what my will is!"[61] At another point in the text, a brother actually asks Francis why, if lately the "purity and perfection" of the brothers have begun to "change into something different," he does not do something to "correct them."[62] Francis's response: "As long as I held office for the brothers, and they remained faithful to their calling and profession . . . I satisfied them by my example and preaching. But afterwards I realized that the Lord multiplied the number of the brothers daily and that through tepidity and lack of spirit they began to turn away from the straight and sure way on which they used to walk." Once his health had finally failed him, Francis continued, he could no longer "correct them by preaching and example" and so he "entrusted the religion to the Lord and to the ministers." Not wanting to become "an executioner, who beats and scourges, like a power of this world," Francis chose to trust in the "Lord's police" to correct the friars and bring them back into the fold. Still, Francis vowed to continue to remind his brothers about the path they had left behind. "Thus, they will have no excuse before the Lord, and I will not be bound to render any further account about them or about myself before the Lord."

Toward the end of the *Assisi Compilation*, we find Francis "moved inwardly with a sorrow of heart" at the brothers who were "turning aside from the highest summit of their profession." But Jesus consoled him, saying:

> I have placed you as a sign to them, so that the works that I work in you, they should see in you, emulate, and do them. Those who walk in my way have me and will have me more abundantly. Those who refuse to walk in my way, that which they seem to have will be taken away from them. Therefore, I tell you, don't be so sad; do what you do, work as you work, for I have planted the religion of the brothers in everlasting love. Know that I love it so much that if any brother, returning to his vomit, dies outside religion I will replace him with another in religion who will have his crown in his place.[63]

This revelation lifted a huge burden off of Francis's shoulders, allowing him, in a very real sense, to wash his hands of the order that he had begun, taking responsibility only for his own behavior. By extension, it also lifted a burden off of the shoulders of the more radical Franciscans whose visions of the order informed the *Assisi Compilation*.

The third source that can be traced directly back to Crescentius's request for information about Francis is the one produced by Thomas of Celano when he was asked to edit the collected reminiscences as a supplement to the original *Life of St. Francis*. The resulting text, which Thomas called the *Remembrance of the Desire of a Soul*, was completed in 1247.[64] The first part of the work covers the events leading up to the saint's conversion, relying in part on information contained in the *Legend of the Three Companions* and the *Anonymous of Perugia*. The second and larger portion is thematic, dedicated to anecdotes illustrating different aspects of Francis's way of life, and borrows liberally from the *Assisi Compilation*. Given the ever-widening chasm between the Conventuals and the Spirituals at the time Thomas was writing the *Remembrance*, it would have been difficult for him to pretend, the way he had twenty years earlier, that there was no conflict within the order.[65] But even allowing for this, it is still surprising how "radical" Thomas of Celano became over the course of the two decades separating his two main biographical contributions. In marked contrast to the *Life*, the *Remembrance* does not shy away from criticizing the order or from co-opting the memory of Francis to voice the concerns of the rigorists, who were being left behind as the order evolved.

The differences in tone between the *Life of St. Francis* and the *Remembrance of the Desire of a Soul* are in part a function of Thomas's sources.

The memories of Francis that Crescentius had solicited from Leo and the other "companions" were shaped by their profound concerns over the relaxation of the *Rule* and their commitment to the *Testament*. And the same concerns remained attached to the new hagiographical data about Francis as it was processed and incorporated into the *Remembrance*. But there are clear indications, beyond Thomas's very decision to use so many of the biting *Assisi Compilation* anecdotes with so little modification, that Thomas shared the sentiments of the companions. On more than one occasion, Thomas gave voice to his own concerns about the order, concerns that were consistent with the rigorism reflected in the *Assisi Compilation*. In a prayer directed to Francis, Thomas lashed out against the idle friars of his own day: "Allow me today, holy father, to raise a complaint about those who claim to be yours! The exercise of virtue has become hateful to many who want to rest before they work, proving they are sons of Lucifer, not of Francis."[66] Elsewhere, after recounting Francis's prediction of a famine, Thomas reflected:

> All of us who saw those days know well how quietly and peacefully those times passed, as long as the servant of Christ was alive, and what rich abundance there was of all good things. There was no famine of the word of God, for the word of preachers in those days was especially full of power, and the hearts of all their listeners were worthy of God's approval. Examples of holiness were shining brightly in religious life, and the hypocrisy of whitened sepulchres had not yet infected so many holy people, nor had the teaching of those who disguise themselves excited so much curiosity.[67]

Considering Thomas's candidness about the changes in the order since he joined it three decades before, it is perhaps less surprising that his work was ultimately superseded than that it took almost twenty years for it to happen.

In any case, when the general chapter met in Narbonne in 1260, it authorized Bonaventure, the minister general at the time, to go back to the drawing board and compose a new official *Life* of Francis. Though Bonaventure had never known Francis personally—he was just a child when Francis died in 1226—he nevertheless felt a special bond to the saint, to whom he attributed his miraculous recovery from a childhood disease.[68] In his prologue, Bonaventure claimed to have relied on the oral testimony of Francis's closest companions. But the resulting *Major Legend of St. Francis* is in fact constructed largely out of information available in the *Life of St. Francis* and the *Remembrance of the Desire of a Soul*.[69] Bonaventure's reliance on Celano's works was, however, a selective and creative reliance, reflecting on the one hand his background as a theologian with a personal interest in mysticism and on the other his task as minister general trying to promote unity within the order the way Thomas of Celano originally had: by focusing on the founder and ignoring the controversies that flared up in his wake.

A comparison of the *Major Legend* and the *Remembrance* reveals that Bonaventure was careful to leave out anything that might suggest that the "evolution" of the order was, in fact, a corruption of the order. Thomas's references to Francis's own concern about the future of the order are missing from the *Major Legend*.[70] Bonaventure also chose to leave out the passage that cautioned the brothers against provoking the jealousy of the clergy with their preaching.[71] In the same spirit, he toned down the rancor of the saint's reaction to building projects and avoided any mention of the *Testament*.[72] Not surprisingly, given Bonaventure's university training, the dire warnings about the distractions of higher education in the *Remembrance* are nowhere to be found in the *Major Legend*.[73]

At the same time, however, Bonaventure retained a good deal of what Thomas had to say about Francis's own extreme commitment to poverty, despite the fact that none of the Conventual friars, least of all Bonaventure himself, maintained anything like this level of asceticism. Bonaventure's logic in this regard comes across clearly in a letter that he addressed to an unnamed university master, in which he drew revealing parallels between the evolution of the Franciscan order—whose "simple and illiterate" original membership had given way to university-trained preachers—and that of the church as a whole, "which began with simple fishermen and grew to include the most illustrious and learned doctors."[74] This evolutionary view of the Friars Minor as a microcosm of the church as a whole was easily extended from the realm of education to that of material possessions, allowing Bonaventure to retain the bulk of what Thomas had said about Francis's virtuoso asceticism without incriminating himself or his order.

Bonaventure finished the *Major Legend* in 1262, and it was approved as the official life of the saint the very next year at the chapter meeting in Pisa. The friars who assembled in Paris in 1266 took the endorsement of Bonaventure's work one step further, ordering all previous accounts of Francis's life burned. Their hope was to promote unity within the increasingly divided order by standardizing the image of its founder.[75] But the rifts were already too deep, and the conflicting images of Francis lived on.

I have gone to some lengths to provide a sense of the historical context within which the earliest Franciscan sources were produced and, in the process, to show how the poverty controversies influenced what Francis's earliest biographers had to say about him. It is important, however, to keep in mind the limitations of this kind of contextualization. For one thing, it is difficult to locate with any precision the individual references to Franciscan poverty on the "timeline" of the poverty controversy. While it makes sense, for instance, to place textual references to the distinction between "use" and "dominion" sometime after the publication of *Quo elongati* in 1230, there is no equally logical *terminus ad quem*. The *dominium* issue remained a bone of contention up through the period of the academic debates and was conceptually indispensable to Bonaventure as he crafted his *Defense of the Poor* (1269).

Second, the proponents of a strict interpretation of the *Rule* never cornered the market on anecdotes that either highlighted the extreme nature of Francis's poverty or identified it explicitly with the poverty of Christ and the disciples. Whether a particular biographer's intent was to criticize the order by constructing a Francis who spoke out against the dangers of compromise (the Spiritual position) or alternatively to glory in the order's evolution by constructing a Francis who embodied the heroic, early stages of a movement that had inevitably and appropriately evolved into something quite different (the Conventual position), the saints that emerge from their texts end up looking much the same in terms of their absolute dedication to lives of voluntary poverty in imitation of Christ.

Finally, it should be noted that the poverty problems about which the various factions argued over the course of the first three decades after Francis's death are quite different from the ones with which this study is concerned. The main points at issue during this early phase of the poverty controversy were: the legitimacy of the papal interventions that had allowed for compromises of the *Rule*; the appropriateness of appealing to the *Testament* and other evidence of the founder's original intentions in response to such compromises; the utility of the distinction between *usus* and *dominium* as a way of addressing the material needs of the order without undermining its official commitment to poverty; the appropriateness of the same distinction as a basis for claiming a higher order of poverty than that practiced by the monastic orders; and, finally, the precise nature of Christ's own poverty. In the midst of all these pressing issues, questions about the relationship between Francis's poverty and the poverty of the poor rarely surfaced.

When comparisons between Francis's poverty and the poverty of the poor did enter the picture, they did so invariably in conjunction with criticisms of Franciscan begging. In the *Assisi Compilation*, Francis is quoted as saying to his brothers: "I have never been a thief, that is, in regard to alms, which are the inheritance of the poor. I always took less than I needed, so that other poor people would not be cheated of their share. To act otherwise would be theft."[76] Elsewhere in the same source, Francis dismisses a brother's efforts to prevent him from giving his mantle to another poor man: "I do not want to be a thief; we will be accused of theft if we do not give to someone in greater need."[77] That the Francis of the *Assisi Compilation* should be so wary of being perceived as a "thief" for accepting alms (unless he is able to convince himself that there is no one more needy than he) indicates that questions about the diversion of charitable goods away from the involuntary poor actually did arise for some contemporary observers of the new order. Other sources include accounts of would-be benefactors hesitating to give alms to the friars on the separate but related grounds that their poverty was a matter of choice. According to the *Anonymous of Perugia*, when the brothers first "went about the city begging alms, scarcely anyone was willing to give to them; instead they would tell them: 'you got rid of your own possessions, and now you want to eat those of others.'"[78] The stress that many of the early sources—beginning with Francis's *Testament* itself—place on the value of manual labor as part of the brothers' daily regimen may itself have been a reaction to early public disdain for Franciscan mendicancy.[79]

One might have expected the relationship between Franciscan poverty and the poverty of the poor to have played a larger role once the academic debates began in 1253, since one of the many prongs of the attack on the friars was precisely the appropriateness of mendicancy as a means for supporting a religious order. The fact that the Gospels never actually say that Jesus and the apostles engaged in begging was not lost on the secular academics, who figured that they could discredit the friars by tracing their mendicancy to the same vices that led ordinary poor people to beg. The twelfth book of Bonaventure's *Defense of the Poor*, which is devoted in large part to a defense of Franciscan begging, allows us to reconstruct these arguments.[80] First of all, Bonaventure's opponents scoffed at the idea that mendicancy could ever serve as a source of "spiritual consolation" when begging had always been so closely associated with degradation and punishment. Bonaventure had to agree that most forms of mendicancy, in particular those that originated from vices such as greed or sloth, had no spiritually redeeming features. But, Bonaventure countered, the special kind of mendicancy practiced by "those who are poor of their own will" actually served an important spiritual function, insofar as it instilled the purest forms of humility.[81] Though he had some trouble adducing actual biblical or patristic references to the kind of begging that is "born of righteousness," Bonaventure found it easy enough to extrapolate from examples of holy men (including Christ himself) who were dependent on the spontaneous generosity of others for their sustenance. Second, Bonaventure's opponents questioned the appropriateness of Franciscan mendicancy on the grounds that the friars begged voluntarily without having been forced to do so by any "dire necessity or calamity." From Bonaventure's perspective, however, it was precisely the fact that the Franciscans deliberately embraced mendicancy that set it apart from and above the begging of ordinary poor people; "for poverty is much more praiseworthy when freely chosen than when imposed by necessity," just as the death of a martyr is to be preferred to that of a robber executed for his crimes.[82] A third criticism to which Bonaventure felt obliged to respond was that the Franciscans, as beggars, found themselves at the wrong end of charitable giving. On the biblical grounds that "it is more blessed to give than to receive,"[83] the critics of the Franciscans argued that the friars "would have been more blessed and perfect if they had been in the state of those who give alms, instead of the state of those who receive them."[84] Again Bonaventure disagreed, on the grounds that for those who voluntarily embraced poverty, receiving was the greater blessing, it being "more perfect to be in need with Christ and to receive alms together with him than to be a friend of the poor and to sustain them."[85]

Most significantly, for the purposes of this study, Bonaventure had to contend with the criticism that Franciscan mendicancy effectively diverted needed resources away from the truly poor. As his opponents saw it, the friars had "received alms by means of which the helpless poor, unable to work, should have been sustained." Their critics went so far as to accuse the Franciscans of murder because they "impiously defrauded these poor of the alms that compassion owed them."[86] Bonaventure's somewhat convoluted response is worth quoting at length:

> Let us say, in defense of the mendicants, that these evangelical men, who gave up their fortune for the sake of the salvation of souls, are not men of blood, but godly men whose virtues have not been forgotten, for in the abundance of their mercy, they have lavishly furnished temporal goods for sustaining the bodies of the poor, and have continually provided spiritual goods for sustaining their souls. Therefore, these mendicants are worthy of the support of the church, for they do not burden it. Instead they relieve it of its charge much better than do those who fatten themselves on an abundance of ecclesiastical revenues, since most of these mendicants would have had the opportunity to enjoy such revenues but preferred to do without them for the sake of Christ. And so when men such as these beg for alms and receive them, they are not defrauding the poor. Through their holy examples and counsels, they are inducing impious men to perform works of mercy. None of the poor are being injured in the least, for in begging the mendicants are within their right and receive nothing but their due.[87]

From Bonaventure's perspective, then, the friars had a right to their share of alms not only as poor people but as members of an order that had not "burdened" the church by requesting regular revenues. His defense against the charge that the friars diverted alms from the "helpless poor" is also twofold. On the one hand, he highlighted their "lavish" provision of "temporal goods for sustaining the bodies of the poor"—presumably in reference to the Franciscan custom of "selling all one's belongings and . . . giving everything to the poor"[88]—and their continuous provision of unspecified "spiritual goods" once they had no more material goods to distribute. On the other hand, he pointed to the positive effect that the Franciscans had on those "impious men" who would not otherwise have considered performing "works of mercy." The implication seems to be that the resulting increase in the pool of alms more than made up for what the Franciscans took from it.

Despite the great care with which Bonaventure countered his opponents' attacks on Franciscan mendicancy in the *Defense of the Poor*, the issue left no obvious mark on his biography of Francis. Granted, Bonaventure finished his life of Francis seven years before he finished the *Defense of the Poor*. But we know that Bonaventure had already responded to this particular criticism of Franciscan poverty in the wake of Alexander IV's condemnation of the views of William of St. Amour in 1256.[89] If the *Major Legend* does contain traces of the author's defense of mendicancy, they are subtle ones. If, for instance, Bonaventure had already come to the conclusion that it was "more perfect to be in need with Christ . . . than to be a friend of the poor and to sustain them," it would help explain why he condensed all of the anecdotes about Francis's charity that he found in Thomas of Celano's works into a single paragraph of the *Major Legend*.[90] Yet without these anecdotes, it is very difficult to get any sense for the distinctions in Bonaventure's own mind between Francis and the poor people with whom he interacted. The closest we get to this is when the Francis of the *Major Legend* voices a very Bonaventuran distinction between "perfect poverty" and ordinary poverty when advising a would-be friar: "If you want to join *Christ's poor*, distribute what you have to *the poor of the world*."[91]

The fact that the relationship between Francis's "holy poverty" and the poverty of the poor never became much of a lightening rod during the controversies that beset the Friars Minor after Francis relinquished control of the order means that whatever information the early sources contain on this subject comes to us more or less "untainted"—or at least not overtly influenced—by the specific political leanings of their authors vis-à-vis the poverty controversy. This important observation provides, I believe, sufficient justification for treating the poverty-related information captured in any one of the early sources as a reflection of a more-or-less consistent idea of Francis's poverty to which the biographers as a whole would have subscribed.

Notes

Introduction

1. Modern interest in Francis owes much to the Calvinist scholar Paul Sabatier, whose *Vie de S. François d'Assise* (Paris: Fischbacher, 1893) became a bestseller in virtually every European language and was the catalyst for a wave of scholarly activity in this area that has now lasted for more than a century. Sabatier's Protestant approach led him to present Francis as the innocent victim of institutionalization at the hands of the papacy, thus insulating the saint from the controversies that soiled the image of the order after his death. Though subsequent scholars have offered various opinions as to who was responsible for the controversial changes in the order, all have followed Sabatier's lead in placing Francis above the fray.

2. Over the last century, many scholars have studied the problems of Franciscan poverty associated with the famous poverty debates that arose after Francis's death (see the appendix), but none to my knowledge has investigated the specific relationship between Francis's own poverty and the poverty of the poor. Jacques Le Goff posed, but did not really answer, one of these questions in a brief overview of Francis's historical context that he first published in 1981 and reissued in 1999: "How should one situate voluntary poverty in comparison with involuntary poverty? Which of the two is 'real' poverty?" Jacques Le Goff, *Saint François d'Assise* (Paris: Gallimard, 1999), pp. 30–31; see also p. 203.

3. Karl Bosi has cautioned medievalists against assuming that the opposite of *pauper* (poor man) in early medieval Europe was *dives* (rich man), when it was, in fact, *potens* (powerful man). To be a *pauper*, in other words, was more likely to mean that you lacked access to social power than to wealth per se. But with the increased urbanization of thirteenth-century Europe—especially Italy—the distinction between *potens* and *dives* became harder to appreciate. Karl Bosl, "*Potens* und *Pauper*: Begriffsgeschichtliche Studien zur gesellschaftlichen Differenzierung im frühen Mittelalter und zum 'Pauperismus' des Hochmittelalters," in *Alteuropa und die moderne Gesellschaft: Festschrift für Otto Brunner* (Göttingen: Vandenhoeck and Ruprecht, 1963), pp. 60–87. It is interesting in this regard that one of the very earli-

est biographers of Francis specifically counterposed *pauperes* and *potentates*. Henri d'Avranches, *Versified Life of St. Francis* 6, l.40, in Regis J. Armstrong, J. A. Wayne Hellmann, and William J. Short, eds. *Francis of Assisi, Early Documents*, 3 vol. (New York: New City Press, 1999–2001), 1:469.

Michel Mollat has provided a more nuanced look at the terminology of poverty in the Middle Ages and offers a broad definition of "pauper" that serves the purposes of this study: "A pauper was a person who permanently or temporarily found himself in a situation of weakness, dependence, or humiliation, characterized by the privation of the means to power and social esteem (which means varied with period and place): these included money, relations, influences, power, knowledge, skill, nobility of birth, physical strength, intellectual capacity, and personal freedom and dignity. Living from hand to mouth, he had no chance of rising without assistance." *The Poor in the Middle Ages: An Essay in Social History*, translated by Arthur Goldhammer (New Haven: Yale University Press, 1986), orig. publ.: *Les Pauvres au Moyen âge* (Paris: Hachette, 1978), p. 5.

4. As Bronislaw Geremek aptly observed, voluntary ascetics like Francis were "doubly privileged, both by the prospect of future salvation and by the aura of sanctity which gave them the respect and dignity of high social status." *Poverty: A History*, translated by Agnieszka Kolakowska (Oxford: Blackwell, 1994); orig. publ.: *Litosc i szubienica: dzieje nedzy i milosierdzia* (Warsaw: Czytelnik, 1989), p. 36. Rodney Stark makes a similar argument with regard to early Christian martyrdom, recognizing the spiritual and secular benefits that rendered the martyr's self-destructive choice a "rational" one. *The Rise of Christianity: How the Obscure. Marginal Jesus Movement Became the Dominant Religious Force in the Western World in a Few Centuries* (San Francisco: HarperCollins, 1996), pp. 163–89.

5. In the preface to his translation of Augustin George et al., eds., *Gospel Poverty: Essays in Biblical Theology* (Chicago: Franciscan Herald Press, 1977), p. xi, M. D. Guinan observes that "poverty, in the sense of economic deprivation, of lacking the necessities of life, is never a Christian virtue." "The only way that we can make 'poverty' a virtue is to spiritualize it." See also Brian Tierney, *Medieval Poor Law: A Sketch of Canonical Theory and its Application in England* (Berkeley: University of Callifornia Press, 1959), p. 11: "Medieval men were quite capable of distinguishing between holy voluntary poverty and squalid involuntary want, and were well aware that the latter state was not likely to be productive of the higher moral virtues." Geremek is, as usual, most sensitive to the irony: "The rule was that poverty could reach its apotheosis only as a spiritual value, while real physical poverty, with its visible degrading effects, was perceived, both doctrinally and by society, as a humiliating state, depriving its victims of dignity and respect, relegating them to the margins of society and to a life devoid of virtue." *Poverty: A History*, p. 31.

6. Jussi Hanska, author of *"And the Rich Man Also Died; and He Was Buried in Hell": The Social Ethos in Mendicant Sermons*, Bibliotheca Historica 28 (Helsinki: Suomen Historiallinen Seura, 1997), has recently argued, on the basis of mendicant sermon collections of the late thirteenth and fourteenth centuries, that the "social ethos" of the Franciscans and Dominicans included a distinct sense that the poor had a spiritual advantage over the rich. But the evidence that Hanska garners does not hold up very well under the weight of this claim. The bulk of the supposedly "pro-poor" rhetoric in the Lazarus sermons is more properly understood as thinly disguised critiques of the wealthy. The fact that—as Hanska himself points out (pp. 58, 93)—so much more attention is focused on the rich man than on Lazarus in these sermons is, in and of itself, telling. That the *sermones ad status* that were directed at the poor made much

of their poverty as a potential ticket to heaven is to be expected, given the point of this particular type of preaching: to provide specific advice to each group within Christian society on how to achieve salvation within the constraints of their specific social niche. But such evidence is not particularly useful as a way of getting at the relative value placed by later medieval Christian society on poverty of this type. Hanska's contention that the mendicant sermons presented poverty in and of itself as a virtue (pp. 92, 103) flies in the face of longstanding Christian interpretations of poverty itself as morally neutral, interpretations that date back at least to the earliest attempts to reconcile the two gospel variations of the first beatitude ("Blessed are you poor" versus "blessed are you poor in *spirit*"). It was, the church fathers agreed, what one did with one's poverty that mattered. Bernard of Clairvaux's concise version of this sentiment—"Poverty is not a virtue, but love of poverty is" (p. 1 15)—is only the most quoted twelfth-century expression of this perspective. See Christine Pellestrandi, "La pauvreté spirituelle à travers les textes de la fin de XIIe siècles—Essai de recherche sémantique," in Michel Mollat, ed., *Études sur l'histoire de la pauvreté*, 2 vols., Études vol. 8 (Paris: Publications de la Sorbonne, 1974), 1:275–91. Neither the arrival of the mendicants nor the development and implementation of *sermones ad status* altered this fundamental perception about the defining role of attitude in the sanctification of the poor man. In my view this notion is best understood as a corollary of the even more fundamental idea that wealth itself cannot be considered the cause of a rich man's damnation but rather how the rich man feels about his wealth and what he does with it. Given the fact that the church fathers (both east and west) typically hailed from the highest levels of secular society, questions about the moral status of the "haves" inevitably received more attention that those directed to the spiritual standing of the "have-nots." But the logic behind the vindication of the wealthy man who did not let himself be seduced by his riches naturally bled into the discussions about poverty and the importance of the poor man's attitude toward it.

To Hanska's credit, he has acknowledged the strengths of various "counter-arguments" to his thesis, in particular those offered by Alexander Murray in *Reason and Society in the Middle Ages* (Oxford: Clarendon Press, 1978). Murray argues (pp. 335–36) that religiously based criticism of the nobility in the later Middle Ages should not be taken at face value but should be read as a "back-handed compliment," on the grounds that Christian society expected more from them. Indeed, as Murray points out (pp. 337–41)—and Hanska concedes—the vast majority of medieval saints came from noble backgrounds. Hanska (*And the Rich Man Also Died*, p. 112) also admits that Murray's own analysis of the sermons of Humbert of Romans turned up as many negative associations with poverty as positive ones. In response to the counter-evidence, Hanska writes "Not always were the rich and powerful assumed to be bad and sinful. Neither were the poor and workers automatically assumed to be good Christians. . . . This obervation, however, does not falsify the basic hypothesis that mendicants tended to think that the poor, the sick and those who worked were better Christians than the nobles, the rich and the powerful. It has not been stated that the mendicant social ethos was monolithic and uncompromising in this respect. . . . The picture of the poor and those who work as potential sinners is indeed a more difficult one, since it appears in the sources much more frequently than that of the virtuous rich man. . . . Evidently the poor and the workers were not *a priori* good Christians" (pp. 124–25). It is also curious that Hanska acknowledges the contributions of Geremek without ever addressing how fundamentally at odds they are with his own conclusions.

As overstated as Hanska's argument about the "mendicant ethos" is, his work nevertheless underscores the fact that Franciscan preachers of the later thirteenth and fourteenth centuries did have something to offer the poor; specifically, advice on how to approach their poverty (with patient resignation) so as to gain spiritual benefits from it. This makes the absence of such advice to the poor in the Francis corpus all the more curious.

7. This distinction between the poor and the holy poor is an old one within the Church. In a letter to the Gallic priest Vigilantius (c. 406), who questioned the practice of sending alms to support ascetic holy men in Jerusalem rather than using them to support the involuntary poor closer to home, Jerome responded: "What! Can those poor creatures, with their rags and filth, lorded over, as they are, by raging lust, can they who own nothing, now or hereafter, have eternal habitations? No doubt it is not the poor simply, but the poor in spirit, who are called blessed. . . . As for his argument that they who keep what they have and distribute among the poor, little by little, the increase of their property, act more wisely than they who sell their possessions, and once and for all give all away, not I but the Lord shall make answer: 'If thou wilt be perfect, go sell all that thou hast and give to the poor, and come, follow Me.' He speaks to him who wishes to be perfect, who, with the Apostles, leaves father, ship, and net. The man whom you approve stands in the second or third rank; yet we welcome him provided it be understood that the first is to be preferred to the second, and the second to the third." *Against Vigilantius* 14, in Jerome, *Letters and Select Works*, Nicene and Post-Nicene Fathers, 2nd series, vol. 6, translated by W. H. Fremantle et al. (Oxford: James Parker, 1893).

8. As Geremek puts it, "Externally . . . the way of life chosen by aspirants to Christian perfection was similar, in its essential features, to the life of the genuinely poor. But poverty is instrumental here: what is important is the spiritual life." *Poverty: A History*, p. 34.

9. In his introduction to the Italian version of Mollat's history of poverty, *I poveri nel Medioevo*, translated by Maria C. De Matteis and Mario Sanfilippo (Bari, Italy: Laterza, 1982), Ovidio Capitani praises the mendicant orders in general for "making available to all the involuntary poor the appellation '*pauperes Christi*,' which had designated only the voluntary poor, the monks." Capitani underemphasizes the extent to which the voluntary poverty of the friars resembled the voluntary poverty of the monks. Quoted by Grado G. Merlo in his introduction to *La Conversione alla povertà nell'Italia dei secoli XII–XIV*, Atti del XXVII Convegno storico internazionale, Todi, 14–17 ottobre 1990 (Spoleto: centro italiano di studi sull'alto medioevo, 1991), pp. 8–9. Alexander Murray's important ideas about the "religious effects of the noble condition" are relevant here. *Reason and Society in the Middle Ages*, pp. 350–82.

10. Hanska, *And the Rich Man Also Died*, is only the most recent and developed expression of a longstanding assumption on the part of historians that the mendicant movement represented a positive step in the direction of appreciating the plight of the involuntary poor. Michel Mollat's enthusiastic portrayal of Francis as one who proclaimed the "dignity of the poor" (p. 11) and set out to restore it after centuries of "poor-bashing" is another: "What was new about the way in which Saint Francis and Saint Dominic looked at the poor? Only the poor themselves can tell us for certain. But as usual they remain silent, stunned perhaps at having been understood and recognized at last. They remain, as always, humble and humiliated. But now at least they are held up as a contrast to the pride, violence, and avarice of the rich and powerful and declared to be not only images of the suffering Christ but as such, and such as they are, capable of playing a role in society (which is not the same thing as being

used by society). For Francis and Dominic the pauper was a living human being, and poverty was a concrete reality. Rather than subscribe to some theoretical notion of what poverty was, they wanted to share the life of the poor. And they went looking for genuine poverty where it had recently found fertile soil in which to grow: in the cities." *The Poor in the Middle Ages*, p. 119. Mollat is, I think, too hasty when he discounts the possibility that the poor may have been "used" by the mendicants.

11. "From a social point of view, saints exist in a Berkeleyan world—if they are not seen they do not exist. [This] means that, for others, saints are what they are seen and believed to be, not what they actually are." Aviad M. Kleinberg, *Prophets in Their Own Country: Living Saints and the Making of Sainthood in the Later Middle Ages* (Chicago: University of Chicago Press, 1992), p. 7. André Vauchez's contribution ("The Saint") to Jacques Le Goff's *Medieval Callings*, translated by Lydia G. Cochrane (Chicago: University of Chicago Press, 1990); orig. publ.: *L'Uomo medievale* (Rome: Laterza, 1987), pp. 312–42, provides a brief but insightful introduction to the formative effects of hagiography as a genre.

As Regis Armstrong has observed, with regard to Francis, "Authors, medieval and modern, have attempted to determine the basic facts, identify the social, ecclesial, and psychological influences on his actions, and define his unique enthusiasm for all that comes from God's hand. They impose different paradigms or patterns of holiness and, in the final analysis, invite others to take up the challenge anew. Thus the 'Francis of legend' emerges, one who straddles the lines between projected history and scientific history, between the acts and the imagination of early thirteenth century Umbria, and between established religious structures and emerging spiritual beliefs. Even a careful reading of the texts . . . will prompt a reader to wonder if it is possible to write an accurate biography of Francis or determine what precisely is at the heart of his vision." Armstrong, Hellman, and Short, *Francis of Assisi*, 1:12–13.

12. For all of their obvious limitations as records of historical events, saint's lives still provide a valuable window into the collective mental framework that encompasses the author as well as the audience. See, for instance, Thomas S. Heffernan, *Sacred Biography: Saints and their Biographers in the Middle Ages* (Oxford: Oxford University Press, 1988), pp. 19–22.

Chapter 1

1. Francis, *Testament* 1–4. Francis may have had Proverbs 27:7 in mind: "to one who is hungry, everything bitter is sweet."

2. Celano, *Life of St. Francis* 17. Compare *Legend of the Three Companions* 11.

3. Celano, *Life of St. Francis* 17.

4. *Legend of the Three Companions* 11–12.

5. Celano, *The Remembrance of the Desire of a Soul* (hereafter *Remembrance*) 9. Bonaventure's version (*Major Legend* 1.5, 2.6) parallels that of the *Remembrance*. According to the *Assisi Compilation*, Francis continued to have a difficult time overcoming his disgust for lepers even after his conversion. On one occasion he instructed a brother not to let the lepers that he was treating leave the hospice with him, knowing how much disgust they would incite among the general population. But the more Francis thought about it, the more upset with himself he became. "Let this be my penance: I will eat together with my Christian brother from the same dish." And this is what Francis did, despite the fact that the man's rotting fingers dripped blood into the bowl every time he reached for food. *Assisi Compilation* 64.

6. Sulpicius Severus, *Life of St. Martin* 5. *The Life of the holy bishop Rabbula of Edessa* (d. 435) contains another early example. See Susan Ashbrook Harvey, "The Holy and the Poor: Models from Early Syriac Christianity," in *Through the Eye of the Needle: Judeo-Christian Roots of Social Welfare*, edited by Emily A. Hanawalt and Carter Lindberg (Kirksville, MO.: Thomas Jefferson University Press, 1994), p. 49.

7. Venantius Fortunatus, *Life of St. Radegund* 19; Helgaud of Fleury, *Life of Robert the Pious*, and Gerald of Wales, *Life of St. Hugh* 46. The *Life of St. Romain of Jura* (c. 435) refers specifically to the example set by Martin as the inspiration for Romain's contact with two lepers. Françoise Bériac, *Histoire des lépreux au Moyen Age: une société d'exclus* (Paris: Imago, 1988), p. 108. Catherine Peyroux discusses the leper kissing episodes in the lives of Martin, Radegund, and Hugh, as well as similar incidents in Caesarius of Heisterbach's *Dialogus Miraculorum* and Aelred of Rievaulx's *Genealogia regum anglorum.* "The Leper's Kiss," in *Monks and Nuns, Saints and Outcasts: Religion in Medieval Society: Essays in Honor of Lester K. Little*, edited by Barbara H. Rosenwein and Sharon Farmer (Ithaca, NY: Cornell University Press, 2000), pp. 180–85.

8. The twelfth and thirteenth centuries witnessed a marked increase in evidence regarding leprosy in Europe. It is not clear whether this was a function of the disease being more widespread or simply a product of the increase in charitable activity aimed at lepers in that period. See Giuseppina de Sandre Gasparini, "Lebbrosi e lebbrosari tra misericordia e assistenza nei secoli XII–XIII," in *La conversione alla povertà nell'Italia dei secoli XII-XIV*, pp. 239–68.

9. For a detailed treatment of medieval notions about the disease, see Bériac, *Histoire des lépreux*, pp. 13–56.

10. Saul Nathaniel Brody, *The Disease of the Soul: Leprosy in Medieval Literature* (Ithaca, NY: Cornell University Press, 1974).

11. Numbers 12.

12. 2 Kings 5:20–27.

13. 2 Kings 15:1-5. For a closer look at leprosy in the Old Testament, see Bériac, *Histoire des lépreux*, pp. 88–91.

14. Matthew 8:2–4, Mark 1:40, and Luke 5:12 depict Jesus healing a leper (who identifies himself as "unclean"), whom he then directs to a priest in accordance with Mosaic law. In Luke 17:12 Jesus heals ten lepers. In Matthew 26:6 and Mark 14:3 he stays at the home of a leper named Simon. In Luke 7:22, leper healing is included among the acts performed by Jesus in fulfilment of Isaiah's prophecy of "good news to the poor" (Isaiah 61:1). There is no mention of leprosy as a function of sin in these New Testament sources. For more detail, see Bériac, *Histoire des lépreux*, pp. 91–94.

15. Bériac, *Histoire des lépreux*, part 2, chapter 1: "La lèpre, allégorie du péché," pp. 87–105. Jerome, for instance, saw Naaman's cure (2 Kings 5:10)—via immersion in the Jordan—as an allegory for baptism and the washing-away of original sin (p. 97). This theme would become very popular over the course of the Middle Ages, thanks to the proliferation of legends about pagan rulers whose leprosy was cured at the font. The eighth-century *Donation of Constantine*, for one, perpetuated the image of paganism as a form of leprosy that could be cured by the waters of baptism. See also Gregory of Tours, *History of the Franks* 2.31: "Like some new Constantine, [Clovis] stepped forward to the baptismal pool, ready to wash away the sores of his old leprosy and to be cleansed in flowing water from the sordid stains which he had borne so long." Translated by Lewis Thorpe (London: Penguin Books, 1974). For other such

references see Hroswitha of Gandersheim, *Gallicanus*, part 1, scene 5; and Notker the Stammerer, *De Carolo Magno* 21.

16. *Peristephanon* 2.229–88; Loeb version: Prudentius, vol. 2 (Cambridge, MA: Harvard University Press, 1959).

17. Quoted in Bériac, *Histoire des lépreux*, p. 102.

18. Brody, *Disease of the Soul*, p. 139. Bériac quotes from the commentary on Luke of Hugh of St. Victor (d. c. 1141), which identifies seven kinds of moral leprosy, corresponding to the number of times that Naamon was required to immerse himself in the Jordan River. Bériac, *Histoire des lépreux*, p. 101.

19. Quoted by Brody, *Disease of the Soul*, p. 135.

20. Bériac, *Histoire des lépreux*, pp. 69–70.

21. In fact, leprosy can be transmitted sexually, but the disease typically requires a three-year gestation period, making it virtually impossible, in the absence of modern scientific techniques, to muster convincing empirical data in support of this position. Brody, *Disease of the Soul*, p. 24.

22. Brody, *Disease of the Soul*, pp. 81–2.

23. Job 2:7.

24. Luke 16:20–22. Origen was the first known Christian exegete to identify Lazarus as a leper. Nicole Bériou and François-Olivier Touati, eds., *Voluntate dei leprosus: Les lépreux entre conversion et exclusion aux XIIe et XIIIe siecles*, Testi, Studi, Strumenti 4 (Spoleto: Centro di studi sull'alto medioevo, 1991), p. 35, n. 3.

25. Hanska has observed that, despite the lack of any explicit reference in Luke to Lazarus's "patience," Christian exegetes were quick to fill in the blank. *And the Rich Man Also Died*, p. 61.

26. See Jerome, *Commentarium in Isaiam prophetam* 14, 53, in *Patrologiae cursus completus: series latina. Sive, Bibliotheca universalis, integra, uniformis, commoda, oeconomica, omnium SS. patrum, doctorum scriptorumque ecclesiasticorum qui ab aevo apostolico ad usuque Innocentii III tempora floruerunt* (hereafter *Patrologia latina*), edited by J.-P. Migne, 221 vols. (Paris: Excudebat Migne, etc., 1844–1902), 24:524–27; esp. 525, for his commentary on this passage, as well as his discussion of the sources for his "quasi leprosum" translation.

27. Caesarius of Heisterbach, *Dialogus Miraculorum* 37. Bériac provides earlier anecdotes about Christ appearing to various saints in the guise of a leper. *Histoire des lépreux*, pp. 128–31.

28. Bonaventure, *Major Legend* 1.6.

29. Celano, *Life of St. Francis* 2. The authors of the *Legend of the Three Companions* (2) concurred with this assessment of Francis's "frivolity" before his conversion. He was, this source reports, "given to revelry and song with his friends. . . . He was most lavish in spending, so much that all he could possess and earn was squandered on feasting and other pursuits." The emphasis placed on Francis's clothing as a sign of his corruption may reflect the story of the rich man, "clothed in purple and fine linen," who ignored the "leper" Lazarus in Luke 16:19–21. Hanska's description of how later mendicants used this part of the Lazarus story to rail against the rich for sartorial extravagance is suggestive of the same linkage. Hanska, *And the Rich Man also Died*, pp. 46–50.

30. Celano, *Life of St. Francis* 8.

31. André Vauchez has used the term *conversatio inter pauperes* to describe the regimen of saints like Francis, who sought, for spiritual reasons, to identify with social outcasts. "Pauvreté et charité aux IXe e XIIe siècles d'après quelques textes hagiographiques," in Mollat, *Études sur l'histoire de la pauvreté*, 1:156.

32. Sulpicius Severus, *Life of St. Martin* 5.

33. Celano, *Life of St. Francis* 146. Bonaventure reports that later in his career Francis cured a leper near Spoleto by kissing him. *Major Legend* 2.6. According to Bonaventure, "this saint . . . had an outstanding power for curing this disease because, out of love for humility and piety, he had humbly dedicated himself to the service of lepers." *Major Legend*, Miracles 8.5.

34. Gerald of Wales, a canon who was present when Hugh of Lincoln kissed his leper, compared Hugh's effort unfavorably with that of Martin, whose kiss had actually cured the leper at the gates of Paris. Hugh responded: "Martin, by kissing the leper, cured him in body, but this leper has, with a kiss, healed me in soul." Gerald of Wales, *The Life of St. Hugh* 46, in *The Life of St. Hugh of Avalon, Bishop of Lincoln 1186–1200*, edited by Richard M. Loomis, Garland Library of Medieval Literature, vol. 31, series A (New York: Garland, 1985), p. 30.

35. As Bonaventure saw it, Francis's healing powers were a byproduct of his service to the lepers: "As a result [of his ministering to them], he received such power from the Lord that he was miraculously effective in healing spiritual and physical illnesses." Bonaventure, *Major Legend* 2.6.

36. Geremek makes a similar point with regard to voluntary poverty: "It is clear that, in medieval Christianity, voluntary poverty commanded respect, and was even enveloped in an aura of sanctity. The very real expulsion from society which it involved was nevertheless accompanied by a high degree of prestige. In cases of genuine poverty there was a direct relation between the pauper's way of life, which infringed generally accepted norms, and the disgust, hostility and rejection of which the poor were objects. In cases of asceticism and voluntary renunciation, on the other hand, the attitudes were reversed: the deliberately 'asocial' condition of ascetic groups evoked the admiration, an admiration sometimes amounting almost to idolatry, of society." *Poverty: A History*, p. 32.

37. Catherine Peyroux alludes somewhat apologetically to this irony when she observes, at the very end of her article: "Thomas' narrative redirected attention away from the agony of the many to valorize the singular and voluntary suffering of Francis. Paradoxically, *and assuredly not by design*, in the act of seeking to represent the power of Francis' spiritual ideal, his first biographer effectively came to displace the experience of those forlorn and desperate bodies who had inspired him." Peyroux, "The Leper's Kiss," p. 188 (emphasis mine).

38. Jacques de Vitry observed, in the *Historia Occidentalis*, that "people consider themselves fortunate if these servants of God [the Franciscans] do not refuse to accept alms or hospitality from them." In Armstrong, Hellman, and Short, *Francis of Assisi*, 1:584.

39. In *The Praise of Folly* (1509), Erasmus notes how the "voluntarily poor" friars of his day were "doing a great deal of injury to common highway beggars by interloping in their traffic of alms." Quoted in *The Protestant Reformation*, edited by Lewis W. Spitz (Englewood Cliffs, NJ: Prentice-Hall, 1966), p. 18.

Chapter 2

1. Celano, *Life of St. Francis* 2. Compare *Legend of the Three Companions* 2.
2. Celano, *Life of St. Francis* 5.
3. Celano, *Life of St. Francis* 8–9.
4. Celano, *Life of St. Francis* 15.

5. The authors of the *Legend of the Three Companions* noted, in this regard, that Francis "was lavish, indeed prodigal . . . in spending more money on expensive clothes than his social position warranted. He was so vain in seeking to stand out that sometimes he had the most expensive material sewed together with the cheapest cloth onto the same garment." *Legend of the Three Companions* 2.

6. Celano, *Life of St. Francis* 16.

7. Celano, *Life of St. Francis* 16.

8. Celano, *Life of St. Francis* 16. According to Bonaventure, the bishop of Assisi gave Francis "a poor, cheap cloak of a farmer who worked for the bishop." Francis drew a cross on it with a piece of chalk, "thus designating it as the covering of a crucified and half-naked poor man." *Major Legend* 2.4.

9. Celano, *Life of St. Francis* 76. The Latin reads: "Pater pauperum pauper Franciscus, pauperibus omnibus se conformans." Job also considered himself a "pater pauperum." Job 29:16.

10. Celano, *Life of St. Francis* 11. The *Anonymous of Perugia* is full of references to the disdain with which Francis's contemporaries at first held him. He and his followers were variously considered "good-for-nothings" (23), "impostors," "fools," rogues" (20), and "wildmen" (19). Aside from the mud-throwing and jeers, the friars faced many other indignities: "They shoved dice in their hands, inviting them to play. One brother was carried by the *capuche* across someone's back, for as long as he pleased" (23). It should be noted that being regarded as a madman was one of the definitive aspects of the "holy fool" form of sanctity. John Saward, *Perfect Fools: Folly for Christ's Sake in Catholic and Othodox Spirituality* (Oxford: Oxford University Press, 1980), pp. 25–26, 85.

11. Celano, *Life of St. Francis* 21.

12. Mark 6:8–9, 12; this lesson is traditionally read on the feast of St. Matthias, February 24. Lawrence sees this moment as the beginning of the final, apostolic phase of Francis's poverty, to be distinguished form his original "life-style of an impoverished hermit." C. H. Lawrence, *The Friars: the Impact of the Early Mendicant Movement on Western Society* (London: Longman, 1994), p. 31.

13. Celano, *Life of St. Francis* 84. It is indicative of Francis's focus on the gospel that the earliest form of the Franciscan "rule" was nothing more than a series of quotations from the Gospels. Francis, *Testament* 14–15. Francis was not the first holy man to treat the gospel as his "rule." Stephen of Muret (d. 1124), for one, had told his followers at Grandmont: "If anyone should ask you to what religious order you belong, tell him the order of the gospel." Quoted by M.-D. Chenu, *Nature, Man, and Society in the Twelfth Century: Essays on New Theological Perspectives in the Latin West*, edited and translated by Jerome Taylor and Lester K. Little (Chicago: University of Chicago Press, 1968); orig. publ.: *Le Théologie au douzième siècle* (Paris: J. Vrin: 1957), p. 239.

14. Celano, *Life of St. Francis* 22.

15. Celano, *Life of St. Francis* 22.

16. According to Bonaventure, Francis, inspired by the asceticism of John the Baptist, would sew pieces of rope to the inside of any tunic that seemed too soft. *Major Legend* 5.2.

17. Celano, *Life of St. Francis* 2.

18. In the words of one contemporary observer, Francis's "clothing was filthy" and "his whole appearance contemptible." Thomas of Spalato, quoted by Little, *Religious Poverty*, p. 163.

19. Celano, *Life of St. Francis* 76.

20. According to the *Assisi Compilation* (90), Francis's insistence that his tunic be just so meant that it became something of a challenge for his brothers to keep him clothed, given the saint's habit of giving his clothes away. "Very often [Francis] endured great need and hardship when he gave away his tunic or a part of it to someone, because he could not quickly find or have another one made. This was true especially since he always wished to have and to wear a poor tunic made of bits and pieces, and occasionally he wanted it patched inside and out." The same source (8) also describes how Francis designed his own death shroud: "He himself ordered the brothers to sew pieces of sackcloth on the outside of it as a sign and example of most holy humility and poverty." See also *Assisi Compilation* 30. Francis felt the same way about his hermitage and so ordered his brothers to make it less attractive. *Assisi Compilation* 57.

21. As Little observed, "basic traits of personality are not lost in the process of exchanging one cultural identity for another." *Religious Poverty*, p. 149. Likewise: "A young man raised in wealth may, when he comes of age, give his fortune away and live in poverty. His character, however, will remain that of a man raised in wealth, for he cannot give his history away." Jack Miles, *God: A Biography* (New York: Vintage Books, 1995), p. 3.

22. Celano, *Life of St. Francis* 63. See also *Remembrance* 98.

23. Some even made tea from the fibers of his rope belt and drank it to cure their ailments. Celano, *Life of St. Francis* 64. According to the *Remembrance* (42), Francis was careful to dispose of all his nail clippings so as not to contribute to the already lively trade in his own relics.

Chapter 3

1. Also known as "father of the poor" and "lover of the poor." Celano, *Life of St. Francis* 76; Celano *Remembrance* 8.

2. Celano, *Life of St. Francis* 14.

3. Celano, *Life of St. Francis* 14.

4. Celano, *Life of St. Francis* 8; 57. See also *Assisi Compilation* 96. The *Rule of 1221* (ch. 8) simply prohibited the friars from touching coins. For more detail, see Little, *Religious Poverty*, pp. 164–65.

5. Celano, *Life of St. Francis* 9; 14.

6. Celano, *Life of St. Francis* 35.

7. Celano, *Life of St. Francis* 76. See also *Remembrance* 8: "He often stripped himself to clothe the poor. Although he had not yet made himself one of them, he strove to be like them with his whole heart." The *Legend of the Three Companions* (10) recounts how the young Francis, seeing all of the poor people begging for alms in front of St. Peter's in Rome, "secretly exchanged clothes with one of those poor people and put them on. Standing on the steps of the church with the other poor, he begged for alms. . . . Elaborating on this episode, Thomas of Celano wrote that "[Francis] took off his fine clothing and dressed himself in a poor man's clothes. He happily settled among the poor in the square in front of the church of St. Peter, a place where the poor are abundant. Considering himself one of them, he eagerly ate with them. If his embarrassed friends had not restrained him, he would have done this many times." Celano, *Remembrance* 8. At one point in the *Major Legend* (1.6), Bonaventure observed with regard to Francis: "To poor beggars he wished to give not only his possessions but his very self."

8. *Legend of the Three Companions* 22.

9. Francis, *Earlier Rule* 9.8. Elsewhere the same document says (2.7): "If the brothers are in need, they can accept, *like other poor people*, whatever is needed for the body excepting money" (emphasis mine). See also: Francis, *Earlier Rule* 7.8, and *Assisi Compilation* 69. The friars once responded to the request of a beggar (who turned out to be Francis in disguise) at their door: "Brother, we are also poor, and because we are so many, we need these alms we are eating. But, for the love of that Lord you invoked, come into the house, and we will give you some of the alms that the Lord has given us." *Assisi Compilation* 74. Nevertheles, Francis seems to have been aware of the criticisms that the Franciscans were diverting alms from those poor who had not chosen their poverty. *Assisi Compilation* 15, 32.

10. Lester Little once explored a different aspect of this theme by noting how differently the poverty of Francis and the poverty of the poor were depicted by artists. "In some representations of Francis, the voluntarily poor man is shown together with involuntary poor people; these images depict the startling contrast between the conditions of voluntary and involuntary poverty. Francis is healthy and handsome, and adequately dressed in his friar's robe. He makes a generous, inviting gesture. Meanwhile, the poor, as depicted in a fresco in Lombardy, are miserable; they are shown reduced to a wretched state, dehumanized by hunger, their gaunt faces filled only with submission, and their bony hands barely able to hold the bowls with which they beg for food." "Religion, the Profit Economy, and St. Francis," in Hanawalt, *Through the Eye of a Needle*, p. 162.

11. Celano, *Life of Francis* 24. Matthew 19:21.

12. *Earlier Rule* 2.4. According to Bonaventure. "only those who had given up everything and kept nothing would he admit to the Order." *Major Legend* 7.3.

13. Celano, *Life of St. Francis* 51. The *Legend of the Three Companions* (15) has Francis explaining that he used ashes this way "because 'Brother Ash' was chaste."

14. Celano, *Life of St. Francis* 52. Francis also publicly confessed for having eaten, during a fast, foods prepared with lard. *Assisi Compilation* 81.

15. For instance: *Assisi Compilation* 68, 71; Celano, *Remembrance* 43, 51. This led Bonaventure to conclude that Francis's was a "wealthy poverty" that was "abundantly sufficient." Bonaventure, *Major Legend* 7.10, 7.12.

16. Celano, *Life of St. Francis* 39.

17. Celano, *Life of St. Francis* 35.

18. Bonaventure, *Major Legend* 5.2.

19. "This is the paradox of poverty as an ideal: it is so easy to be poor by chance, so difficult by policy." Richard W. Southern, *Western Society and the Church in the Middle Ages*, Pelican History of the Church, vol. 2 (London: Penguin Books, 1970), p. 288.

20. This may, in fact, have been the case for the very first follower of Francis, whose name is left out of the *Life of St. Francis*. Celano, *Life of St. Francis* 24. The *Assisi Compilation* (70) contains a telling anecdote about a young nobleman from Lucca who, after flirting with the idea of joining Francis, ultimately "returned to the world" and rejoined his relatives.

21. *Earlier Rule* 1.1.

22. *Earlier Rule* 2.13.

23. *Earlier Rule* 9.1–2. 1 Timothy 6–8.

24. Celano, *Life of St. Francis* 36.

25. Celano, *Life of St. Francis* 62.

26. Jacques de Vitry observed that the Franciscans "are grieved, indeed troubled,

by the fact that they are honored by both clergy and laity more than they would wish."
Jacques de Vitry, letter I, in Armstrong, Hellman, and Short, *Francis of Assisi* 1:580.

27. Celano, *Remembrance* 133.

28. Celano, *Life of St. Francis* 53. In his *Letter to the Entire Order* (47; 2) Francis referred to himself as "a worthless and weak man" and "a useless man and an unworthy creature of the Lord God." See also Celano, *Remembrance* 140.

29. Celano, *Life of St. Francis* 92.

30. *Assisi Compilation* 10.

31. *Assisi Compilation* 81. The same source recounts how Francis publicly confessed eating "meat and broth flavored with meat" when he was ill (80). Later in his life, whenever anyone prepared a special meal for him in consideration of his failing health, he would make a point of announcing the fact: "He did not wish to conceal from people what was known to God" (80).

32. *Assisi Compilation* 81.

33. Celano, *Remembrance* 135–39.

34. As Peter Berger has observed, "one of the inherent difficulties of masochism in human relations is that the other may not play the sadistic role to satisfaction." *The Sacred Canopy: Elements of a Sociological Theory of Religion* (New York: Doubleday, 1967), p. 57.

35. Celano, *Life of St. Francis* 53.

36. Thomas's Francis is fearful that he will lose his divine rewards if he accepts any earthly ones. Hence his attempts to hide the marks of the stigmata "so that human favor would not rob him of the grace given him." Celano, *Life of St. Francis* 95; 96. Thomas was well aware that the more Francis fled from public adulation, the more he attracted it. "He would zealously expose himself to insults," wrote Thomas, "so that he would not be forced by self-love to lust for anything temporal. . . . To what end? He was honored by all and merited high marks from everyone." (53). Francis once described to Brother Leo what true joy for him really was: "I return from Perugia and arrive here in the dead of night. It's winter time, muddy, and so cold that icicles have formed on the edges of my habit and keep striking my legs and blood flows from such wounds. Freezing, covered with mud and ice, I come to the gate and, after I've knocked and called for some time, a brother comes and asks: 'Who are you?' 'Brother Francis,' I answer. 'Go away!' he says. 'This is not a decent hour to be wandering about! You may not come in!' When I insist, he replies: 'Go away! You are simple and stupid! Don't come back to us again! There are many of us here like you—we don't need you!' I stand again at the door and say: 'For the love of God, take me in tonight.' And he replies: 'I will not! Go to the Crosiers' place and ask there!'" "I tell you this: If I were patient and did not become upset, true joy, as well as true virtue and the salvation of my soul, would consist in this." Francis, *True and Perfect Joy* 8–11.

37. When asked what he would want to be if could not be a Cistercian, the holy Abbot John of Montmirail (d. 1217) responded: "a *ribaldus*" (wastrel, good-for-nothing). In response to his interlocuter's astonishment ("You'd want to belong to the class of men most contemptible to God and men, and be counted as one of them?") John reasoned: "there are *ribaldi* and *ribaldi*. Many of them have habits very different from those you describe. And after all, look at the jobs they have to do: some have to clean stables, or carry sewage, and humbly submit to doing and carrying all sorts of nasty things, and eat their bread in the sweat of their brow. Their life may be degraded and despicable by men. But it is praiseworthy and very precious in God's sight." Quoted by Murray, *Reason and Society*, pp. 392–93.

38. Celano, *Life of St. Francis* 17. The meaning of this reference to the "king" is made clear in the *Legend of the Three Companions* (3): "You are generous and courteous," Francis once admitted to himself, "to those from whom you receive nothing except passing and worthless approval. Is it not right that, on account of God who repays most generously, you should be courteous and generous to the poor?" See also the *Anonymous of Perugia* 4. For more examples of Francis's generosity, see *Legend of the Three Companions* 8–9.

39. Celano, *Life of St. Francis* 76. See also *Assisi Compilation* 93. Francis was not the first saint whose voluntary poverty challenged his ability to be charitable toward the poor. According to his hagiographer, St. Bernard the Penitent (d. 1182) "visited paupers and the sick with the greatest diligence and charitably distributed to the beggars whatever he was able to secure through his own begging." Quoted by André Vauchez, "Pauvreté et charité aux IXe e XIIe siècles d'après quelques textes hagiographiques," in Mollat, *Études sur l'histoire de la pauvreté*, 1:157.

40. Celano, *Remembrance* 83. "Although extreme poverty abounded in them, [Francis and his brothers] were always generous, and spontaneously shared the alms given with all who asked for the love of God. When they went along and came upon poor people begging from them, some of the brothers would give them some of their clothing, since they had nothing else to give. One of them even tore the *capuche* from his tunic and gave it to a poor beggar; while another tore off a sleeve and gave it away; and still others gave away a part of their tunic to observe the Gospel passage: 'Give to all who ask of you.'" *Anonymous of Perugia* 27–28; Luke 6:30. See also the *Legend of the Three Companions* 43–44.

41. The Latin reads: *ditissimus pauper.* Celano, *Life of St. Francis* 76.

42. Celano, *Life of St. Francis* 76. Once Francis asked the doctor who was accompanying him to give alms on his behalf to three poor women whom they met. Celano, *Remembrance* 93.

43. Francis was, as I have already noted, a very attractive focus of charity. Thomas of Celano describes how Francis and brother Paul, seeing a particularly meek lamb grazing among a flock of goats, decided that they must take it with them, but lacked the funds to purchase it: "suddenly a traveling merchant arrived to pay for what they wanted." Celano, *Life of St. Francis* 78.

44. Geremek recognizes this "conflict between two incompatible ideals: the heroic life of renunciation on the one hand, and the duty to help the poor on the other." *Poverty: A History*, p. 20.

45. Celano, *Life of St. Francis* 14.

46. Celano, *Remembrance* 66.

47. Celano, *Remembrance* 68. In the *Assisi Compilation* (27) we find Francis punishing a brother who had touched money by ordering him " to pick up the money from the windowsill with his own mouth, take it outside the fence of that place, and with his mouth put it on the donkey's manure pile."

48. Francis, *Earlier Rule* 8.8–11.

49. Tierney, among others, noted the element of "self-interest in the Christian doctrine of charity, even in its scriptural form. A man was urged to give alms generously with the assurance that his action would be pleasing to God and would merit a heavenly reward." Tierney, *Medieval Poor Law*, p. 46. By Francis's time, there was already a long history of Christian charitable activity toward the poor aimed more at serving the spiritual needs of the benefactors than the physical needs of the beneficiaries. The institution of the *register pauperum* ("register of the poor"), whereby a specified (and often very limited) number of poor people became the recipients of

ritualized monastic charity, is a case in point. Pierre-André Sigal, "Pauvreté et charité aux XIe et XIIe siècles d'après quelques textes hagiographiques," in Mollat, *Études sur l'histoire de la pauvreté*, 1:145–46, 151–52; 159. In Sigal's own words, "one gets the impression that the poor are no more than a pretext for charitable acts in which the benefits accrue to those who perform them more than to those who are the recipients of them" (p. 159). See also, in the same collection: Michel Rouche, "La Matricule des pauvres: Evolution d'une institution de charité du Bas Empire jusqu'à la fine du Haut Moyen Age," 1:83–110; and Willabrord Witters, "Pauvres et pauvreté dans les coutumiers monastiques du moyen âge," 1:198–200.

50. Celano, *Remembrance* 132. Based on *Assisi Compilation* 82.

51. Celano, *Remembrance* 139. The passage continues: "We do not discern initiatives; we do not test spirits. And so when vanity drives us to do something, we imagine it was prompted by charity. Furthermore, if we do even a little good, we cannot bear its weight, while we are living we keep unloading it, and let it slip away as we approach the final shore. We can patiently accept not being good. What we cannot bear is not being considered good, not appearing good. And so we live only for human praise, since we are only human."

52. An envy that Thomas regarded as a most "enviable envy." Celano, *Remembrance* 84.

53. Celano, *Remembrance* 83. Thomas of Celano seems to have been sensitive to the potential for criticism on this point: "The father of the poor, the poor Francis, conforming himself to the poor in all things, was distressed to see anyone poorer than himself, *not out of any desire for empty glory*, but from a feeling of simple compassion." Celano, *Life of St. Francis* 76 (emphasis mine). According to the *Assisi Compilation* (51), the early friars competed with one another to see who could collect the most alms, a crude but effective measure of their relative humility.

54. Celano, *Remembrance* 84.

55. Even when Francis was in a position to perform acts of charity, he was always more concerned, with regard to almsgiving, about "profit for souls rather than support for the body." Celano, *Remembrance* 78. Lester Little recently observed: "Some historians saw the friars as administering directly to the poor, as speaking to them and as offering material help to them. Modern research has not been able to sustain this agreeable notion, thus demoting it to a romantic myth." And later: "They raised money for the 'poor,' meaning themselves . . . but what we see little of is direct, material aid passing from the friars to poor people." "Religion, the Profit Economy, and St. Francis," in Hanawalt, *Through the Eye of a Needle*, pp. 157, 158.

56. According to the *Legend of the Three Companions* (22), Francis was himself initially disgusted by the idea of actually eating the food that he had collected from begging.

57. Celano, *Remembrance* 71. According to Bonaventure, Francis himself had to "put aside all embarrassment" before he could bring himself to beg. *Major Legend* 2.7. He felt sympathy for his new brothers in this regard, initially shielding them from the humiliation by doing all of the begging himself. *Assisi Compilation* 51.

58. "The holy father was much happier to use alms begged from door to door rather than offerings." Celano, *Remembrance* 71.

59. Celano, *Remembrance* 74; *Assisi Compilation* 51. Based on 2 Corinthians 8:9 and Philippians 2:5–9.

60. *Assisi Compilation* 51. Francis's logic reflects that of the commentary of Gregory I on the rich man and Lazarus, in which Gregory wondered why beggars approached potential benefactors with such trepidation when they were in the posi-

tion to offer them their invaluable services as heavenly intercessors. *Homiliarum in evangelia* 2:40, in *Patrologia latina*, 76:1310.

61. Matthew 25:40.

62. Celano, *Remembrance* 71. Compare Bonaventure, *Major Legend* 7.8. The *Earlier Rule* (9.9) says: "The brothers who work at acquiring [alms] will receive a great reward and enable those who give them to gain and acquire one." In the *Assisi Compilation* (101) Francis quotes from Matthew 25 and then interprets: "Although the Lord may be understood to be speaking of all the spiritually poor, he was never-theless predicting the religion of the Lesser Brothers that was to come in his church."

63. Hanska poses this question, without ever really answering it: "An interesting problem is how much the sanctity of voluntary poverty was transmitted to actual and less voluntary poverty." *And the Rich Man Also Died*, p. 13.

64. In his thorough study of late medieval sanctity, André Vauchez marveled at the resilience of the notion that wealth and power were virtual prerequisites for sanc-tity, a notion that held sway even after the sea-change of the mid-twelfth century, when for about a century Christian perfection was specifically defined in terms of "evangelical virtues such as humility, poverty and asceticism." "Their exaltation ought to have allowed members of the lower ranks of society to accede in their turn to the honours of the local cult." But, Vauchez observes, this did not happen. "The content and forms of sanctity may have changed, but the new saints still mostly came from the high nobility." "With very few exceptions, it was as if the perception of saint-hood could only operate to the benefit of the social elites. All nobles were certainly not seen as saints, but almost all saints came from the nobility. For a long time to come, the celestial court only opened its doors to people who already occupied high positions on earth." André Vauchez, *Sainthood in the Later Middle Ages*, translated by Jean Birrell (Cambridge: Cambridge University Press, 1997); orig. publ.: *La sainteté en Occident aux derniers siècles du moyen âge* (Paris: École Française de Rome, 1988), pp. 175–76. See also Murray, *Reason and Society*, pp. 331–404.

65. Celano, *Remembrance* 73 (italics mine). See also Bonaventure, *Major Legend* 7.7. The author of the *Assisi Compilation* (98) recounts how Francis kissed the arm of a brother whom he saw "return happy and joyful" from almsgiving. Celano's version (*Remembrance* 76) records how Francis was overjoyed at the sight of one of his friars singing as he returned from an alms-collecting expedition: "Blessed be my brother who goes willingly, begs humbly, and returns joyfully!" For his part, Geremek writes: "It would be natural to suppose that the recognition of poverty as a spiritual value entailed a similar recognition of the dignity of the pauper as such. . . . Clearly there was a link between [external signs of poverty] and the moral valuation of poverty as a condition. However, in placing too much emphasis on this valuation, we are liable to overlook the realities of a world in which the pauper is no more than an object of charity and the bearer of a humiliating condition." *Poverty: A History*, p. 25. Elsewhere: "The exalta-tion of poverty as a spiritual value conflicted with the low social status of the truly poor" (p. 27). Augustine recognized the same dynamic when he observed, with regard to the sorrow of the rich man whom Jesus told to sell all that he had and give it to the poor: "For it is one thing to forbear from appropriating what is wanting to us; it is another thing to rend away that which has become a part of ourselves: the former action is like declining food, the latter is like cutting off a limb." Augustine, *Letters* 31.5.

66. *Legend of the Three Companions* 44.

67. *Assisi Compilation* 33.

68. Francis himself was not above contributing to this subtle form of "poor bash-ing." In his *Admonitions* (27.3) we read that "where there is poverty with joy, there

is neither greed nor avarice." Its logical corollary: where there is poverty *without* joy, there is cupidity and avarice. In other words, people who do not willingly embrace their poverty and recognize it as a path toward spiritual fulfillment are not simply poor: they are sinful. Similarly, Bonaventure observed, "Because when begging alms, [Francis] was motivated not by greed for profit but by liberty of spirit, God, the father of the poor, seemed to have a special care for him." *Major Legend* 7.9.

69. Celano, *Remembrance* 78–79.

70. *Assisi Compilation* 114.

71. Suspicions about the moral quality of beggars often clouded acts of medieval charity. Geremek characterized the attitude of the wealthy this way: "Poverty goes hand in hand with greed: if one is content with what one has, one is not poor. In this context the only connotations of poverty are pejorative ones." *Poverty: A History*, p. 30.

72. Celano, *Remembrance* 35; based on *Assisi Compilation* 74.

73. Celano, *Remembrance* 36.

74. *Legend of the Three Companions* 38–39. For another version of the same story, see: *Anonymous of Perugia* 20–22.

75. Celano, *Life of St. Francis* 76. 2 Corinthians 8:9 and Philippians 2:5–9.

76. In a later chapter I look more closely at this idea of the Incarnation as an act of voluntary poverty.

77. Lester Little noted the same irony: "The friars were not really the poor, but rich people dressed up as the poor." "Religion, the Profit Economy, and St. Francis," in Hanawalt, *Through the Eye of a Needle*, p. 162. The *Earlier Rule* hints that there was already some criticism of the order along these lines. In the section that addresses the friar's clothing, it (2.13) reads: "Even though they may be called hypocrites, let them nevertheless not cease doing good nor seek expensive clothing in this world."

Chapter 4

1. Habig, *St. Francis of Assisi*, p. 563.

2. Celano, *Life of St. Francis* 5. See the *Legend of the Three Companions* (5) for a variation on this theme.

3. Celano, *Life of St. Francis* 1, 2.

4. Celano, *Life of Francis* 5.

5. Le Goff, *François d'Assise*, pp. 196–98.

6. Habig, *St. Francis of Assisi*, p. 563.

7. *Legend of the Three Companions* 5, 6.

8. Celano, *Life of St. Francis* 9, 11. According to the authors of the *Assisi Compilation* (103), Francis once referred to his faithful brothers as "my knights of the round table" and made reference to the main characters of the *Song of Roland*. See also Bonaventure, *Major Legend* 1.5.

9. Bonaventure, *Major Legend* 1.4. See also 5.1.

10. Celano, *Life of St. Francis* 7. The *Legend of the Three Companions* (7) is more explicit: "The bride was the true religion that he later embraced, a bride more noble, richer and more beautiful because of her poverty." Bonaventure wrote: "He had chosen to glory above all in the privilege of poverty which he was accustomed to call his mother, his bride, and his lady." Bonaventure, *Major Legend* 7.6.

11. Francis's *Salutation of the Virtues* begins: "Hail, Queen Wisdom! May the Lord protect you, with your sister, holy pure Simplicity! Lady holy Poverty, may the Lord protect you, with your sister, holy Humility!" Thomas of Celano saved most of

his references to Lady Poverty for the *Remembrance* (55, 82, 93). The allegorization of Poverty as a woman to whom Francis was betrothed became a popular theme in Franciscan art and literature, as is evidenced by Giotto's fresco in the Lower Church in Assisi, as well as Dante's description of Francis and Poverty as "lovers." *Paradiso*, canto 11, line 74.

12. Plato, *Symposium* 9.

13. Especially Proverbs 8:1–36 and Wisdom 6–8.

14. Proverbs 8:23, 30; *Sacred Commerce* 25, in Armstrong, Hellman, and Short, *Francis of Assisi* 1:537.

15. Thomas of Celano mirrored this sentiment when he wrote: "My sons, know that poverty is the special way to salvation; its fruits are many, and known only to a few." Celano, *Remembrance* 200.

16. Matthew 5:3.

17. *Sacred Commerce* 1, 19.

18. *Sacred Commerce* 2.

19. *Sacred Commerce* 16.

20. *Sacred Commerce* 12.

21. Proverbs 8:18.

22. In Proverbs, this goes no further than Wisdom's declaration: "I love those who love me, and those who seek me diligently find me." Proverbs 8:17.

23. For more on this topic, see Denys Turner, *Eros and Allegory: Medieval Exegesis of the Song of Songs* (Kalamazoo, MI: Cistercian Publications, 1995).

24. *Sacred Commerce* 5.

25. *Sacred Commerce* 9; Song of Songs 2:5.

26. *Sacred Commerce* 15.

27. *Sacred Commerce* 25. It is interesting that Eve is left out of the picture in Lady Poverty's reworking of the Genesis story, presumably so as not to complicate Lady Poverty's own special relationship with the first man.

28. *Sacred Commerce* 26.

29. *Sacred Commerce* 30.

30. *Sacred Commerce* 31; Exodus 3:17.

31. *Sacred Commerce* 21.

32. *Sacred Commerce* 22.

33. *Sacred Commerce* 17. See also *Sacred Commerce* 4.

34. *Sacred Commerce* 33.

35. *Sacred Commerce* 34.

36. *Sacred Commerce* 39. Lady Poverty defined greed as an "immoderate desire to acquire or retain riches."

37. *Sacred Commerce* 39.

38. *Sacred Commerce* 40. Matthew 5:14. This mirrors the sentiments found in the *Earlier Rule* 8.8–11, which prohibited the Franciscans from soliciting money in support of leper colonies.

39. *Sacred Commerce* 47.

40. Isaiah 5:8.

41. *Sacred Commerce* 49.

42. *Sacred Commerce* 49.

43. *Sacred Commerce* 60–62.

44. *Sacred Commerce* 63. The authors of the *Assisi Compilation* (26) noted that in the early days of the order, "if a brother had a ragged sheet over some straw he considered it a bridal couch."

45. *Sacred Commerce* 52.
46. *Sacred Commerce* 54.
47. *Sacred Commerce* 5.
48. Wisdom 2:1.
49. *Sacred Commerce* 6. Elsewhere the author noted: "Poverty is the only thing that everyone condemns, so that it cannot be discovered in the land of those living comfortably." *Sacred Commerce* 10.
50. *Sacred Commerce* 17.
51. *Sacred Commerce* 3.
52. *Sacred Commerce* 18.

Chapter 5

1. There are countless parallels between the *Life of St. Francis* and the Gospels. According to Thomas, Francis's miracles included healing cripples, casting out demons, giving sight to the blind, and even turning water into wine. Celano, *Life of St. Francis* 61–70, 119–50. Francis and his followers referred to themselves as "new disciples of Christ." When Francis composed their earliest rule, "he used primarily words of the holy gospel, longing only for its perfection." *Life of St. Francis* 13. When he sent his brothers out two by two to preach repentance, he did so with Christ's commission to his apostles in mind. *Life of St. Francis* 34. Upon his conversion, he declared: "Until now I have called Pietro Bernardone my father . . . But . . . from now on [I say]: 'Our Father, who art in heaven,' and not 'my father, Pietro di Bernardone.'" *Legend of the Three Companions* 20. In the *Assisi Compilation* (22), the dying Francis celebrates a Last Supper with his brothers.
2. Celano, *Remembrance* 26.
3. Celano, *Life of St. Francis* 84.
4. Celano, *Life of St. Francis* 115.
5. Celano, *Life of St. Francis* 115. See also *Legend of the Three Companions* 68.
6. Celano, *Life of St. Francis* 82.
7. Celano, *Life of St. Francis* 77.
8. Celano, *Life of St. Francis* 77. See also Celano, *Remembrance* 111.
9. Celano, *Life of St. Francis* 78.
10. Francis, *Testament* 6–11. This explains Francis's frenetic concern for how priests handled the eucharistic elements. Francis, *Exhortations to the Clergy, First Letter to the Custodians, A Letter to the Entire Order* 12–29. Francis's respect for members of the clergy was built on the same basic principle: they were the only ones who could effect the miracle of turning bread and wine into the body and blood of Christ. See also Francis, *Admonitions* 2.9, 26.2.
11. Celano, *Life of St. Francis* 86.
12. Celano, *Life of St. Francis* 84. In his *Remembrance* (35), Thomas refers to Greccio as "the place where [Francis] had earlier recalled the birth of the child of Bethlehem, becoming a child with the child."
13. Celano, *Remembrance* 200.
14. Celano, *Remembrance* 199.
15. Celano, *Life of St. Francis* 55.
16. Celano, *Remembrance* 11.
17. *Legend of the Three Companions* 14.
18. *Legend of the Three Companions* 14. See also *Major Legend* 9.2.

19. Celano, *Life of St. Francis* 115. 1 Corinthians 2:2.

20. Celano, *Life of St. Francis* 95. See also 90, 113.

21. "True love of Christ transformed this lover into [Christ's] very image," concluded Thomas of Celano, *Remembrance* 135.

22. Bonaventure, *Major Legend* 14.4. Chapter 13 of Bonaventure's work is devoted in its entirety to the stigmata, as is the first section of his appendix regarding Francis's miracles.

23. Celano, *Life of St. Francis* 36. Thomas added that Francis "gleamed like a shining star in the darkness of night and like the morning spread over the darkness" (37).

24. Celano, *Life of St. Francis* 90, 37. "I became all things to all men, that I might by all means save some." I Corinthians 9:22.

25. Celano, *Life of St. Francis* 22. See also Bonaventure, *Major Legend* 7.1.

26. *Assisi Compilation* 8.

27. Matthew 8:20, Luke 9:58.

28. Matthew 10:9–10.

29. Matthew 6:25–26.

30. Matthew 6:24.

31. Matthew 4:8–10.

32. Matthew 4:20–22.

33. Matthew 9:9–13, Luke 5:27–28, Mark 2:13–17.

34. Matthew 19:16–29, Luke 18:18–30, Mark 10:17–30. See also Matthew 8:19 and 8:21 for other would-be disciples who were apparently discouraged by the sacrifices that Jesus asked of them.

35. 2 Corinthians 8:9.

36. Philippians 2:5–9.

37. It is interesting to note that from the perspective of early Christian exegetes, Jesus' form of voluntary poverty (the Incarnation) did nothing to diminish the fundamental "riches" of his own divinity. Jean Leclercq, "Les controverses sur la pauvreté du Christ," in Mollat, *Études sur l'histoire de la pauvreté*, 1:50. But this strains the analogy between the Incarnation and any act of deliberate self-impoverishment on the part of a rich man, because the wealth from which the rich man is distancing himself is considered anything but divine. Still one could argue that the rich man does retain (or better, acquires) "riches" in a new spiritual form.

38. For a brief history of early Christian commentaries on these passages, see ibid., 1:45–52.

39. Of the 196 biblical passages cited in Francis's own writings, all but 32 come from the New Testament, with the four Gospels accounting for 115 of them. Based on the calculations of H. Boehmer, cited by Le Goff, *François d'Assise*, p. 112.

40. See chapter 2.

41. By so doing, Francis was following in the footsteps of a number of late twelfth-century monastic reformers who used 2 Corinthians 8:9 as the principal theological justification for their experiments in voluntary poverty; in particular Peter of Blois, Alan of Lille, and the apologists for the Order of Grandmont. Christine Pellestrandi, "La Pauvreté spirituelle à travers les textes de la fin du XIIe siècle," 1:279–85.

42. *Later Admonition and Exhortation to the Brothers and Sisters of Penance* 5. The reference to Mary's poverty follows from Luke 1:52 (the Magnificat): "he has put down the mighty from their thrones, and exalted those of low degree."

43. Francis, *Admonitions* 1:16–18. "The Lord of the universe, God and the Son of God, so humbles himself that for our salvation he hides himself under an ordinary piece of bread." Francis, *A Letter to the Entire Order* 27.

44. Celano, *Remembrance* 74. See also *Later Rule* (7).

45. Celano, *Remembrance* 73. See also *Assisi Compilation* 97.

46. This is consistent with the image of Christ, in the *Sacred Commerce* (14; compare 4), who "left behind all the ranks of angels and the immense powers—of which there is a great abundance in heaven—when he came to look for you [Lady Poverty] in the lowest regions of the earth." Susan Harvey suggests the same kind of connection between voluntary poverty and the Incarnation in the Syriac *Life of the Man of God*. Harvey, "The Holy and the Poor: Models from Early Syriac Christianity," in Hanawalt, *Through the Eye of a Needle*, p. 65.

47. Celano, *Life of St. Francis* 76.

48. Nothing, that is, short of following the example of St. Alexis (also known as the "Man of God"), the legendary fifth-century Roman who suddenly left home on his wedding day and made his way to Edessa, where he lived a life of poverty without ever telling anyone that he used to be rich. This act of "social suicide" assured Alexis that he would never know the social benefits that came with a life of renunciation. Though none of the early biographers of Francis mention the story of Alexis, it is hard to imagine, given the popularity of the legend in the West, that Francis would have been unfamiliar with it. Extant manuscripts tell us that the story spread to every corner of Europe between the eleventh and the thirteenth centuries. And we can deduce from the literary form of the earliest vernacular versions that it must have been something of a standard in the repertoire of the troubadours and jongleurs who made their living on the street corners and squares of every medieval city. For summaries of scholarly opinion on the provenance of the legend of St. Alexis, see Alexander Gieysztor, "La legende de saint Alexis en occident: un ideal de pauvreté," in Mollat, *Études sur l'histoire de la pauvreté*, 1:125–26; and Carl J. Odenkirchen, *The Life of St. Alexius, in the Old French Version of the Hildesheim Manuscript: The Original Text Reviewed with Comparative Greek and Latin Versions*, Medieval Classics, 9 (Brookline, MA.: Classical Folia Editions, 1978), pp. 29–32. It is interesting to note, in this regard, that when the young Francis was trying to sort out his spiritual stirrings, he was known, from time to time, to pretend to be poor. According to Bonaventure, Francis's career as a beggar began at a monastery outside of Assisi where no one recognized him. *Major Legend* 2.6. Once while in Rome, Francis "secretly exchanged clothes with one of those poor people" whom he encountered outside of St. Peter's "and put them on. Standing on the steps of the church with the other poor, he begged for alms." *Legend of the Three Companions* 10 (see Celano, *Remembrance* 8, and Bonaventure, *Major Legend* 1.6). But as much as the Francis seems to have enjoyed this masquerade, he decided against making it a permanent feature of his holy life. "After taking off the beggar's clothes and putting on his own, he returned to Assisi and began to pray that the Lord would direct his way."

49. In his creative reconstruction of Francis's life, Nikos Kazantzakis includes an episode that speaks directly to this tension. Francis, en route to Rome to secure the pope's approval for his way of life, happens upon a "fat, jovial monk with red sandals and a wide, red hat." Spreading a silk handkerchief on a rock so that he might sit without soiling his robe, the monk asked Francis why he was heading to Rome and learned that he intended to ask the pope to grant him the privilege of pursuing a life of absolute poverty. The monk found this amusing: "'I can see arrogance peeping through the holes in your robes,' he said. 'Nothing and everything are the same, and whoever seeks to have nothing also seeks to have everything—which you know

well enough, you sly foxes, but you pretend to be poor, miserable devils just so that you can dig your claws into everything without meeting any opposition and without anyone realizing what you are up to—not even God. . . . You possess everything already, hypocrite! You are the richest man on earth. . .for the simple reason that you have placed your hopes in God." The monk went on to challenge the befuddled Francis: "What I want to see is this: for you to become so poor that you must renounce even the hope that one day you will see God. Can you do it? Can you? That is what perfect Poverty means; what it means to be a perfect ascetic. That is the highest form of sainthood. Can you do it?" Concluding from this unexpected interchange that he was not dealing with any ordinary monk, Francis quickly made a sign of the cross, and the apparition disappeared with "a screeching, jeering laugh." But it was not as easy for Kazantzakis's Francis to make the sting of the monk's criticism go away. Having concluded that "the words of the Tempter and the words of God are often identical," he whispered, "Lord . . . give me the strength to enable me one day to renounce hope, the hope, O Lord, of seeing Thee. Who knows: perhaps this, and only this, constitutes absolute poverty." Nikos Kazantzakis, *St. Francis* (New York: Simon and Schuster, 1962), pp. 159–61.

50. Many scholars have observed that Francis's poverty was, first and foremost, an *imitatio Christi*, not an *imitatio pauperis*. For instance, Raoul Manselli, "La Povertà nella vita di Francesco d'Assisi," in *La povertà del secolo XII e Francesco d'Assisi* pp. 270, 272, wrote: "St. Francis did not simply want to be poor, but to be an imitator of Christ." The radicalness of Francis's life "is not a function of poverty per se, but of the manner in which poverty is understood, inserted into a global vision of an exemplary Christian life. Being poor did not matter to him; it was being poor in the humiliation and pain of the crucified Christ that mattered." What few seem to have noticed or addressed is: (1) the connection between voluntary poverty and the Incarnation, and (2) how antithetical voluntary and involuntary poverty really are.

51. Stephen R. Munzer makes this point in "Beggars of God: The Christian ideal of Mendicancy," *Journal of Religious Ethics* 27 (1999): 310. Bonaventure was forced to defend this Franciscan innovation in his *Defense of the Poor* 12.25–41.

52. The Christian relationship between poverty as a socioeconomic condition and poverty as a spiritual attitude has its roots in the Old Testament, where the people of Israel were expected to be charitable toward people who were poor, humble, and dependent at the same time that they were supposed to see themselves collectively as poor, humble, and dependent on God's charity. Just as God was imagined to defend the poor from abuse by the rich, so he defended Israel when it behaved humbly, in its relations with its God. Jean Leclerq, "Aux origines bibliques du vocabulaire de la pauvreté," in Mollat, *Études sur l'histoire de la pauvreté*, 1:36. The Book of Psalms is the *locus classicus* for this dual significance of poverty. For instance, Psalm 69:5: "But I am poor and needy; hasten to me, O God! You are my help and my deliverer; O lord, do not delay!"

53. Luke 4:18.

54. Matthew 9:3, 12:7. In Matthew 26:6–13, we find Jesus contradicting this logic when his disciples objected to the woman's "waste" of an expensive ointment that could have been sold to help the poor. "Why do you trouble the woman? For she has done a beautiful thing to me. For you will always have the poor with you, but you will not always have me."

55. Luke 6:20–21. Much ink has been spilled trying to identify the poor, hungry, and weeping Judaeans to whom Jesus made these promises. Most New Testament

scholars see close parallels between the justice passages in the Gospels and those of Isaiah and the rest of the prophets. Some interpret the "poor" to be the chastened people of Israel as a whole. Others take them to be those Jews—whether economically rich or poor—who were spiritually aware enough to appreciate how utterly dependent they were on the mercy of God. Still others want to see the "poor" as a reference to the poor, that is, the defenseless, dependent sectors of society.

56. Luke 6:24. There is a distinct sense in Jesus's message that any social benefits that might accrue from perceived acts of piety would take away from the spiritual benefits. Matthew 6.5, 6.16.

57. Luke 18:25.

58. Luke 16:20–25.

59. Luke 1:46–55.

60. Matthew 25:35–6.

61. Matthew 5:17–19: "Think not that I have come to abolish the law and the prophets; I have come not to abolish them but to fulfil them. For truly, I say to you, till heaven and earth pass away, not an iota, not a dot, will pass from the law until all is accomplished."

62. Matthew 19:16–29, Luke 18:18–30, Mark 10:17–30.

63. Max Weber, *The Sociology of Religion*, translated by Ephraim Fischoff (Boston: Beacon Press, 1993), p. 162.

64. Matthew 19:27–18.

65. Celano, *Life of St. Francis* 17. His breach with his father, in fact, began when he sold cloth in Foligno and tried to donate the profits to a poor priest at the ramshackle church of San Damiano. Celano, *Life of St. Francis* 9.

66. Celano, *Remembrance* 9 (based on *Legend of the Three Companions* 11–12). According to the *Remembrance*, Francis also made of point of being generous to the needy, as evidenced by the story of his clothing a half-naked knight (5).

67. *Legend of the Three Companions* 9.

68. Celano, *Remembrance* 71.

69. In his study of poverty in hagiographical literature, Sigal has distinguished between saints whose lives were distinguished by a high level of *liberalitas erga pauperes* (liberality toward the poor) and those who sought more of a *conversatio inter pauperes* (interaction among the poor). The twelfth-century saints Stephen of Muret and Bernard of Tiron are his principal examples of the latter. Sigal, "Pauvreté et charité," 1:156–57.

70. Francis, *Testament* 14.

71. Celano, *Life of St. Francis* 84.

72. Celano, *Life of St. Francis* 84. Compare the *Earlier Rule* 1.1 and Celano, *Remembrance* 90.

Chapter 6

1. Christian exegetes from very early on understood the story of the sisters Mary and Martha to be a lesson in the relative merits of the *vita passiva* (Mary) and the *vita activa* (Martha). "Martha, Martha, you are anxious and troubled about many things. One thing is needful. Mary has chosen the good portion, which shall not be taken away from her." Luke 10:41–42. For more on this matter, see Giles Constable, "Interpretation of Mary and Martha," in *Three Studies in Medieval Religious and Social Thought* (Cambridge: Cambridge University Press, 1995), pp. 1–141.

2. Justin (d. 155), in his *First Apology* (1.15), reported that "many men and women, now in their sixties and seventies who have been disciples of Christ from childhood, have preserved their purity; and I am proud that I could point to such people in every nation. Then what shall we say of the uncounted multitude of those who have turned away from incontinence and learned these things?" in *Early Christian Fathers*, translated and edited by Cyril C. Richardson (New York, Macmillan: 1970), p. 250. Chastity was perhaps the most socially visible sign of membership in the Christian community. As such, it left an impression on pagan observers as well. Galen, for one, observed that the Christians' "contempt for death is patent to us every day, and likewise their restraint from intercourse. For they include not only men but also women who refrain from intercourse all through their lives." Quoted by Peter Brown in *The Body and Society: Men, Women, and Sexual Renunciation in Early Christianity* (New York: Columbia University Press, 1988), p. 33.

3. I Corinthians 7:25–40.

4. Ignatius, *Letter to Polycarp*; in Richardson, *Early Christian Fathers*, p. 119 (emphasis mine).

5. The treatise *On the Glory of Martyrdom*, traditionally attributed to Cyprian of Carthage (d. 257), typifies this kind of argument.

6. Indeed from the perspective of the early church, Christian sanctity was, for all intents and purposes, synonymous with martyrdom.

7. The Donatist movement of Roman Africa, which insisted that bishops be free of the taint of collaboration with the imperial authorities during the persecutions, illustrates how difficult this transition from beleaguered sect to imperial cult could be.

8. Athanasius, *Life of St. Antony* 47, translated by Robert T. Meyer, Ancient Christian Writers, 10 (New York: Newman Press, 1950). "Indeed," as Antony put it, "if we live as if we were to die each new day, we shall not sin" (p. 19).

9. *The Sayings of the Desert Fathers* 2.16, in *Western Asceticism*, edited by Owen Chadwick (Philadelphia: Westminster Press, 1958).

10. Jerome once observed: "A monk's function is not to teach, but to lament." *Against Vigilantius* 15, in *Letters and Select Works*, Nicene and Post-Nicene Fathers, 2nd series, vol. 6, translated by W. H. Fremantle (Oxford: James Parker, 1893).

11. See, for example, Cyprian, *Letters* 10, 20–21, 27.

12. Athanasius, *Life of St. Antony* 87.

13. *Life of St. Daniel the Stylite* 36.

14. For the classic study of the power of late antique holy men, see Peter Brown, "The Rise and Function of the Holy Man in Late Antiquity," *Journal of Roman Studies* 61 (1971): 80–101. Susan Harvey has observed that insofar as the ascetics of late antiquity modeled their behavior on the Old Testament prophets, advocacy on behalf of the poor in the interests of promoting justice was part and parcel of their religiosity. Harvey, "The Holy and the Poor," p. 54.

15. *The Sayings of the Desert Fathers* 2.7. It should come as no surprise, given the magnetism that drew less ascetically minded Christians to the cells of these desert saints, that at some point, in the midst of all of this competitive asceticism, someone would imagine a saint who outdid all of his peers by depriving himself not only of the material pleasures of this world but of the adulation of his coreligionists; that is, by going into the desert without letting anyone know that he was there. The life of the Alexandrian prostitute-turned-hermit Mary of Egypt, who roamed the desert for decades without anyone ever seeing her until shortly before her own death, is one such example from this period. The life of the "Man of God" (later dubbed "St. Alexis"), who fled his Roman aristocratic household on the day that he was to marry

and lived out his life anonymously as a beggar in Edessa, is another. The case of the "Man of God" is particularly interesting in this regard. What better way to underscore the effort required to protect himself from adoration than by having him live out his life, not in the desert, but in the middle of a city, where every day he would have to struggle with the temptation to share his pathetic story and reap the benefits of communal adulation? See Harvey, "The Holy and the Poor," pp. 43–66.

16. Athanasius, *Life of St. Antony* 87.

17. Athanasius, *Life of St. Antony* 84.

18. Athanasius, *Life of St. Antony* 84.

19. Athanasius, *Life of St. Antony* 85.

20. Athanasius, *Life of St. Antony* 70.

21. Athanasius, *Life of St. Antony* 44. Elsewhere: the desert was "populated with monks who left their own people and registered themselves for citizenship in heaven" (14).

22. Leontius, *Life of St. John the Almsgiver* 5, translated by Elizabeth Dawes and Norman H. Baynes, *Three Byzantine Saints: Contemporary Biographies*, translated from the Greek (Oxford: Basil Blackwell, 1948).

23. Leontius wrote his *Life* as a supplement to an earlier one written by John Moschus and Sophronius, which is no longer extant.

24. Leontius, *Life of St. John the Almsgiver*, Supplement 2. John was referring to the classic exchange between the rich and the poor in any act of charity: the poor person receives material assistance, while the rich one gains the spiritual benefits of the poor person's blessing.

25. Leontius, *Life of St. John the Almsgiver*, Supplement 2.

26. Leontius, *Life of St. John the Almsgiver*, Supplement 7.

27. Leontius, *Life of St. John the Almsgiver*, Supplement 6.

28. Leontius, *Life of St. John the Almsgiver*, Supplement 9.

29. Leontius, *Life of St. John the Almsgiver*, Supplement 7. Other eastern bishop-saints who distinguished themselves by their mobilization of resources for the poor were Rabbula of Edessa, Basil of Caesarea, and John Chrysostom. See Harvey, "The Holy and the Poor," p. 51. Harvey's article summarizes in particular the many dimensions of Rabbula's charity-oriented career, making the point that what distinguished him from other late antique bishops was his unwillingness to distinguish between the voluntary and the involuntary poor (p. 51).

30. Possidius, *Life of St. Augustine* 7, translated by F. R. Hoare, in Thomas F. X. Noble and Thomas Head, *Soldiers of Christ: Saints and Saints' Lives from Late Antiquity and the Early Middle Ages* (University Park: Penn State University Press, 1995), p. 39.

31. Possidius, *Life of St. Augustine* 24; 27.

32. Possidius, *Life of St. Augustine* 23–24.

33. Possidius, *Life of St. Augustine* 19. Ezechiel 3:17; 2 Timothy 4:2.

34. Leontius, *Life of St. John the Almsgiver*, Supplement 42.

35. Leontius, *Life of St. John the Almsgiver*, Supplement 42.

36. Susan Harvey has observed that for all of his efforts on the part of the poor, "Rabbula, like many of the great bishops of his time, was first and foremost an ascetic—a holy man." "The Holy and the Poor," p. 55.

37. Possidius, *Life of St. Augustine* 4.

38. Possidius, *Life of St. Augustine* 5. This monastic community, which emphasized chastity and poverty, served as something of a training ground not only for the clergy of Hippo but for bishops who were "exported" to other parts of the province (11).

39. Sulpicius Severus, *Dialogues* 24, in *The Western Fathers*, translated by F. R. Hoare (New York: Harper, 1954).

40. Sulpicius Severus, *Dialogues* 24.

41. Sulpicius Severus, *Life of St. Martin* 10, in *The Western Fathers*. According to Sulpicius, the young Martin "longed for the desert" even as a young catechumen (2) and, before he became bishop, lived in at least four different hermitages (6–9). Like many of the most famous hermits in Egypt, Martin attracted a large number of like-minded ascetics to his cell, "many among them of noble rank," who "had been brought up to something quite different before forcing themselves to this lowliness and endurance." *Life of St. Martin* 10; *Lives of the Desert Fathers* 2, 3, 7, 10, 18. Many of Martin's fellow monks ultimately found themselves drafted into the episcopacy.

42. Sulpicius Severus, *Life of St. Martin* 9.

43. Sulpicius Severus, *Life of St. Martin* 20.

44. Sulpicius Severus, *Life of St. Martin* 27.

45. Sulpicius Severus, *Life of St. Martin* 9.

46. Sulpicius Severus, *Letter 1: To the Priest Eusebius*.

47. This is not to say that monks never engaged in missionary activity. Augustine, Gregory I's choice to lead the Roman mission to England, and Boniface, the "apostle to the Germans," both began their careers as monks. See Chenu, *Nature Man, and Society*, p. 212.

48. Sulpicius Severus, *Life of St. Martin* 12–16.

49. Sulpicius Severus, *Life of St. Martin* 1.

50. Augustine, *Letters* 211, translated by Wilfrid Parsons, Fathers of the Church 32 (New York: Fathers of the Church, 1956), pp. 50–51.

51. Cassian, *Conferences* 19, translated by Edgar C. S. Gibson, A Select Library of the Nicene and Post-Nicene Fathers of the Christian Church, 2nd series, vol. 11, edited by Henry Wace and Philip Schaff (Oxford: James Parker, 1894), p. 491.

52. Benedict, *Rule*, prologue, in *The Rule of St. Benedict*, translated by Anthony C. Meisel and M. L. del Mastro (New York: Doubleday, 1975).

53. Benedict, *Rule* 1. Cassian, *Conferences* 18.

54. Benedict, *Rule* 1.

55. According to his earliest biographer, Gregory fled "with great humility," upon learning that he had been elected pope, and hid in an empty cask and then in a forest. *The Earliest Life of Gregory the Great by an Anonymous Monk of Whitby* 7, translated by Bertram Colgrave (Cambridge: Cambridge University Press, 1968), pp. 85–87.

56. Gregory, *Pastoral Rule* 1.5, translated by Henry Davis, Ancient Christian Writers 11 (Westminster, MD: Newman Press, 1950), p. 31.

57. Gregory, *Dialogues*, prologue, translated by Odo John Zimmerman, Fathers of the Church 39 (New York: Fathers of the Church, 1959), p. 4.

58. For the author's extended *apologia* on the lack of miracles, see *Earliest Life of Gregory the Great* 3–7, pp. 77–85.

59. Bede, *Ecclesiastical History of the English People* 2.1, translated by Leo Sherley-Price, rev. ed. (London: Penguin Books, 1990).

60. Ibid.

61. *Earliest Life of Gregory* 5, p. 81. "Among other signs of this man's holiness, one very true and wholly admirable sign is that in all his writings there shone forth an outstanding heavenly skill, for, as we have already said, Christ spoke through him.

This is clear to all who study his *Homilies*. It is Christ himself who says, 'Preach the gospel to every creature.' Gregory inherited this abundant skill as well as his wisdom from Him who is the 'wisdom of God in a mystery, even the hidden wisdom which God ordained before the world unto our glory': therefore he was called the 'golden-mouthed' by the Romans" (24, pp. 117–18).

62. Cluny foundation charter, in *Select Historical Documents of the Middle Ages*, edited by Ernest F. Henderson (London: George Bell, 1910), pp. 329–33.

63. For a broad, insightful treatment of this relationship between the landed elite and the monasteries of this time, see Barbara Rosenwein, *Rhinoceros Bound: Cluny in the Tenth Century* (Philadelphia: University of Pennsylvania Press, 1982).

64. This type of *vita activa*, aimed at the souls of benefactors, operated alongside the other kind, aimed at providing for the needs of those who came to the monastery in search of food and other essentials. The theory behind such monastic hospitality was that each visitor should be treated as if he were Christ himself. Benedict, *Rule* 53, 66. The *Rule* (4) also included "refreshing the poor" among the "instruments of good works," though the precise meaning of this and its relationship to almsgiving was never very clear. By the time of the Cluniac reform, the duties of the *eleemosynarius* (almoner) were defined specifically in terms of visitors who came to the monastery on foot, as opposed to those of the *custos hospitum* (hospitaler), who was charged with tending to guests who arrived on horseback. This same period saw the incorporation of the *mandatum* of the poor into the liturgical life of the monastery, whereby a certain specified number of poor people were fed on a daily basis as a way of ritually fulfilling the institution's responsibilites toward the poor as defined in the *Rule*. In an effort to protect the *vita passiva* of the institution, the monks were carefully insulated from both kinds of service to the world: only the abbot and other appropriate officers had direct access to outsiders. Willabrord Witters, "Pauvres et pauvreté dans les coutumiers monastiques du moyen âge," 1:179–83, 194–95, 198–200.

65. The founders of Grandmont in particular made a concerted effort to avoid any compromise of their "poverty" posed by the traditional privileges of monastic orders. Pellistrandi, "La Pauvreté dans la regle de Grandmont," 1:229–44.

66. Particularly interesting, in this regard, is the fact that Benedictine monks were accustomed to interpreting their *vita communis* (modeled on the description of the Christians in Jerusalem living in common provided by Acts 4:32) as the basis for their own distinctively monastic claim to be living the *vita apostolica*. Chenu singles out the *De vita vere apostolica* of Rupert of Deutz (d. 1130) to illustrate this point: "There is nothing here of the apostolate, of the preaching of the word of God which characterized the role of the apostles in the primitive church." As Chenu points out, Luke 10 (Christ's commission to the apostles) began to challenge Acts 4 as the theoretical basis for the *vita apostolica* over the course of the twelfth century. Chenu, *Nature, Man, and Society*, pp. 205–6, 211; 213–14.

67. That is, living according to a "rule" (Latin: *regula*).

68. The so-called Rule of St. Augustine is attested to for the first time in 1076. Little, *Religious Poverty*, pp. 102–3. For another take on the significance of the Augustinian canons, see: Richard W. Southern, *Western Society and the Church in the Middle Ages*, Pelican History of the Church, vol. 2 (London: Penguin Books, 1970), pp. 241–44. According to Peter Damian, "the only men fit for the office of preaching are those who lack the support of earthly riches and who, because they possess nothing whatever of their own, hold everything in common." Quoted by Chenu, *Nature, Man, and Society*, p. 215.

69. Little, *Religious Poverty*, p. 104.

70. Ibid., p. 107.

71. As Little notes, very little is known about Pope Urban I (222–30), yet regulations pertaining to canons were attributed to him centuries later, so that by the time of the papal reform in the eleventh century he was considered a "principal founder of the regular life for canons." Ibid., p. 104.

72. The roughly 120 surviving letters of Jerome (c. 340–420) cover a wide array of subjects, including virginity and the ascetic life.

73. *Patrologia latina* 151:338–39. Quoted by Little, *Religious Poverty*, p. 103. The anonymous *Liber de diversis ordinibus* (1122–30) draws the firmest lines not between monks and canons but between the *ordo antiquus* and the *ordo novus*, the latter (defined by its dedication to a more ascetic discipline) including both Cistercian monks and canons regular. Bernard Metz, "La Pauvreté religieuse dans le *Liber de diversis ordinibus*," in Mollat, *Études sur l'histoire de la pauvreté*, 1:247–54.

74. Sulpicius Severus, *Life of St. Martin* 10.

75. Little, *Religious Poverty*, p. 108.

76. In the midst of the beatings that his father gave him, Francis proved that he would "gladly suffer anything for the name of Christ." Celano, *Life of Francis* 13. He was also "exhilarated with great joy" after being beaten and thrown into a ditch by brigands (16). The litany of ascetic practices that Thomas ascribes to Francis (39–40) and his followers is reminiscent of the classic eremitic literature of the desert.

77. Celano, *Life of Francis* 40. Elsewhere: "The resolute knight of Christ never spared his body. As if it were a stranger to him, he exposed it to every kind of injury, whether in word or in deed. If anyone tried to enumerate everything this man underwent, the list would be longer than that passage where the apostle recounts the tribulation of the saints [2 Corinthians 11:23–29; Hebrews 11:33–38]." Celano, *Remembrance* 21. Bonaventure seconded Francis's love of persecution: "In different parts of the world many insults were hurled against [the friars] as persons unknown and looked down upon, but true love of the gospel of Christ had made them so patient, that they sought to be where they would suffer physical persecution rather than be where their holiness was recognized and where they could glory in worldly favor." Bonaventure, *Major Legend* 4.7.

78. Celano, *Life of Francis* 55–57. *Remembrance* 30.

79. Celano, *Life of Francis* 57.

80. Celano, *Life of Francis* 55.

81. Other early friars did achieve martyrdom at the hands of the Muslims, for instance the lay brother described in Celano, *Remembrance* 208, and the five friars who died in Morocco, as described in the *Chronicle* (7) of Jordan of Giano. In should be noted that as enamored as Francis was with martyrdom, he was leery of the tendency to elevate martyrs to the status of heroes. Hence, according to Jordan, Francis would not let the brothers read the *passiones* of the Franciscan martyrs of Morocco: "Everyone should glory in his own suffering and not in that of another." Hermann, *Thirteenth-Century Chronicles*, p. 24. This mirrors Francis's sentiments as recorded in his *Admonitions* (6.3): "Therefore, it is a great shame for us, the servants of God, that the saints have accomplished great things and we want only to receive glory by recounting them."

82. Celano, *Life of Francis* 93.

83. Bonaventure, *Major Legend* 9.9.

84. Celano, *Life of Francis* 107. When his brothers urged Francis to seek medical help, "he absolutely refused to do this. His noble spirit was aimed at heaven and he only desired to be set free and to be with Christ" (98).

85. This was despite the fact that from very early on (as evident from references in the writings of Bonaventure and Matthew Paris, for instance), the Franciscans had come to be associated in the minds of their observers with cities. Le Goff, *Saint François d'Assise*, p. 164.

86. Celano, *Life of Francis* 6. Given his focus on the mystical aspects of Francis's holy life, Bonaventure is a particularly good source for this kind of "retreat from the world" imagery. "Released now from the chains of all earthly desires, this scorner of the world left the town and in a carefree mood sought the secret of solitude so that alone and in silence he would hear the mystery of the divine eloquence." Bonaventure, *Major Legend* 2.5.

87. Celano, *Life of Francis* 9. San Damiano was, in fact, only the first of three churches that Francis repaired, all of which lay in the countryside outside of the city. (21).

88. Celano, *Life of Francis* 42.

89. Celano, *Life of Francis* 44. It was Francis's wish to die at the Portiuncula (106, 108).

90. Celano, *Life of Francis* 97, 81. Jacques Le Goff discusses the mix of small, concentrated settlements dispersed over largely rural areas that was typical of central Italy at the time. Le Goff, *Saint François d'Assise*, p. 129.

91. Celano, *Remembrance* 35.

92. Celano, *Life of Francis* 71. According to Bonaventure, Francis could also achieve a remarkable level of detachment via prayer: "His mind was so fixed on heavenly splendors that he was not aware of the differences of place, time, and people that passed." *Major Legend* 10.2.

93. Celano, *Life of Francis* 91. Later Thomas observed that Francis, laid low by his illness, sought to "flee human company and go off to the most remote places, so that, letting go of every care and putting aside anxiety about others, for the time being only the wall of the flesh would stand between him and God" (103). "Saint Francis usually passed the whole day in an isolated cell, returning to the brothers only when pressed by necessity to take some food. He did not leave it for dinner at the assigned time because his hunger for contemplation was even more consuming, and often completely overwhelmed him." *Remembrance* 45; see 46, 49. Francis was also overjoyed to learn that the friars in Spain "set up the following way of life for themselves: half of them take care of the household chores and half remain free for contemplation. In this manner each week the active half moves to the contemplative, and the repose of those contemplating returns to the toil of labor" (178).

94. In 1224, Honorius III issued a bull (*Quia populares*, 1224) granting the new order the right to celebrate mass in their own oratories rather than having to attend public, parish services. One would think, from the wording of the justification. that the bull was addressing monks rather than mendicants: "Fleeing the tumult of the crowds as something that impedes your proposed way of life, you eagerly seek separate places so that you can give yourself more freely to the sacred quiet of prayer. Because of this, we are most attentive to this opportune request of your many prayers. For your intercession before God will be all the more efficacious to the extent that, living perfectly, you become all the more worthy of graces from him." In Armstrong, Hellman, and Short, *Francis of Assisi*, 1:562.

95. Celano, *Life of St. Francis* 35.

96. Bonaventure, *Major Legend* 12.1.

97. Gregory IX once compared Francis to Jacob, who, despite being struck by

the beauty of Rachel (representing the *vita passiva*), felt obliged to seek out Leah (representing the *vita activa*). "Not wishing to benefit only himself by remaining on the mountain, clinging to Rachel's embraces alone, that is to a contemplation that is beautiful but sterile, he came down to Leah's forbidden bedchamber, to lead his flock, now fertile with twins, to the interior of the desert to seek the pleasures of life." Gregory IX, *Mira circa nos* 5 (1228), in Armstrong, Hellman, and Short, *Francis of Assisi*, 1:568.

98. Francis and the movement that he inspired was part of a much broader phenomenon in twelfth- and thirteenth-century Europe in which laymen of many different stations claimed some control over their own spiritual fates. This watershed in Latin spirituality has been the focus of countless studies, some of the more seminal being Chenu, *Nature, Man, and Society*, esp. pp. 259–65; Vauchez, *Sainthood in the Later Middle Ages*; and Little, *Religious Poverty*.

99. As Daniel Lesnick has observed, "earlier Christian preaching had served the need of the Church to spread its authority by teaching fundamental doctrine to the untutored laity, but the new style of preaching [embodied by Francis] . . . focused more on meeting spiritual needs as perceived by the laity." "The new preaching was an attempt to provide an increasingly spiritually anxious and self-assertive urban laity with the tools to work for their own salvation." *Preaching in Medieval Florence*, p. 36, 37. See also Chenu, *Nature, Man, and Society*, pp. 231–32.

100. Celano, *Life of St. Francis* 17. Sulpicius Severus, *Life of St. Martin* 18.

101. Celano, *Life of St. Francis* 16. Sulpicius Severus, *Life of St. Martin* 5.

102. Celano, *Life of St. Francis* 9, 46. Sulpicius Severus, *Life of St. Martin* 5, 20.

103. Celano, *Life of St. Francis* 43. Sulpicius Severus, *Life of St. Martin* 20.

104. Celano, *Life of St. Francis* 72. Sulpicius Severus, *Life of St. Martin* 26.

105. Sulpicius Severus, *Life of St. Martin* 18. Bonaventure quoted from the antiphon traditionally read at the feast of St. Martin when he observed: "O truly and fully blessed man, I say, whose life 'the persecutor's sword did not take away, and who yet did not lose the palm of martyrdom.'" In Armstrong, Hellman, and Short, *Francis of Assisi*, 2:604.

106. According to Sulpicius Severus, Martin "had nothing with him but the cape that he had on, for he had already used up what else he had, in similar good works." *Life of St. Martin* 3.

107. Celano, *Remembrance* 5.

108. More on this in chapter 8.

109. It is worth noting in this regard that the early lives of Francis do record, if only in passing, continued contact between the friars and lepers long after Francis's fateful embrace. Thomas of Celano tells us that those of the brothers "who knew how worked with their own hands, staying in houses of lepers or other suitable places, serving everyone humbly and devoutly." Celano, *Life of St. Francis* 39. The author of the *Assisi Compilation* (9) reports that "at the beginning of the religion, after the brothers grew in number, [Francis] wanted the brothers to stay in hospitals of lepers and serve them. At that time whenever nobles and commoners came to the religion, they were told, among other things, that they had to serve lepers and stay in their houses." The same source (63) reveals that the early friars sometimes made use of leprosaria for lodging purposes as they made their way through Italy. The *Assisi Compilation* (64) also records Francis's hesitation about allowing the lepers that he was treating to leave the hospice with him, knowing how much disgust they would incite among the general population.

Chapter 7

1. Robert S. Lopez, *The Commercial Revolution of the Middle Ages, 950–1350* (Cambridge: Cambridge University Press, 1976).

2. Mollat, *Études sur l'histoire de la pauvreté*, and *Povertà e ricchezza nella spiritualità dei secoli XI e XII*, Convegni del Centro di studi sulla spiritualità medievale 8, Todi, 15–18 ottobre 1967 (Todi: Presso l'Accademia Tudertina, 1969), are the best collections of studies regarding such institutions as they relate to the poor. Bériou and Touati, *Voluntate dei leprosus*, and Bériac, *Histoire des lépreux*, are the most up-to-date studies of this phenomenon as it relates to the leprosaria. See also Guiseppina de Sandre Gasparini, "Lebbrosi e lebbrosari tra misericordia e assistenza nei secoli XII–XIII," pp. 239–68.

3. Jacque de Vitry's close attention to the activities of the Augustinian canons betrays his own former ties with the group. *Historia Occidentalis* 16–20.

4. This and the following excerpts are taken from Jacques de Vitry, *Historia Occidentalis* 29 (*The Historia Occidentalis of Jacques de Vitry: A Critical Edition*, edited by John F. Hinnebusch [Fribourg, Switzerland: University of Fribourg Press, 1972] pp. 146–48). While serving the needs of the poor and sick, the canons lived, as Jacques de Vitry explains, "according to the Rule of St. Augustine in common without private possessions under obedience to one master and, upon receiving their regular habit, promise perpetual continence to the Lord."

5. Jacques de Vitry devoted another chapter of his *Historia Occidentalis* to the Humiliati, a tripartite order originating in Lombardy that was officially approved by Innocent III in 1201. The lay members of the Humiliati were directed by the pope to live simple, honest lives of penance without leaving their homes or occupations. Jacques de Vitry observed that although the lay Humiliati "remained physically in the world . . . [and] continued to live with their wives and their daughters," they "removed themselves from all worldly business . . . wore religious habits, ate with sobriety, and performed acts of charity." Jacques de Vitry, *Historia Occidentalis* 28, p. 145. Though the *Historia Occidentalis* says nothing about the Beguines and Beghards that emerged in the Netherlands at about the same time that the Humiliati were forming in Lombardy, we know that Jacques de Vitry—while serving as bishop of Liège—was closely connected to the Beguine Marie d'Oignies, whose *Life* he authored.

6. Lesnick, *Preaching in Medieval Florence*, pp. 36, 37.

7. The logic behind the *sermones ad status* is summarized neatly by Jacques de Vitry: "it is not only those who renounce the world and go into religion who are *regulares* [that is, Christians living in accordance with a "rule"] but all the faithful of Christ who serve the Lord under the gospel's rule and live by the orders of the single greatest Abbot or Father of all." Quoted by Chenu, *Nature, Man, and Society*, pp. 221–22. The *sermones ad status* as a genre can, in a sense, be traced back to the *Pastoral Rule* of Gregory I (d. 604), which contains a section on "diversity" in the art of preaching. In it, Gregory distinguished between preaching techniques most suitable for "men and women, the poor and the rich, the joyful and the sad, prelates and subordinates, servants and masters," and so on. Gregory, *Pastoral Rule* 3.1. As Christoph Maier recently observed, the proliferation of *ad status* sermons in the thirteenth century was one manifestation of a broad "pastoral reform movement" that began in Paris in connection with Peter the Chanter and quickly spread to other universities. The goal of the movement was to "apply moral theology as it was studied in the academic circles of the schools to society at large." Though this movement predates the foundation of the mendicant orders, the Franciscans and Dominicans are largely responsible for its

success because they were actually trained to preach. Maier, *Crusade Propaganda and Ideology: Model Sermons for the Preaching of the Cross* (Cambridge: Cambridge University Press, 2000), pp. 4–5; and D. L. D'Avray, *The Preaching of the Friars: Sermons Diffused from Paris before 1300* (Oxford: Clarendon Press, 1985), p. 21. As D'Avray observes (p. 15), the tenth canon of the Fourth Lateran Council (1215), calling on bishops to enlist the aid of preachers to help them carry out their pastoral duties, is a good indication of how highly the church leadership of the time—particularly Innocent III—regarded preaching as a means of moral reform.

8. For an edition of thirteenth-century sermons to lepers written by Jacques de Vitry, Guibert de Tournai, and Humbert de Romans, see the appendix to Bériou and Touati, *Voluntate dei leprosus*, pp. 81–163. For a study of these sermons, see Bériou, "Les lépreux sous le regard des prédicateurs d'après les collections de sermons *ad status* du XIIIe siècles," pp. 33–80. Jussi Hanska also discusses the *ad status* sermons delivered *ad pauperes* and *ad leprosos* in *And the Rich Man Also Died*, pp. 92–95.

9. François-Olivier Touati, "Les léproseries aux XIIe et XIIIe siècles, lieux de conversion?" in Bériou and Touati, *Voluntate dei leprosus*, pp. 1–32. For a more general treatment of the spread of leprosaria in this period, see Bériac, *Histoire des lépreux*, pp. 151–70. Canon 23 of Lateran III (1179) called for tending to the spiritual needs of lepers by making sure that their colonies were equipped with churches, cemeteries, and clergy.

10. Vauchez, *Sainthood in the Later Middle Ages*, p. 199, categorizes this type of saint under the heading "saints of charity and labor" ("saints de la charité et du travail"). Vauchez concluded from his extensive survey of late medieval hagiography that lay, charity-oriented saints were to be found in many northern and central Italian cities between the years 1180 and 1280. Why they emerged at this particular time and in this particular region is not entirely clear, though in general terms it is perhaps safe to say that the rapid urbanization of Italy in this period resulted in new kinds of social and economic problems that in turn spawned creative spiritual responses. The reasons for the sudden disappearance of the "civic saint" type in the late thirteenth century are harder to imagine, though Vauchez suggests that it had something to do with efforts on the part of the mendicant orders themselves to control lay forms of religious life and channel such energies into the lay tertiary orders that the Franciscans and Dominicans both sponsored (p. 206). Robert Favreau, "Fondations charitables laiques au XIIe siècle: L'exemple de l'Anjou," in Mollat, *Études sur l'histoire de la pauvreté*, 2:564–610, provides a close look at the twelfth-century transition from the primarily ecclesiastical to the primarily lay foundation of charitable institutions in the French county of Anjou. Aside from the shift in patronage, Favreau notes the increase in services aimed at the local poor as opposed to the itinerant pilgrim.

11. Sicard's *Life* of Omobono is no longer extant, but it presumably informed the summary of the saint's activities that is found in the bull *Quia pietas* (1199). Vauchez, *Sainthood in the Later Middle Ages*, p. 37, n. 18. A number of lives and liturgical recognitions of the saint were composed in the succeeding centuries, the earliest probably being an office (*Cum orbita solis*) written in the thirteenth century (p. 356, n. 366). See F. Zanoni, "Vita metrica dei SS. Imerio e Omobono," *Annali della Biblioteca e Libreria civica di Cremona* 9 (1956): 29–32.

12. Omobono would come to be known as a patron of clothworkers and tailors, suggesting that he, like Francis, participated in the Italian cloth industry. *Oxford Dictionary of Saints*, edited by David Hugh Farmer, 3rd ed. (Oxford: Oxford University Press, 1992), p. 234.

13. F. Zanoni, "Vita metrica dei SS. Imerio e Omobono," pp. 29, 30.

14. *Hospitalis pauperum.* The word *hospitalis* (and its variants) was used to describe an institution more akin to a modern hospice than a hospital. Its function was to provide food, shelter, and medical attention to people who had no other place to go. This included pilgrims as well as the involuntary poor and the infirm. Institutionally, the *hospitalis* grew out of the Benedictine monastic obligations to tend to the needs of guests, rich and poor alike. But over time a clear distinction developed between the monastic hospitality that was shown to "guests" (*hospitium hospitum*) and that that was extended to the "poor" (*hospitium pauperum*) See Witters, "Pauvres et pauvreté dans les coutumiers monastiques du moyen âge," in Mollat, *Études sur l'histoire de la pauvreté*, 1:177; and, in the same collection, Martine Peaudecerf, "La Pauvreté a l'abbaye de Cluny d'apres son cartulaire," 1:225.

15. For other examples of saints going out of their way to find and treat the poor and sick, see Sigal, "Pauvreté et charité," 1:156.

16. *Acta Sanctorum quotquot toto orbe coluntur* (Antwerp: Joannem Mevrsium, 1643–), Jun 1:756.

17. For a detailed study of this saint and his relationship to the foundation of hospices in this part of Italy, see Giuliana Albini, "Fondazioni di ospedali in area padana (secoli XI-XIII)," in *La conversione alla povertà nell'Italia dei secoli XII–XIV*, Atti del XXVII Convegno storico internazionale, Todi, 14–17 ottobre 1990 (Spoleto: Centro italiano di studi sull'alto medioevo, 1991), pp. 269–323.

18. *Acta Sanctorum* Jul 5:323.

19. *Acta Sanctorum* Mar 3:53–55.

20. I have chosen to highlight the activities of male Italian civic saints so as to emphasize the parallels to Francis's own example. The most famous contemporary female (non-Italian) poverty saint was Elizabeth of Thuringen (1207–31), the young widow of Landgrave Ludwig IV; inspired by the Franciscan movement, she not only founded a hospice for the poor in Marburg but lived a life of intense austerity while she tended to the needs of her sick and impoverished guests. Taxonomically speaking, she fits somewhere between the "holy queen" category (compare her, for instance, to St. Radegund) and that of the "civic saint." Vauchez, "Charité et pauvreté chez Sainte Elisabeth de Thuringe d'apres les acts du proces de canonisation," 1:163–73.

21. *Acta Sanctorum* Jul 6:645–57. For the most up-to-date treatment of Raymond, see Luigi Canetti, *Gloriosa Civitas: culto dei santi e società cittadina a Piacenza nel medioevo, Cristianismo antico e medievale*, 4 (Bologna: Pàtron Editore, 1993), pp. 167–285. The original Latin version of Rufino's life (written in 1212), housed in archives of the convent of St. Raymond in Piacenza, was misplaced sometime after it was loaned (1525) to the nearby Dominican house for the purposes of producing a vernacular version. A futile search for the original in 1728 ultimately led the Bollandist Peter Bosch to translate the Italian version back into Latin for inclusion in the *Acta Sanctorum*. Canetti, *Gloriosa Civitas*, p. 169, n. 6. Raymond's existence is corroborated by the chronicler Giovanni de Mussis, whose *Chronicon Placentinum* records the death of the saint—"a man of great charity and hospitality"—in 1202 (p. 172).

22. *Acta Sanctorum* Jul 6:646.

23. It was this pilgrimage that earned for Raymond the nickname "Palmario," the palm frond being the symbol traditionally associated with pilgrimages to the Holy Land.

24. *Acta Sanctorum* Jul 6:648.

25. *Acta Sanctorum* Jul 6:650.

26. *Acta Sanctorum* Jul 6:650.

27. *Acta Sanctorum* Jul 6:653.

28. *Acta Sanctorum* Jul 6:651.

29. *Acta Sanctorum* Jul 6:652.

30. *Acta Sanctorum* Jul 6:653. Matthew 10:28.

31. "Non unum hoc os mihi est, quod quidem inedia vexari non invitus pariar, sed ora tot sunt, quot hic videtis fame peruentia." Acta Sanctorum Jul 6:651.

32. *Acta Sanctorum* Jul 6:652. Matthew 7:1–2.

33. Raymond, who effectively became the conscience of Piacenza, even spoke out against the evils of violent entertainment in the form of military contests. "Our Savior does not want you to occupy yourselves with uncleanness in the form of games of war which provoke the passions; he wants you to apply yourselves to decent, peaceful, civil games designed to restore your souls from weariness." *Acta Sanctorum* Jul 6:653.

34. *Acta Sanctorum* Jul 6:652.

35. *Acta Sanctorum* Jul 6:653.

36. *Acta Sanctorum* Jul 6:654.

37. *Acta Sanctorum* Jul 6:651. Matthew 25:34–36.

38. It is telling, for instance, that neither the date nor the circumstances of Raymond's canonization are known. It seems most likely that Bishop Grimerio of Piacenza was gathering evidence for the process when he died in 1210. His successor, Fulco, armed with Rufino's *Life* (which was written in 1212), probably secured Raymond's place on the canon of saints during the early years of the pontificate of Honorius III (1216–27). There is little evidence of an active cult dedicated to Raymond. The "Statutes of the College of Notaries" (1454) contain a reference to yearly poor relief, distributed "in festo S. Raymundi." But by then, the hospital that Raymond had founded, as well as the chapel that housed his body, had been in ruins for decades. The effort on the part of the Cistercian nuns (1525) to have his *Life* translated into the vernacular seems to have been aimed at reviving a moribund cult. Canetti, *Gloriosa Civitas*, pp. 173–74; 233. Raymond was not alone in his anonymity. Of all the civic saints, only Omobono is reasonably well known, and that is because he has a claim to the distinction of being the first saint canonized strictly by papal decree. See Vauchez, *Sainthood in the Later Middle Ages*, pp. 33–57, and Eric W. Kemp, *Canonization and Authority in the Western Church* (Oxford: Oxford University Press, 1948), pp. 82–106.

Chapter 8

1. Celano, *Life of St. Francis* 5.

2. Celano, *Life of St. Francis* 14. Bonaventure distinguished the young Francis from the "greedy merchants," even though he was, at the time, " intent on making a profit." *Major Legend* 1.1. He also elaborated on the father's "thirst" for money by describing how he "gulped down the money" that his son returned to him. (2.3). See Lester K. Little, "Pride Goes before Avarice: Social Change and the Vices in Latin Christendom," *American Historical Review* 76 (1971): 16–49. For a history of the sin of avarice (and a critique of Little), see Richard Newhauser, *The Early History of Greed: The Sin of Avarice in early Medieval Thought and Literature*, Cambridge Studies in Medieval Literature 41 (Cambridge: Cambridge University Press, 2000).

3. Celano, *Life of St. Francis* 1.

4. Celano, *Life of St. Francis* 1. Along the same lines, the author of the *Legend of the Three Companions* (34) observed: "Lust for the flesh, greed for the world, and

pride of life was so widespread, that the whole world seemed to be engulfed in these three malignancies."

5. Celano, *Life of St. Francis* 2.

6. Celano, *Life of St. Francis* 2.

7. Celano, *Life of St. Francis* 14–15.

8. As Moorman observed: "To [Francis] poverty became an ideal, a state of bliss to be worked hard for and paid for. Just as it took hard work, effort, and concentration in order to get rich, so it required the same qualities in order to get poor and stay poor." Moorman, *Richest of Poor Men*, p. 82.

9. Celano, *Remembrance* 55. For other instances of the pearl metaphor (based on Matthew 13:46), see Celano, *Life of St. Francis* 3, and Bonaventure, *Major Legend* 7.1.

10. By "burghers" I am referring to a wide band of the urban social spectrum ranging from shopkeepers and artisans at the lower end to members of the most powerful burgher and noble families at the upper end; that is, everyone who participated successfully in the urban (commercial-industrial) economy. In his study of late thirteenth- and fourteenth-century Florence, Daniel Lesnick makes a firm distinction between the "comfortable and aspiring" *populo* (craftsmen, artisans, professionals, etc.), with their close ties to the Franciscans, and the *populo grasso* (those involved in banking, international trade, etc.), with their connections to the Dominicans. During Francis's lifetime, however, it appears that he and his brothers appealed to both categories of city dwellers. Lesnick, *Preaching in Medieval Florence*, pp. 172–81.

11. The *Anonymous of Perugia* (16) recorded the following observation about the friars: "Either they are clinging to the Lord for the sake of the highest perfection, or they have gone mad, for their physical life seems reckless." See also the *Legend of the Three Companions* 21. In his bull *Mira circa nos* 2 (1228), Gregory IX described Francis as a "beacon whom the rich viewed with contempt." In Armstrong, Hellman, and Short, *Francis of Assisi*, 2:40, 1:566.

12. Little's version of this dynamic places more emphasis on Francis's role as a pioneer, blazing a trail that others would have much less difficulty following. "When a sensitive person like Francis penetrates the unknown on his own, with no guide or model to follow, he undergoes severe torments of doubt and uncertainty, as we have seen. Such a painful individual crisis can then serve the needs of others who need not suffer again the same agonies. The precise model was given by those whom Francis himself converted. These listened to him, made a firm resolve, and then took all their possessions, sold them, and distributed the money to poor people." *Religious Poverty*, p. 162.

13. As Little has observed, with regard to the mendicant orders as a whole, "the unique achievement of the friars was their creation of new forms of religious expression specifically for the urban sector of society and those people dominant within it." *Religious Poverty*, p. 173. This fits what Le Goff has observed with regard to changing opinions about traditionally "sinful" professions in the twelfth and thirteenth centuries. Jacques Le Goff, *Time, Work and Culture in the Middle Ages*, translated by Arthur Goldhammer (Chicago: University of Chicago Press, 1980); orig. publ.: *Pour un autre Moyen Age: temps, travail et culture en Occident* (Paris: Gallimard, 1977). Hanska's consideration of the Lazarus exegesis in the same period has led him to conclude: "all these commentaries . . . seem to confirm the opinion of Lester K. Little, that it was the mendicant doctors who made it morally acceptable, or at least legal . . . to earn money and become rich." Hanska, *And the Rich Man Also Died*, pp. 32, 88–92, 106–9. See also Jean Longère, "Pauvreté et richesse chez quelques

predicateurs durant le seconde moitie du XIIe siècle," in Mollat, *Études sur l'histoire de la pauvreté*, 1:255–72.

14. For more on the rise of preaching in the twelfth and thirteenth centuries, see Chenu, *Nature, Man, and Society*, p. 247; and Little, *Religious Poverty*, pp. 184–92.

15. Celano, *Life of St. Francis* 35.

16. Celano, *Life of St. Francis* 23. He would, according to Thomas, address a large group "as if it were a single person," telling it "the most amazing things" (72).

17. *Legend of the Three Companions* 54. "His words were neither hollow nor ridiculous," the same source continues, "but filled with the power of the Holy Spirit, penetrating the marrow of the heart, so that listeners were turned to great amazement" (25). This source (21) also describes Francis as "burning with enthusiasm" and "inebriated with the spirit."

18. *Anonymous of Perugia* 36.

19. Celano, *Remembrance* 107. Psalm 67:34. The same part of the *Remembrance* describes Francis's sermons as simple yet profound: "With few words he would suggest what was inexpressible, and, weaving movements together with fiery gestures, he carried away all his hearers toward the things of heaven."

20. Quoted by Little, *Religious Poverty*, pp. 162–63.

21. *Legend of the Three Companions* 54.

22. Celano, *Remembrance* 107. Psalm 67:34.

23. As Francis himself wrote: "Let us hold our bodies in scorn and contempt because, through our own fault, we are all wretched and corrupt, disgusting and worms." Francis, *Later Admonition and Exhortation* 46.

24. Matthew 4:17. Celano, *Life of St. Francis* 23.

25. Celano, *Life of St. Francis* 33. As laymen, Francis and his nonclerical followers would not have been permitted to preach anything but penance. It was not unheard of for bishops to permit laymen to preach penitential sermons on an ad hoc basis. A century earlier (in 1116), Bishop Hildebert of Le Mans authorized the charismatic hermit Henry of Lausanne to preach penance in the cathedral during Lent. As R. I. Moore points out, "The hermits were regarded as men especially fit to call the world to repentance." R. I. Moore, *The Origins of European Dissent*, rev. ed. (Oxford: Blackwell, 1985), p. 84.

26. Celano, *Life of St. Francis* 36.

27. Celano, *Life of St. Francis* 29.

28. As Thomas put it succinctly, he struck at their sinful lives "with a sharp blow." Celano, *Life of St. Francis* 36.

29. Celano, *Life of St. Francis* 97. See also *Remembrance* 107. "He said that a simple tongue-tied brother, who challenges others to good by his own example, must be preferred" to a preacher seeking his own praise. Bonaventure, *Major Legend* 8.2.

30. Celano, *Life of St. Francis* 54.

31. Celano, *Life of St. Francis* 52.

32. Celano, *Remembrance* 207.

33. Celano, *Life of St. Francis* 53. In the *Earlier Rule* (17.3), Francis advised: "Let all the brothers preach by their deeds."

34. Lester Little is right on target here when he observes that "the friars were not staid in their public appearances. Francis himself willingly lived in the image of the jongleur." Little, *Religious Poverty*, p. 200. His fascination with troubadour performances may explain why it was that Francis often broke into French ("the language par excellence of poetry and chivalric sentiments") when he sang. This, in turn, may

be the reason why Francis, who was originally named Giovanni (after John the Baptist) came to be called "Francesco." Le Goff, *Saint François d'Assise*, p. 49. For other references to Francis and his use of the French language, see Celano, *Life of St. Francis* 16; *Remembrance* 127; *Assisi Compilation* 38; and *Legend of the Three Companions* 10. John Saward's identification of Francis as the classic example of the "holy fool" type of saint in the Latin West is relevant here. *Perfect Fools: Folly for Christ's Sake in Catholic and Othodox Spirituality* (Oxford: Oxford University Press, 1980), pp. 84–89. Daniel Lesnick locates the more emotive aspects of Franciscan preaching specifically within the *sermo humilis* tradition. Lesnick, *Preaching in Medieval Florence*, pp. 234–71.

35. Celano, *Life of St. Francis* 2.

36. *Assisi Compilation* 38.

37. *Assisi Compilation* 66.

38. *Assisi Compilation* 83. Another of Francis's early followers had been a lute player, whom Francis invited to play for him. He politely refused: "I fear the people will suspect me of being tempted to my old levity." *Remembrance* 126, based on *Assisi Compilation* 66.

39. Celano, *Life of St. Francis* 73.

40. Little, *Religious Poverty*, p. 197. Little lays out his "rejection-reflection" thesis in the pages that follow: "we have seen how the friars confronted the chief problem of the new society, namely money-making. In the first place, they rejected money-making for themselves, turning instead to the recently matured ideal of voluntary poverty. Secondly, however, they persisted in the linguistic and formal mode of the money-makers, while avoiding the spiritually harmful aspects of such people's work. And thirdly, having themselves demonstrated part of the way, they provided for the leaders of urban society a revised moral theology that approved of money-making in certain, carefully defined circumstances. The friars' spirituality was both determined by, and a determining factor within, the new urban society" (pp. 201–2).

41. Little, *Religious Poverty*, pp. 199, 200.

42. Lester Little has made the most of this important observation in a number of studies, including: Barbara Rosenwein and Lester Little, "Social Meaning in the Monastic and Mendicant Spiritualities," *Past and Present* 63 (1974), 23–24; and Little, *Religious Poverty*, pp. 197–200.

43. Contemporary observers recognized the connection between mendicant preaching and urban audiences, even if their reasoning was different. Humbert of Romans explained that it was in the cities that "preaching is more efficacious because there are more people and the need is greater, for in the city there are more sins." Quoted by Lawrence, *The Friars*, p. 102.

44. In his study of thirteenth-century preaching manuals, D'Avray offers some examples of the use of "market-place vocabulary" on the one hand and the justification of commercial activities on the other. *The Preaching of the Friars*, pp. 208–16. But D'Avray is quick to point out that these examples must be considered within a broader context. First of all, even rurally based, monastic authors of sermons relied to some extent on merchant imagery. Second, thirteenth-century urban society was defined by more than simply a commercial economy, a fact that helps explain the wide range of metaphors and images found in the sermons (pp. 216–25). D'Avray concludes: "Commercial imagery is only a subset of social imagery, but social imagery in its turn is only a subset of a more general tendency in thirteenth-century preaching to use images, comparisons, or 'similitudes' more freely that we are accustomed to expect from prose" (p. 225). Lawrence concurs with D'Avray, for different rea-

sons: "Some Mendicant preachers identified with their city audiences by using the vocabulary and imagery of commerce to make their points; but to judge from the sermons that survive, this obvious trick of the trade was not as common as has sometimes been suggested. In collections of Mendicant sermons the themes that recur most frequently are the need for repentance and contrition, reconciliation with enemies, confession of sins, and the obligation to give alms to the poor." Lawrence, *The Friars*, pp. 121, 123.

45. Hughes de Saint-Cher's influential commentary on Luke (c. 1235) is a case in point. Hughes underscored how the rich man in the Lazarus story was not criticized for *having* riches but for *loving* them. Quoted, along with a number of other pertinent examples from later mendicant thinkers, by Hanska, *And the Rich Man Also Died*, pp. 29–31.

46. "Do not lay up for yourselves treasures on earth . . . but lay up for yourselves treasures in heaven. . . . For where your treasure is, there will your heart be also." Matthew 6:19–21. "The kingdom of heaven is like treasure hidden in a field, which a man found and covered up; then in his joy he goes and sells all that he has and buys that field. Again, the kingdom of heaven is like a merchant in search of fine pearls, who, on finding one pearl of great value, went and sold all that he had and bought it." Matthew 13:44–6. "Every one who has left houses or brothers or sisters of father or mother or children or lands, for my name's sake, will receive a hundredfold, and inherit eternal life." Matthew 19:29. The parable of the talents is a particularly good example: the servants who invested their money and presented their master with the returns were rewarded, while the one who buried his in fear was reprimanded: "You slothful and wicked servant! . . .you ought to have invested my money with the bankers, and at my coming I should have received what was my own with interest." Matthew 25:26–27.

47. Francis, *Earlier Rule* 1.1–2.

48. Francis, *Earlier Rule* 2.15.

49. Francis, *Earlier Rule* 8.5.

50. Francis, *Later Admonition and Exhortation* 30. The same source (72) contrasts this salutary kind of investment with the kind that many rich men of Francis's day made on their deathbeds, signing all their worldly possessions over to their families so that they would not be in a position to "make satisfaction . . . out of [their] wealth, for what [they] have done and the ways in which they have cheated and deceived people." Francis once rejected a would-be friar for giving his material goods away to some of his relatives "who needed them." *Assisi Compilation* 62.

51. Celano, *Life of St. Francis* 6. Matthew 13:46. See also Bonaventure, *Major Legend* 1.4, where Francis is described as a "spiritual merchant."

52. Celano, *Life of St. Francis* 14, 44.

53. Celano, *Remembrance* 55, 72; 12.

54. Bonaventure, *Major Legend* 6.3.

55. Bonaventure, *Major Legend* 7.1; see also 1.1.

56. *Anonymous of Perugia* 15.

57. *Anonymous of Perugia* 29.

58. *Legend of the Three Companions* 3.

59. *Assisi Compilation* 96.

60. *Assisi Compilation* 83. See also Celano, *Remembrance* 213. Along these same lines are the words spoken by a friar to a deathly ill Francis: "You will sell all your sackcloth to the Lord for a good price! Many canopies and silk coverings will hang over this body of yours now clothed in sackcloth." *Assisi Compilation* 4. Jacques de

Vitry made use of the same kind of investment metaphors in his descriptions of the Franciscan order. At one point, he observed that the friars "happily traded their commerce in temporal riches for spiritual ones." *Historia Occidentalis* 32. Elsewhere he summarized their mission in the following terms: "Not only by their preaching, but also by their example of a holy life and perfect conversion, they invite many men, not only of lower station but also high-born nobles, to a contempt of the world, to leave behind their estates, their castles and their very ample possessions, and in a blessed exchange to trade their temporal wealth for spiritual treasure." Armstrong, Hellman, and Short, *Francis of Assisi*, 1:583. In a sermon that he delivered to the Franciscans sometime between 1229 and 1240, Jacques de Vitry summed up the point of one of his anecdotes as follows: "How much more stupid and miserable does our [worldly] life seem to the lovers of the true life and of eternal glory. When compared with heavenly treasure, they would judge our splendid palaces and clothing and riches as dung and our glory as wind, nothing when compared to the ineffable beauty and glory of the saints which is in heaven." Armstrong, Hellman, and Short, *Francis of Assisi* 1:588.

61. A common feature of hagiographic literature, as illustrated by Murray, *Reason and Society*, p. 399.

62. *Legend of the Three Companions* 54.

63. Celano, *Life of St. Francis* 31.

64. Celano, *Remembrance* 107.

65. In the *Assisi Compilation* (72), we find the high-born friar Leonard resenting the fact that the infirm Francis (whose "parents were never at the same level as mine") rode a donkey while he himself was forced to walk.

66. Nor does the logic of Thomas's observation that people of all stripes were "moved by what they saw and heard" rule out the possibility that some "stripes" of people were moved more by what they "saw" than by what they "heard." As D'Avray has observed, in a world in which "almost any kind of wandering preacher, it would seem, had a chance of winning a following . . . the medium was probably more powerful than the precise message." D'Avray, *The Preaching of the Friars*, pp. 25–26. In any case, there was presumably no lack of poor people who would have regarded Francis as a saint regardless of the implications of his "holy poverty," simply because their ideas of what constituted sanctity would have been influenced by the dominant images of sanctity that were presented to them by the church. Vauchez explains this well: "That [saints drawn from the elite] were so prominent and so overwhelmingly preponderant at the level of local sainthood owes something to the barrier opposed by the ruling classes to devotions concerning saints of modest extraction. But it must also be recognized that the poor had, to a degree, adopted the scale of values which the church and the lay aristocracy had taught them, by common accord, through innumerable channels, not least legends and works of art." *Sainthood in the Later Middle Ages*, p. 177.

67. Chenu imagined Francis preaching to people of all economic levels (including the poor), but he, too, realized that the "poverty" of Francis's audience was more likely to be social than economic, as in the case of the merchants who, for all their wealth, were socially disadvantaged, in the sense that there was no clear place for them within the feudal structures that still dominated medieval society. Evangelical poverty represented a way out of this restrictive world. Chenu, *Nature, Man, and Society*, pp. 243–44. Murray has described medieval saints as being typically from the upper classes but freed from the normal class restraints by their religious conversions. Murray could have pushed his analysis a bit further by noting that despite the universal, cross-class appeal

that saints often enjoyed, their messages were still directed at the elite levels of society that produced them. *Reason and Society*, pp. 383–401.

68. Hanska makes the point: "If we take a closer look into Saint Bernard's key phrase: 'Poverty is not virtue, but love of poverty is,' we perceive that it does not exclude *les pauvres proprement dits*. It was quite possible to be poor through necessity and still love one's poverty and be happy with one's position. Rejecting riches could mean giving away one's riches but also not desiring to have them. The latter way of rejecting them was open to the actual poor." Hanska, *And the Rich Man Also Died*, p. 133. See also Pellistrandi, "La Pauvreté spirituelle a travers les textes de la fin du XIIe siècle," 1:287–91. The late twelfth-century canonist Huguccio "divided the poor into three categories. Some were born poor but willingly endured their poverty for the love of God. Others joined themselves to the poor by giving up all their possessions to follow Christ. These two kinds of poverty were called voluntary. But there was a third sort of poor who were filled only with 'the voracity of cupidity.' That sort of poverty was called necessary or involuntary." Tierney, *Medieval Poor Law*, p. 11.

69. This is a variation on what Peter Berger observed, when he wrote: "whatever else the constellations of the sacred may be 'ultimately,' empirically they are products of human activity and human signification—that is, they are human projections." *Sacred Canopy*, p. 89.

70. The twelfth-century theologian Gerhoch of Reichersberg distinguished between the *pauperes cum Petro* and the *pauperes cum Lazaro*, the former term referring to those who had voluntarily assumed a life of poverty (like the apostle Peter) and the latter to those who had not. The "Peter" category provided a model for the nonpoor of how to live a holy life detached from the things of the world. The "Lazarus" category provided them with a focus for charitable activity, thus allowing them to turn their material wealth into spiritual treasure. Geremek, *Poverty: A History*, pp. 24–25.

Paul Freedman's explanation for the paucity of peasant saints is relevant here: "If the peasant's way of life removed him from temptation, it also allowed him little opportunity for heroic abstinence. The peasantry was widely considered to hold certain privileges with respect to salvation, but not with respect to individual spiritual distinction meriting sainthood. The individual heroic piety requisite to sainthood was manifest and dramatic when there was more to renounce." Paul Freedman, *Images of the Medieval Peasant*, p. 222.

71. Parallel to this logic is the exegetical tendency to use the example of Job— "who was like a king, a very rich man," yet lost it all—to console victims of other twists of fortune. What right did they have to complain, given how much more Job had lost? Humbert of Romans, *Sermo ad leprosos*, quoted by Hanska, *And the Rich Man Also Died*, p. 94.

72. Catholic scholars who study poverty typically fail to take into account this sociological phenomenon when addressing the issue of access to the spiritual rewards associated with poverty. In the words of Philip F. Mulhern, "The poverty of spirit that [Jesus] urged on all His hearers pertained to every one of them, and to all of the possessions of every one." That the rich have a distinct advantage when it comes to *demonstrating* their proper disdain for material possessions does not figure into his analysis. *Dedicated Poverty: Its History and Theology* (Staten Island, NY: Alba House, 1973), p. 27.

73. Jacques de Vitry, *Letters* 1. Armstrong, Hellman, and Short, *Francis of Assisi*, 1:579. See also *Anonymous of Perugia* 47.

74. Little went on to observe that "besides a large group of nobles (who enjoyed a disproportionate representation in the sources), the largest groups were made up of ministerials, knights, patricians, and burghers. These were groups that commanded vast material resources but lacked commensurate social prestige and political power." Little, *Religious Poverty*, p. 161. His conclusions are supported by the more recent work of Jacques Paul, "La signification social du Franciscanisme," in *Mouvements franciscains e société française XIIe–XXe siècles*, edited by André Vauchez (Paris: Beauchesne, 1984), pp. 9–25.

75. Lawrence, *The Friars*, p. 34.

76. *Assisi Compilation* 61. See Celano, *Remembrance* 190.

77. For medieval distinctions between "peasants" and "paupers," see Freedman, *Images of the Medieval Peasant*, p. 11.

78. Little, *Religious Poverty*, p. 206.

79. Ibid., 205.

80. Le Goff has noted that, with few exceptions, those of Francis's "hôtes" that can be identified come from "groupes supérieurs." *Saint François d'Assise*, p. 132. Le Goff also points out that of the 62 beneficiaries of Francis's miracles that can be identified by social standing (in the 197 miracle accounts reported by Celano in his *Treatise on Miracles*), 28 (by far the single largest category) are noble. But this kind of data is not particularly useful, given the general hagiographical tendency to favor the testimony of nobly born witnesses when it comes to identifying miracles.

81. Little, *Religious Poverty*, p. 205. It should also be noted that Francis's biographers record relief on the part of the new order when the most prominent citizens began to show interest in their mission. According to the *Legend of the Three Companions* (27), Francis was "overjoyed" when Bernard joined him, "especially since Lord Bernard was a person of great stature." Later (36), Francis would console his early disciples: "Do not fear, because after not much time many learned and noble men will come to us, and will be with us preaching to kings and rulers and great crowds."

82. As André Vauchez has observed, "in a society where wealth and power were regarded as signs of divine favour and election, the great of this world were *a priori* best placed to achieve salvation and distinction in the eyes of the world at large. Their eminent social position and the means at their disposal enabled them to construct places of worship and distribute alms, defend and propagate the Christian faith, and support the clergy. The aristocracy was even in an advantageous position with regard to re-nunciation, since only those with possessions were in a position to dispossess them-selves; paradoxically, their temporal power only rendered their spiritual success more striking." *Sainthood in the Later Middle Ages*, p. 175.

83. Rosenwein and Little, "Social Meaning in the Monastic and Mendicant Spiri-tualities," pp. 4–32.

84. On the "spiritual rehabilitation" of merchants in the twelfth and thirteenth centuries, see Hanska, *And the Rich Man Also Died*, pp. 88–92; and Lesnick, *Preach-ing in Medieval Florence*, pp. 93–81, esp. p. 176. One of the principal strategies that the later mendicant preachers used was to argue for the "public utility" of trade. This allowed them to claim that there was nothing inherently bad about commerce as long as its practitioners steered clear of the sins—greed, deception, fraud—that were tra-ditionally associated with it.

85. Geremek writes: "The Christian social ethic which exalted poverty as a search for perfection through humility varied in its translation into practice according to the social setting. For the working masses it meant accepting one's lot with humility; for

them, abandoning their social role by renouncing work would be an act not of humility but of pride." *Poverty: A History*, p. 21.

86. Luke 16:19–23.

87. Francis, *Earlier Rule* 10.3.

88. Francis, *The Canticle of Exhortation for the Ladies of San Damiano* 5–6.

89. Hanska's study of Lazarus sermons shows that Franciscan and Dominican preachers in the late thirteenth and early fourteenth centuries regularly held up Lazarus as an example of the kind of patient, long-suffering poverty that could potentially open the doors of heaven to a truly poor person. Many of the sermons went so far as to present poverty as a kind of blessing, insofar as it served to test a person's spiritual quality. Hanska, *And the Rich Man Also Died*, pp. 61–2, 92–95, 103. But Lesnick's findings in his study of mendicant preaching in Florence caution us against reading too much into the apparently sympathetic sermons directed at the poor. "Neither the Dominicans nor the Franciscans in Florence, despite their large percentages of members from beneath the patriciate, expressed genuine concern for the plight of the poor, nor did they develop anything approaching a nuanced analysis of 'the poor' as a socioeconomic category." "Like the Dominican preacher, the Franciscan encouraged charitable acts not for their social utility but for the salvation they bring to the bestower." "There is [in these sermons] no reference whatsoever to the chronic indigence that many have assumed accompanies a commercial-capitalist economy." Lesnick, *Preaching in Medieval Florence*, pp. 174; 146–49.

90. It is noteworthy in this regard that even Jacques de Vitry, a great admirer of the relief efforts of the Augustinian canons, saved his most lavish praise for Francis and his followers, who, as he saw it, were responsible for "lifting up and resuscitating a religion that was downcast and almost dead." Jacques went so far as to describe them collectively as a "new kind of athlete" that God had raised up to do battle against the devil in the time of Antichrist. Yet while Jacques made much of Franciscan poverty, calling Francis and his brothers *pauperes Christi* and extolling their efforts to recapture the "religion of the primitive church," he was silent when it came to Franciscan interactions with the other *pauperes*, the very ones who filled the hospices that were being quietly administered by his beloved Augustinian canons, among others. Jacques de Vitry, *Historia Occidentalis* 32.

Appendix

1. For a useful overview of the poverty disputes as a whole, see: Malcolm D. Lambert, *Franciscan Poverty: The Doctrine of the Absolute Poverty of Christ and the Apostles in the Franciscan Order, 1210–1323*, rev. ed. (St. Bonaventure, NY: Franciscan Institute, 1998).

2. "Let the brothers be careful not to receive in any way churches or poor dwellings or anything else built for them unless they are according to the holy poverty we have promised in the *Rule*." "I strictly command all the brothers . . . not to dare to ask any letter from the Roman curia . . . whether for a church of another place . . ." Francis, *Testament* 24–25. In 1224 Honorius III issued his *Quia populares*, in which he granted to the friars the right to celebrate mass using portable altars in their own oratories, rather than having to rely on parish services. This marked a step not only toward the clericalization of the order but toward the accumulation of material possessions. Armstrong, Hellman, and Short, *Francis of Assisi*, 1:562.

3. Honorius III's bulls *Cum dilecti* (1219) and *Pro dilectis* (1220) asked bishops throughout Christendom to receive the friars with respect and allow them to "sow the seed of the word of God." Armstrong, Hellman, and Short, *Francis of Assisi* 1:558–60. Francis was well aware of the episcopal resistance that his order faced and did his best to forestall conflicts by submitting himself without question to the authority of bishops: "I would not preach in parishes against their will." "Were they to persecute me, I would still want to have recourse to them." Francis, *Testament* 6.

4. Francis, *Testament* 35.

5. Francis, *Testament* 34, 35.

6. *Quo elongati* 2–3. Armstrong, Hellman, and Short, *Francis of Assisi*, 1:571.

7. *Quo elongati* 5. Armstrong, Hellman, and Short, *Francis of Assisi*, 1:572–73.

8. *Quo elongati* 6. Armstrong, Hellman, and Short, *Francis of Assisi*, 1:573. This, as Malcolm Lambert has observed, was the beginning of a "quiet shift in emphasis away from the renunciation of actual goods . . . to the renunciation of rights." Lambert, *Franciscan Poverty*, p. 107.

9. For background, see Decima L. Douie, *The Conflict between the Seculars and the Mendicants at the University of Paris in the Thirteenth Century* (London: Blackfriars, 1954); and Penn R. Szittya, *The Antifraternal Tradition in Medieval Literature* (Princeton: Princeton University Press, 1986), pp. 11–61. See also: Philippe Grand, "Gerard d'Abbeville et la pauvreté voluntaire," in Mollat, *Études sur l'histoire de la pauvreté*, 1:389–409.

10. John 12:6 and 13:29. Szittya, *Antifraternal Tradition*, pp. 49–50. This interpretation was much more in line with traditional Christian commentary, which saw the bag as evidence that Christ and the apostles held property in common. It was Francis's contention that the "bag" attested to Judas's status as a false apostle that was the novelty, exegetically speaking.

11. *Apologia pauperum*. This has often been translated "Defense of the Mendicants," but that obscures the important double-entendre of *pauperum*.

12. As will become clear later, some of the sources resist precise dating. I have chosen to follow in the steps of Regis Armstrong and the other editors of the recent English edition of the Franciscan corpus, as far as the chronology of the sources is concerned.

13. *Chronicle of Brother Jordan* 19. For a convenient English version of this chronicle (and the two other early Franciscan chronicles by Salimbene and Thomas of Eccleston) see *Thirteenth-Century Chronicles*, translated by Placid Hermann, (Chicago: Franciscan Herald Press, 1961).

14. *Chronicle of Brother Jordan* 30–31.

15. Francis was officially canonized on July 16, 1228.

16. John R. H. Moorman, *A History of the Franscican Order from its Origins to the Year 1517* (London: Oxford University Press, 1968), pp. 279–80.

17. Thomas's *Life of St. Francis* is traditionally referred to as the *Vita Prima* or *First Life*. Shortly after he completed it, Thomas of Celano also prepared a set of readings about Francis's life for liturgical use by the Franciscan community. Armstrong, Hellman, and Short, *Francis of Assisi*, 1:172.

18. Celano, *Life of St. Francis* 92.

19. Thomas regarded the miracle of the stigmata as "a great sacrament and evidence of the grandeur of a special love." For him it confirmed that Francis's holy life "revealed in even brighter light the perfection of earlier saints." Celano, *Life of St. Francis* 90.

20. Celano, *Life of St. Francis* 33.

21. Thomas admits that the cardinal bishop of Sabina, upon meeting Francis, initially urged him to become a hermit or a monk. Likewise Innocent's initial "blessing" carried a probationary undertone: "When the almighty Lord increases you in numbers and grace, come back to me with joy and I will grant you more things than these and, with greater confidence, I will entrust you with greater things." Celano, *Life of St. Francis* 33. It was by no means a foregone conclusion that Francis, as a layman, would be given permission to preach. On the contrary, the institutional church had always been suspicious of lay preachers. Valdès, the merchant from Lyons who, in 1173, gave away all of his possessions and begin an itinerate life of preaching, is a case in point. While the pope at the time (Alexander III) "applauded the vows of voluntary poverty which he had taken, he forbade him and his companions to assume the office of preaching except at the request of the priests." R. I. Moore, *Birth of Popular Heresy* (New York: St. Martin's Press, 1976), p. 112. Indeed it was Valdès's irrepressible desire to preach that ultimately led to his condemnation by Lucius III in 1184. For his part, Francis benefited from the fact that the pope whom he solicited for premission to preach happened to be Innocent III, who was willing to take a chance on a new kind of order, one that might be able to contribute to his own "top-down" program of revitalization and centralization within the church.

22. Elsewhere: "Blessed Francis, with the consent and approval of the Lord Pope Honorius, chose this man [Ugolino] as father and lord over the whole religion and order of his brothers because blessed poverty greatly pleased him and holy simplicity received his greatest reverence." Celano, *Life of St. Francis* 99; 100.

23. Celano, *Life of St. Francis* 75.

24. Celano, *Life of St. Francis* 74.

25. Celano, *Life of St. Francis* 126.

26. Celano, *Life of St. Francis* 74. At the same time, Thomas was careful to present Francis's mission as one aimed at revitalizing the church, not challenging it: "The first work that blessed Francis undertook, after he had gained his freedom from the hands of his carnally minded father, was to build a house of God. He did not try to build a new one, but he repaired an old one, restored an ancient one. He did not tear out the foundation, but he built upon it." (18). Throughout the *Life*, in fact, Francis comes across as a dutiful son of the church with an inordinate respect for clerics of all ranks. Francis's attempt to give money to the poor priest at San Damiano is the first of many instances of Francis's great deference to the clergy (9). According to Thomas, this unmitigated respect led the brothers to continue confessing their sins to a particular priest "even when his wickedness had been reported to them by many people" (46). Likewise Francis held churches in the highest esteem. "In whatever place a church had been built, even when they were not near it, but could glimpse it from a distance, they would turn toward it. Prostrate on the ground, bowing inwardly and outwardly, they would adore the Almighty saying, 'We adore you, O Christ, in all your churches'" (45).

27. Celano, *Life of St. Francis* 15. Later, Thomas tells us, Francis ran into Guido in Rome and benefited from his support and advice in anticipation of the fateful papal audience (32).

28. Celano, *Life of St. Francis* 28.

29. Celano, *Life of St. Francis* 104.

30. Celano, *Life of St. Francis* 108.

31. Celano, *Life of St. Francis* 102.

32. Celano, *Life of St. Francis* 95.

33. Upon returning from his sojourn in the East, Francis relinquished his control of the order (at the chapter meeting in September 1220) to his vicar, Peter Catani. When Catani died a few months later, Francis appointed Elias to replace him.

34. Celano, *Life of St. Francis* 98, 109, 108.

35. Armstrong, Hellman, and Short, *Francis of Assisi*, 1:423–25.

36. Armstrong, Hellman, and Short, *Francis of Assisi*, 1:363–64.

37. This view, espoused by Michael Cusato, is summarized in Armstrong, Hellman, and Short, *Francis of Assisi*, 1:525–27. I first heard Cusato's ideas on this subject at the celebration of the publication of *Francis of Assisi: The Early Documents*, in Berkeley, California, April 6–7, 2000. Cusato's talk was titled: "Talking about Ourselves: The Shift in Franciscan Writing from Hagiography to History, 1235–1247."

38. *Sacred Commerce* 39.

39. This dating is based on the fact that the text refers to the death of brother Sylvester (March 4, 1240) but does not mention the death of Gregory IX (August 22, 1241). Armstrong, Hellman, and Short, *Francis of Assisi*, 2:31–58. The traditional name of the manuscript stems from the fact that it was discovered in Perugia (in 1671).

40. Armstrong, Hellman, and Short, *Francis of Assisi*, 2:61.

41. For useful summaries of the debates regarding this source, see: Armstrong, Hellman, and Short, *Francis of Assisi*, 2:62–64; and Théophile Desbonnets' introduction to the *Legend of the Three Companions* in *St. Francis of Assisi, Writings and Early Biographies: English Omnibus of the Sources for the Life of St. Francis*, edited by Marion A. Habig, 3rd rev. ed. (Chicago: Franciscan Herald Press, 1973), pp. 855–80.

42. *Legend of the Three Companions* 22.

43. Otherwise known as the *Legend of Perugia* and the *Ancient Legend*, among other aliases. Armstrong, Hellman, and Short, *Francis of Assisi*, 2:113–16. Large portions of the *Assisi Compilation* follow verbatim Thomas of Celano's *Remembrance of the Desire of a Soul* (see hereafter). For convenience sake, I have treated these passages as if they were originally part of the *Remembrance* and subsequently borrowed by the author(s) of the *Assisi Compilation*, even though it is possible that the vectors of influence pointed in the opposite direction.

44. *Assisi Compilation* 16.

45. *Assisi Compilation* 56.

46. *Assisi Compilation* 56. Francis's desire that the Portiuncula serve as a model for the rest of the Franciscan communities made him particularly unyielding when it came to requests for new buildings (56). If, as even Francis came to realize, buildings were necessary, they were to be "poor little houses . . . of mud and wood" (58).

47. *Assisi Compilation* 23.

48. *Assisi Compilation* 101–5.

49. *Assisi Compilation* 25.

50. *Assisi Compilation* 105. *Earlier Rule* 2.13. The anecdote leaves the distinct impression that the minister to which Francis referred the novice would not have shared Francis's determination to uphold the *Rule*.

51. *Assisi Compilation* 93.

52. *Assisi Compilation* 43.

53. *Assisi Compilation* 47.

54. *Assisi Compilation* 104.

55. *Assisi Compilation* 104.

56. *Assisi Compilation* 103. "There are many who willingly climb to the heights of knowledge. May that person be blessed who renounces it for the love of God." *Assisi Compilation* 104.

57. *Assisi Compilation* 102.

58. *Assisi Compilation* 17.

59. *Assisi Compilation* 106.

60. *Assisi Compilation* 44. The "ancients" (as is clear from *Assisi Compilation* 18) are none other than Augustine, Benedict, and Bernard, founders of the three most prominent regular orders of the time: the Augustinian canons, the Cluniac Benedictine monks, and the Cistercian Benedictine monks. The point here is that the mendicant Franciscan order was being transformed into a kind of monastic order, complete with buildings and other property.

61. *Assisi Compilation* 44.

62. *Assisi Compilation* 106.

63. *Assisi Compilation* 112.

64. The official name of the work (*Memoriale in desiderio animae*) is based on Isaiah 26:8: "Your name and your memory are the desire of my soul." Armstrong, Hellman, and Short, *Francis of Assisi*, 2.241. It is more widely known today as the *Vita Secunda*, or *Second Life*. Thomas was also commissioned to prepare a book of miracles associated with Francis (the *Tractatus de Miraculis* or *Treatise on the Miracles*), which he compiled between 1250 and 1254. Armstrong, Hellman, and Short, *Francis of Assisi*, 1:172.

65. There are many ways in which the *Remembrance* reflects the climate of the 1240s. One of the more telling signs of the times is the fact that Elias, who had been deposed as minister general in 1239, is never mentioned by name in the *Remembrance* despite the frequent and positive references to him in the *Life*. Another is the fact that Thomas had so little to say, this time around, about Clare and her "Poor Ladies of San Damiano." Indeed he even added a number of anecdotes about the perils of associating with women while underscoring Francis's own impeccable conduct in this area. *Remembrance* 112–14, 204–7. Thomas's choice of anecdotes also suggests that he was aware of the growing discord within the order. Thus the Francis of the *Remembrance* comes down hard on brothers who stray from the flock (32, 34, 39; 190). It is also clear from Thomas's stories that some friars were serving as private chaplains and in some cases living in palaces (119–21). Others had their eyes on prelacies, putting their humility at risk (145). Thomas is also more specific about the tensions between the friars and the secular clergy, with regard to preaching rights (146–47).

66. Celano, *Remembrance* 162. See also 177, 179, 209.

67. Celano, *Remembrance* 52.

68. Bonaventure, *Major Legend*, prologue, 3.

69. Not to mention Thomas's *Treatise on Miracles*. Moorman estimated that 85 percent of the *Major Legend* was taken directly from the works of Celano. *Sources*, p. 142. Taking his organizational cues from the *Remembrance*, Bonaventure opted to "maintain a more thematic order, relating to the same theme events that happened at different times." *Major Legend*, prologue, 4.

70. Celano, *Remembrance* 188. On the contrary, Francis's begrudging authorship of the *Rule* is depicted as an untroubled act of divine revelation. Francis, like a modern-day Moses, withdrew to a quiet place and "dictated everything just as it had been revealed by God." The stigmata appeared shortly thereafter as a sign of divine affirmation. Bonaventure, *Major Legend* 4.11.

71. "We have been sent to help clerics for the salvation of souls so that we may make up whatever may be lacking in them. . . . Know then, brothers, that the good of souls is what pleases God the most, and this is more easily obtained through peace with the clergy than fighting with them. If they should stand in the way of people's salvation, revenge is for God, and he will repay them in due time. So, be subject to prelates so that, as much as possible on your part, no jealousy arises. If you are children of peace, you will win over both clergy and people for the Lord, and the Lord will judge that more acceptable than only winning over the people while scandalizing the clergy. Cover up their failings, make up for their many defects, and when you have done this, be even more humble." Celano, *Remembrance* 146.

72. Bonaventure, *Major Legend* 7.2. Moorman, *Sources*, p. 145.

73. Celano, *Remembrance* 185, 194–95. Bonaventure's intellectual fascination with the mystical aspects of Francis's holy life account for a number of creative additions to the *Major Legend*. For example, when describing Francis's church repair efforts, Bonaventure wrote: "At the bidding of divine providence, which guided Christ's servant in everything, he built up three material churches before he preached the gospel and began the order, not only to ascend in an orderly progression from the sensible to the intelligible, from the lesser to the greater, but also to symbolize mystically in external actions perceived by the senses what he would do in the future." Bonaventure, *Major Legend* 2.8. See also 3.6, 4.4.

74. Armstrong, Hellman, and Short, *Francis of Assisi*, 2:497.

75. Ibid., 1:18.

76. *Assisi Compilation* 15.

77. *Assisi Compilation* 32.

78. *Anonymous of Perugia* 16–17, 19–24. The *Anonymous of Perugia* is the best source for capturing the full range of criticisms that Francis and the brothers elicited from the people they encountered before they were widely accepted as holy men.

The film *Brother Sun, Sister Moon* (1972, screenplay: Suso Cecchi D'Amico, Lina Wertmüller, Franco Zeffirelli; English version: Kenneth Ross), captures this potential conflict. Trying to justify his inclination to share his meager rations with Francis and his brothers, a poor peasant observes: "But they're poorer than we are." "Poorer?! What poorer?" responds another. "They're the sons of landowners, sons of the rich. Go look for bread in your own home. Why do you have to come and steal from us, the real poor?"

79. Loosely quoting the *Testament* (20–22), the *Assisi Compilation* (48) reads: "He would often say: 'I want all my brothers to work and keep busy, and those who have no skills to learn some so that we may be less of a burden to people, and that in idleness the heart and tongue may not stray.'"

80. Bonaventure, *Defense of the Poor* 12.25–29. The quotations that follow are from José de Vinck's translation, *The Works of Bonaventure*, v. 4: *Defense of the Mendicants* (Paterson, NJ: St. Anthony Guild Press, 1966).

81. Bonaventure, *Defense of the Poor* 12.26–27.

82. Bonaventure, *Defense of the Poor* 12.29.

83. Acts 20:35.

84. Bonaventure, *Defense of the Poor* 12.30.

85. Bonaventure, *Defense of the Poor* 12.33.

86. Bonaventure, *Defense of the Poor* 12.36. Jean de Meun's (1277) poetic criticism of the mendicant movement closely mirrors the academic one: "But, by the letter of the law, I think / That one who eats the alms which ought to go / To people spent and feeble, naked, poor, / Covered with sores and old, unfit to earn / Their bread

because they are too weak to work, / His own damnation eats." *The Romance of the Rose*, translated by Harry W. Robbins (New York: Dutton, 1962) 54, ll. 101–6.

87. Bonaventure, *Defense of the Poor* 12.37.

88. Francis, *Earlier Rule* 2.4.

89. Christian Wenin, "Saint Bonaventure et la travail manuel," in *Le Travail au moyen âge: une approche interdisciplinaire*, edited by Jacqueline Hamesse and Collette Muraille-Samaran (Louvain-la-neuve: Institute d'études médiévales, 1990) p. 148.

90. Bonaventure, *Defense of the Poor* 8.5. As Charles M. de la Ronciere has noted, the later Franciscan biographers (beginning with Bonaventure) tended to downplay the charitable activity of Francis on the grounds that the Franciscans were the only ones who were "truly poor" (*pauperes Christi*) and therefore the only worthy recipients of alms. La Ronciere, "Pauvres et Pauvreté a Florence au XIV siecle," in Mollat, *Études sur l'histoire de la pauvreté*, 2:725–26.

91. Bonaventure, *Major Legend* 7.3 (emphasis mine).

References

Sources Related to the Life of Francis

Francis's Own Writings

Latin: Théophile Desbonnets, Thaddée Matura, Jean-François Godet, and Damien Vorreux, eds. *François d'Assise, Écrits.* Sources Chrétiennes, n. 285. Paris: Les éditions du Cerf, 1981.
English: Armstrong, Hellmann, and Short, *Francis of Assis,* 1:33–167.

Early Biographies and Other Literature Pertaining to Francis, in Chronological Order

Thomas of Celano, The Life of St. Francis

Latin: *Vita Sancti Francisci. Analecta Franciscana* 10.1–3 (1926–28).
English: Armstrong, Hellmann, and Short, *Francis of Assisi,* 1:169–308.

The Sacred Commerce of St. Francis with Lady Poverty

Latin: Stefano Bruni, ed. *Sacrum Commercium sancti Francisci cum domina Paupertate.* S. Maria degli Angeli: Edizioni Porziuncula, 1990.
English: Armstrong, Hellmann, and Short, *Francis of Assisi,* 1:521–54.

Henri d'Avranches, The Versified Life of St. Francis

Latin: *Legenda Versificata. Analecta Franciscana* 10.4 (1936).
English: Armstrong, Hellmann, and Short, *Francis of Assisi* 1:421–520.

Julian of Speyer, The Life of St. Francis

Latin: *Vita Sancti Francisci. Analecta Franciscana* 10.4 (1936).
English: Armstrong, Hellmann, and Short, *Francis of Assisi,* 1:361–420.

The Anonymous of Perugia

Latin: Lorenzo di Fonzo. *"l'Anonimo Perugino* tra le Fonti Francescane del secolo XIII: Rapporti letterari e testo critico." *Miscellanea Franciscana* 72 (1972): 117–483.
English: Armstrong, Hellmann, and Short, *Francis of Assisi,* 2:34–58.

The Legend of the Three Companions

Latin: Théophile Desbonnets, ed. "Legenda Trium Sociorum: Édition Critique." *Archivum Franciscanum Historicum* 67 (1974): 38–144.
English : Armstrong, Hellmann, and Short, *Francis of Assisi,* 2:66–110.

The Assisi Compilation

Latin: Marino Bigaroni, ed. *"Compilatio Assisiensis" dagli Scritti di fr. Leone e Campagni su S. Francesco d'Assisi. Dal Ms. 1046 di Perugia. Il edizione integrale redduta e correta con versione italiana a fronte e variazioni.* Assisi: Pubblicazioni della Biblioteca Franciscana Chiesa Nuova, 1992.
English: Armstrong, Hellmann, and Short, *Francis of Assisi,* 2:118–230.

Thomas of Celano, The Remembrance of the Desire of a Soul

Latin: *Memoriale in desiderio animae. Analecta Franciscana* 10.1–3 (1926–28).
English: Armstrong, Hellmann, and Short, *Francis of Assisi,* pp. 239–393.

Bonaventure, The Major Legend of St. Francis

Latin: *Opera Omnia S. Bonaventurae.* Vol. 8. Ed. Patres Collegii S. Bonaventurae ad Claras Aquas. Quaracchi, Italy: Collegium s. Bonaventurae, 1882.
English: Armstrong, Hellmann, and Short, *Francis of Assisi,* 2:525–683.

Select Bibliography

Acta sanctorum quotquot toto orbe coluntur, vel a catholicis scriptoribus celebrantur, quae ex Latinis & Graecis, aliarumque gentium antiquis monumentis. Ed. Jean Bolland. Antwerp: Joannem Mevrsium, 1643–.
Analacta Franciscana sive chronica aliaque varia documenta ad historian Fratrum Minorum spectantia. Ed. Patres Collegii S. Bonaventurae and Claras Aquas. Quaracchi, Italy: Collegium S. Bonaventurae, 1885–1951.
Armstrong, Regis J., J. A. Wayne Hellmann, and William J. Short, eds. *Francis of Assisi: Early Documents.* 3 vols. New York: New City Press, 1999–2001.
Berger, Peter L. *The Sacred Canopy: Elements of a Sociological Theory of Religion.* New York: Doubleday, 1967.

Bériac, Françoise. *Histoire des lépreux au Moyen Age: une société d'exclus*. Paris: Imago,1988.

Bériou, Nicole. "Les lépreux sous le regard des prédicateurs d'après les collections de sermons *ad status* du XIIIe siècle." In Bériou and Touati, *Voluntate dei leprosus*, pp. 33–80.

Bériou, Nicole, and François-Olivier Touati, eds. *Voluntate dei leprosus: Les lépreux entre conversion et exclusion aux XIIe et XIIIe siecles*. Testi, Studi, Strumenti 4. Spoleto: Centro di studi sull'alto medioevo, 1991.

Bibliotheca hagiographica latina antiquae et mediae aetatis, Brussels: Société des Bollandistes, 1898–1901. Reprinted 1992.

Bibliotheca hagiographica latina. Novum Supplementum. Brussels: Société des Bollandistes, 1986.

Bienvenu, Jean-Marc. "Fondations charitables laiques au XIIe siècle: L'exemple de l'Anjou." In Mollat, *Études sur l'histoire de la pauvreté*, 2:563–69.

Bonaventure. *Defense of the Poor. The Works of Bonaventure: Cardinal, Seraphic Doctor, and Saint*. Tr. José de Vinck. Vol. 4: Defense of the Mendicants. Paterson, NJ: St. Anthony's Guild Pres, 1966.

Bosl, Karl. "*Potens* und *Pauper*: Begriffsgeschichtliche Studien zur gesellschaftlichen Differenzierung im frühen Mittelalter und zum 'Pauperismus' des Hochmittelalters." In *Alteuropa und die moderne Gesellschaft: Festschrift für Otto Brunner*. Göttingen: Vandenhoeck and Ruprecht, 1963, pp. 60–87.

Brody, Saul Nathaniel. *The Disease of the Soul: Leprosy in Medieval Literature*. Ithaca, NY: Cornell University Press, 1974.

Brown, Peter. *The Body and Society: Men, Women, and Sexual Renunciation in Early Christianity*. New York: Columbia University Press, 1988.

———. "Poverty and Power." In *Power and Persuasion in Late Antiquity: Towards a Christian Empire* (Madison:University of Wisconsin Press, 1992), pp. 71–117.

———. "The Rise and Function of the Holy Man in Late Antiquity." *Journal of Roman Studies* 61 (1971): 80–101.

Burr, David. *Olivi and Franciscan Poverty: The Origins of the Usus Pauper Controversy*. Pennsylvania: University of Pennsylvania Press, 1989.

Cahiers de Recherches sur l'Histoire de la Pauvreté. 10 vols. Paris: Sorbonne, 1962–77.

Campagnola, Stanislao da. "La Povertà nelle *regulae* di Francesco d'Assisi." In *La povertà del secolo XII e Francesco d'Assisi*, pp. 219–53.

Canetti, Luigi. *Gloriosa Civitas: culto dei santi e società cittadina a Piacenza nel medioevo*. Cristianismo antico e medievale 4. Bologna: Pàtron Editore, 1993.

Chenu, M.-D. *Nature, Man, and Society in the Twelfth Century: Essays on New Theological Perspectives in the Latin West*. Edited and translated by Jerome Taylor and Lester K. Little. Chicago: University of Chicago Press, 1968. Orig. publ.: *Le Théologie au douzième siècle*. Paris: J. Vrin, 1957.

Comba, Rinaldo. "Dimensioni economiche e sociali dell'indigenza (fine XII–metà XIV secolo)." In *La Conversione alla povertà nell'Italia dei secoli XII–XIV*, pp. 33–51.

Constable, Giles. "Interpretation of Mary and Martha." In *Three Studies in Medieval Religious and Social Thought*. Cambridge: Cambridge University Press, 1995, pp. 1–141.

La Conversione alla povertà nell'Italia dei secoli XII–XIV. Atti del XXVII Convegno storico internazionale, Todi, 14–17 ottobre 1990. Atti dei Convegni dell'Accademia

Tudertina e del Centro di Studi sulla spiritualità medievale, new series: 4. Spoleto: Centro italiano di studi sull'alto medioevo, 1991.

Countryman, L. William. *The Rich Christian in the Church of the Early Empire: Contradictions and Accommodations.* New York: Edwin Mellen Press, 1980.

Dal Pino, Franco. "Scelte di povertà all'origine dei nuovi ordini religiosi dei secoli XII–XIV." In *La Conversione alla povertà nell'Italia dei secoli XII–XIV*, pp. 53–125.

D'Avray, David. L. *The Preaching of the Friars: Sermons Diffused from Paris before 1300.* Oxford: Clarendon Press, 1985.

Douie, Decima L. *The Conflict between the Seculars and the Mendicants at the University of Paris in the Thirteenth Century.* Aquinas Society of London, paper 23. London: Blackfriars, 1954.

Fasciculus Morum: A Fourteenth-Century Preacher's Handbook. Edited and translated by Siegfried Wenzel. University Park: Pennsylvania State University Press, 1989.

Flood, David, ed. *Poverty in the Middle Ages.* Franziskanische Forschungen 27. Paderborn, Germany: D. Coelde, 1975.

Freedman, Paul. *Images of the Medieval Peasant.* Stanford, CA: Stanford University Press, 1999.

George, Augustin, et al., eds. *La Pauvreté évangélique.* M. D. Guinan, trans. *Gospel Poverty: Essays in Biblical Theology.* Chicago: Franciscan Herald Press, 1977.

Geremek, Bronislaw. *Poverty: A History.* Translated by Agnieszka Kolakowska. Oxford: Blackwell, 1994. Orig. publ. *Litosc I szubienica: dzieje nedzy I milosierdzia.* Warsaw: Czytelnik, 1989.

Gieysztor, Alexander. "*Pauper sum et peregrinus*: La légende de saint Alexis en Occident: un ideal de pauvreté." In Mollat, *Études sur l'histoire de la pauvreté*, 1:125–39.

González, Justo L. *Faith and Wealth: A History of Early Christian Ideas on the Origin, Significance, and Use of Money.* San Francisco: Harper and Row, 1990.

Graus, Frantisek. "Poveri della città e poveri delle campagne." In *La concezione della povertà nel medioevo. Antologia di scritti.* Ed., Ovidio Capitani. Bologna: Pàtron: 1983.

Grundmann, Herbert. *Religious Movements in the Middle Ages: The Historical Links between Heresy, the Mendicant Orders, and the Women's Religious Movement in the Twelfth and Thirteenth Century, with the Historical Foundations of German Mysticism.* Translated by Steven Rowan. Notre Dame, IN: University of Notre Dame Press, 1995. Orig. publ.: *Religiöse Bewegungen im Mittelalter: Untersuchungen über die geschichtlichen Zusammenhänge zwischen der Ketzerei, den Bettelorden und der religiösen Frauenbewegung im 12. und 13. Jahrhundert und über die geschichtlichen Grundlagen der deutschen Mystik.* Hildesheim: G. Olms, 1961.

Habig, Marion A., ed. *St. Francis of Assisi, Writings and Early Biographies: English Omnibus of the Sources for the Life of St. Francis.* 3rd rev. ed. Chicago: Franciscan Herald Press, 1973.

Hamesse, Jacqueline, and Collette Muraille-Samaran, eds. *Le Travail au moyen âge: une approche interdisciplinaire.* Louvain-la-neuve: Institute d'études médiévales, 1990.

Hanawalt, Emily Albu, and Carter Lindberg, eds. *Through the Eye of the Needle: Judeo-Christian Roots of Social Welfare.* Kirksville, MO: Thomas Jefferson University Press, 1994.

Hanska, Jussi. *"And the Rich Man Also Died; and He Was Buried in Hell": The Social Ethos in Mendicant Sermons.* Bibliotheca Historica 28. Helsinki: Suomen Historiallinen Seura, 1997.

Heffernan, Thomas S. *Sacred Biography: Saints and their Biographers in the Middle Ages.* Oxford: Oxford University Press, 1988.

Hengel, Martin. *Property and Riches in the Early Church: Aspects of a Social History of Early Christianity.* Philadelphia: Fortress Press, 1974.

Hermann, Placid, tr. *Thirteenth-Century Chronicles.* Chicago: Franciscan Herald Press, 1961.

Hinnebusch, John F., ed. *The Historia Occidentalis of Jacques de Vitry: A Critical Edition.* Fribourg, Switzerland: University of Fribourg Press, 1972.

Kazantzakis, Nikos. *St. Francis.* New York: Simon and Schuster, 1962.

Kemp, Eric W. *Canonization and Authority in the Western Church.* Oxford: Oxford University Press, 1948.

Kleinberg, Aviad M. *Prophets in their Own Country: Living Saints and the Making of Sainthood in the Later Middle Ages.* Chicago: University of Chicago Press, 1992.

Lambert, Malcolm. *Franciscan Poverty: The Doctrine of the Absolute Poverty of Christ and the Apostles in the Franciscan Order, 1210–1323.* Rev. ed. St. Bonaventure, NY: Franciscan Institute, 1998.

La Ronciere, Charles M. de. "Pauvres et pauvreté a Florence au XIVe siècle." In Mollat, *Études sur l'histoire de la pauvreté,* 2:661–774.

Lawrence, C. H. *The Friars: the Impact of the Early Mendicant Movement on Western Society.* London: Longman, 1994.

LeClercq, Jean. "Aux origines bibliques du vocabulaire de la pauvreté." In Mollat, *Études sur l'histoire de la pauvreté* 1: 35–43.

———. "Les controverses sur la pauvreté du Christ." In Mollat, *Études sur l'histoire de la pauvreté,* 1:45–56.

Le Goff, Jacques. *The Birth of Purgatory.* Translated by Arthur Goldhammer. London: Scolar Press, 1984. Orig. publ.: *La naissance du Purgatoire.* Paris: Editions Gallimard, 1981.

———. *Saint François d'Assise.* Paris: Gallimard, 1999.

———. *Time, Work and Culture in the Middle Ages.* Translated by Arthur Goldhammer Chicago: University of Chicago Press, 1980. Orig. publ.: *Pour un autre Moyen Age: temps, travail et culture en Occident.* Paris: Gallimard, 1977.

———. ed. *Medieval Callings.* Translated by Lydia G. Cochrane. Chicago: University of Chicago Press, 1990. Orig. publ.: *L'uomo medievale.* Rome: Laterza, 1987.

Lesnick, Daniel R. *Preaching in Medieval Florence: The Social World of Franciscan and Dominican Spirituality.* Athens, GA: University of Georgia Press, 1989.

Little, Lester. "Pride Goes before Avarice: Social Change and the Vices in Latin Christendom." *American Historical Review* 76 (1971): 16–49.

Little, Lester K. *Religious Poverty and the Profit Economy in Medieval Europe.* Ithaca, NY: Cornell University Press, 1978.

———. "L'Utilite sociale de la pauvreté voluntaire." In Mollat, *Études sur l'histoire de la pauvreté,* 1:447–59.

Longère, Jean. "Pauvreté et richesse chez quelques prédicateurs durant la seconde moitié du XIIe siècle." In Mollat, *Études sur l'histoire de la pauvreté,* 1:255–73.

Maier, Christoph T. *Crusade Propaganda and Ideology: Model Sermons for the Preaching of the Cross.* Cambridge: Cambridge University Press, 2000.

Manselli, Raoul. "La Povertà nella vita di Francesco d'Assisi." In *La povertà del secolo XII e Francesco d'Assisi,* pp. 257–82.

Merlo, Grado G. "La conversione alla povertà nell'Italia dei secoli XII–XIV." In *La Conversione alla povertà nell'Italia dei secoli XII–XIV*, pp. 1–32.

Mollat, Michel. *The Poor in the Middle Ages: An Essay in Social History*. Translated by Arthur Goldhammer. New Haven: Yale University Press, 1986. Orig. pub. *Les Pauvres aux moyen âge*. Paris: Hachette, 1978.

———, ed. *Études sur l'histoire de la pauvreté*. 2 vols. Études vol. 8. Paris: Publications de la Sorbonne, 1974.

Moorman, John R. H. *A History of the Francican Order from Its Origins to the Year 1517*. London: Oxford University Press, 1968.

———. *Richest of Poor Men: The Spirituality of St. Francis of Assisi*. London: Darton, Longman, and Todd, 1977.

———. *Sources for the Life of S. Francis of Assisi*. Publications of the University of Manchester, vol. 274. Manchester: Manchester University Press, 1940.

Moore, R. I. *The Origins of European Dissent*. Rev. ed. Oxford: Blackwell, 1985.

———, ed. *Birth of Popular Heresy*. New York: St. Martin's Press, 1976.

Mulhern, Philip F. *Dedicated Poverty: Its History and Theology*. Staten Island NY: Alba House, 1973.

Munzer, Stephen R. "Beggars of God: The Christian Ideal of Mendicancy." *Journal of Religious Ethics* 27 (1999): 305–30.

Murray, Alexander. "Piety and Impiety in Thirteenth-Century Italy." Edited by G. J. Cuming and Derek Baker. *Popular Belief and Practice*. Studies in Church History 8. Cambridge: Cambridge University Press: 1972.

———. *Reason and Society in the Middle Ages*. Oxford: Clarendon Press, 1978.

Natalis, Hervaeus. *The Poverty of Christ and the Apostles*. Translated by John D. Jones. Toronto: Pontifical Institute of Mediaeval Studies, 1999.

Newhauser, Richard. *The Early History of Greed: The Sin of Avarice in Early Medieval Thought and Literature*. Cambridge Studies in Medieval Literature 41. Cambridge: Cambridge University Press, 2000.

Noble, Thomas F. X., and Thomas Head. *Soldiers of Christ: Saints and Saints' Lives from Late Antiquity and the Early Middle Ages*. University Park: Penn State University Press, 1995.

Odenkirchen, Carl J. *The Life of St. Alexius, in the Old French Version of the Hildesheim Manuscript: The Original Text Reviewed with Comparative Greek and Latin Versions*. Medieval classics 9. Brookline, MA: Classical Folia Editions, 1978.

Patrologiae cursus completus: series latina. Sive, Bibliotheca universalis, integra, uniformis, commoda, oeconomica, omnium SS. patrum, doctorum scriptorumque ecclesiasticorum qui ab aevo apostolico ad usque Innocentii III tempora floruerunt. Edited by J.-P., Migne, 221 vols. Paris: Excudebat Migne, etc., 1844–1902.

Pellestrandi, Christine. "La pauvreté dans la règle de Grandmont." In Mollat, *Études sur l'histoire de la pauvreté*, 1:229–45.

———. "La pauvreté spirituelle à travers les textes de la fin de XIIe siècles (Essai de recherche sémantique)." In Mollat, *Études sur l'histoire de la pauvreté*, 1:275–91.

Peyroux, Catherine. "The Leper's Kiss." *Monks and Nuns, Saints and Outcasts: Religion in Medieval Society: Essays in Honor of Lester K. Little*. Edited by Barbara H. Rosenwein and Sharon Farmer. Ithaca, NY: Cornell University Press: 2000, pp. 172–88.

Pichon, E. "Essai sur le lèpre du haut moyen âge." *Le moyen âge* 90 (1984): 331–356.

A Pobreza e a assistència aos pobres na península Ibérica durante a Idade Média. Actas das primeiras jornadas Lusos-Espanholas de História Medieval, Lisbon, 25–30 setembro, 1972. Lisbon: O Instituto, 1973.

La povertà del secolo XII e Francesco d'Assisi. Società internazionale di studi francescani. Atti del II convegno internazionale. Assisi, 17–19 October, 1974. Assisi: [s.n.], 1975.

Povertà e ricchezza nella spiritualità dei secoli XI e XII. Convegni del Centro di studi sulla spiritualità medievale, 8. Todi, 15–18 ottobre 1967. Todi: Presso l'Accademia Tudertina, 1969.

Renan, Ernest. *Nouvelles études d'histoire religieuse.* Paris: Calmann Lévy, 1884.

Ridley, Matt. *The Origins of Virtue: Human Instincts and the Evolution of Cooperation.* London: Penguin Books, 1996.

Rosenwein, Barbara. "Feudal War and Monastic Peace: Cluniac Liturgy as Ritual Aggression." *Viator* 2 (1971): 129–57.

———. *Rhinoceros Bound: Cluny in the Tenth Century.* Philadelphia: University of Pennsylvania Press, 1982.

Rosenwein, Barbara, and Lester Little. "Social Meaning in the Monastic and Mendicant Spiritualities." *Past and Present* 63 (1974):4–32.

Sabatier, Paul. *Vie de S. François d'Assise.* Paris: Fischbacher, 1894.

Sandre Gasparini, Guiseppina de. "Lebbrosi e lebbrosari tra misericordia e assistenza nei secoli XII-XIII." In *La Conversione alla povertà nell'Italia dei secoli XII–XIV,* pp. 239–268.

Saward, John. *Perfect Fools: Folly for Christ's Sake in Catholic and Orthodox Spirituality.* Oxford: Oxford University Press, 1980.

Sheils, W. J., and Diana Wood, *The Church and Wealth.* Papers presented at the 1986 Summer Meeting and the 1987 Winter Meeting of the Ecclesiastical History Society. In *Studies in Church History.* Vol. 24. Oxford: Blackwell, 1987.

Sigal, Pierre-André. "Pauvreté et charité aux XIe et XIIe siècles d'après quelques textes hagiographiques." In Mollat, *Études sur l'histoire de la pauvreté,* 1:141–62.

Southern, Richard W. *Western Society and the Church in the Middle Ages.* Pelican History of the Church, vol. 2. London: Penguin Books, 1970.

Stark, Rodney. *The Rise of Christianity: How the Obscure, Marginal Jesus Movement Became the Dominant Religious Force in the Western World in a Few Centuries.* San Francisco: HarperCollins, 1996.

Stark, Rodney, and Roger Finke. *Acts of Faith: Explaining the Human Side of Religion.* Berkeley: University of California Press, 2000.

Szittya, Penn R. *The Antifraternal Tradition in Medieval Literature.* Princeton: Princeton University Press, 1986.

Tierney, Brian. *Medieval Poor Law: A Sketch of Canonical Theory and Its Application in England.* Berkeley: University of California Press, 1959.

Touati, François-Olivier. "Les léproseries aux XIIe et XIIIe siècles, lieux de conversion?" In Bériou and Touati, *Voluntate dei leprosus,* pp. 1–32.

Turner, Denys. *Eros and Allegory: Medieval Exegesis of the Song of Songs.* Kalamazoo, MI: Cistereian Publications, 1995.

Vanchez, André, ed. Mouvements franciscains e société française, XIIe–XXe siècles. Paris: Beauchesne, 1984.

Vauchez, André. *Sainthood in the Later Middle Ages*. Translated by Jean Birrell. Cambridge: Cambridge University Press, 1997. Orig. publ.: *La sainteté en Occident aux derniers siècles du moyen age*. Paris: École Française de Rome, 1988.

Witters, Willibrord. "Pauvres et pauvreté dans les coutumes monastique du Moyen Âge." In Mollat, *Études sur l'histoire de la pauvreté*, 1:177–215.

Zweig, Michael, ed. *Religion and Economic Justice*. Philadelphia: Temple University Press, 1991.

Index